Conservation today

David Pearce

D0001550

R

Routledge
London and New York

ARCHITECTURE LIBRARY

008077   c

First published 1989 by Routledge
11 New Fetter Lane, London EC4P 4EE
29 West 35th Street, New York, NY 10001

© 1989 David Pearce

Typeset, printed, and bound in
Great Britain by
Butler & Tanner Ltd, Frome and London

All rights reserved. No part of this book may be reprinted
or reproduced or utilized in any form or by any electronic,
mechanical, or other means, now known or hereafter
invented, including photocopying and recording, or in any
information storage or retrieval system, without
permission in writing from the publishers.

British Library Cataloguing in Publication data
Pearce, David
  Conservation today
  1. Great Britain. Buildings of
    historical importance. Conservation
  I. Title
  363.6′9′0941

Library of Congress Cataloging in Publication Data
also available

ISBN 0–415–00778–X (hb)
      0–415–03914–2 (pb)

Contents

Foreword

In recent years more and more people have derived great pleasure from visiting our historic houses and buildings, and this has made them more aware of the need for conservation in order to preserve them for future generations.

As the Prime Minister, Mrs Margaret Thatcher, stressed when she visited the Royal Fine Art Commission in January this year to launch our report *A New Look for London*, 'We are all no more than life tenants of our heritage and we have a moral duty to pass it on in as good a condition as that in which we received it.'

When we set up the Art and Architecture Education Trust we decided that one of the projects should be devoted to the encouragement of an ever greater awareness of the need for conservation. Hence an exhibition, 'Conservation Today' (for the benefit of tomorrow), which we hope will increase the public's interest and knowledge of what has been done and what is still to be done. The exhibition, generously funded by the Wolfson Foundation, demonstrates ideas and illustrates projects where great efforts have been made to preserve old buildings and groups of buildings and, in the majority of cases, adapt them for imaginative new uses. We are concerned that necessary refurbishments are carried out sensitively and that new buildings associated with them add to the richness of the scene.

To organize the presentation we are fortunate to have secured the services of Peter Murray and, at his suggestion, those of David Pearce. Mr Pearce, originally an architect, has played a significant role in conservation in Britain, as a co-founder and Vice Chairman of SAVE Britain's Heritage and as Secretary – in distant succession to William Morris – of the Society for the Protection of Ancient Buildings. He is also a writer and was engaged upon research for a book which, fortuitously, shared several of the themes in our proposed exhibition. Two projects were brought together; the book provides case studies of the projects illustrated in the exhibition as well as detailed background information on the nuts and bolts of conservation and adaptive re-use.

'Conservation Today' draws on experience in Britain since European Architectural Heritage Year in 1975. As was the case with that event it is our intention to share our experiences with those of our colleagues in Europe, many of whom will be participating in the exhibition and the associated seminar.

Lord St John of Fawsley

Acknowledgements

There is a handful of people without whom this book would not have seen the light of day – Diana Hunt, Peter Murray, Matthew Saunders, and Celia Scott – not to speak of its editor, Andrew Wheatcroft. Very particular thanks are due to them, and also to Sophie Andreae, James Boutwood, Stephen Croad, Sarah Jenkins, Sasha Lubetkin, David Martin, Gordon Michell, Christopher Pearce, Ken Powell, Duncan Simpson, and Marianne Watson-Smyth.

The author and publishers would like to thank the following copyright holders for permission to reproduce illustrations:
Robert Adam for 79; Birmingham City Council for 15, 16a, and 16b; Brighton Pavilion for 89; British Rail Property Board for 20, 41b and 42; Richard Bryant for 34a, 34b and chapter 1 title-page; Cadw for 7; Castle Ashby Estate Office for 57; Martin Charles for 75 and 76; CZWG Architects for 77 and 78; Jim Connell for 9; Conran Roche Architects for 84a; Gillian Darley for 4 and chapter 2 title-page; Gilbert Dennis for 94a, 94b and 95; John Donat Photography for 44a, 50, 51a, 51b, 52, 55 and 56; English Heritage for 14a, 14b, 17, 38, 39, 43, 45 and 60; Essex County Council for 46, 65, 69a and 69b; Tony Evans for 58 and 59; Terry Farrell and Company for 32a and 33b; Mark Fiennes for 53 and 54; Glasgow City Council for 10, 11 and 12; G-MEX Management Ltd for 40; Roderick Gradidge for 83; The Halpern Partnership for 21; Simon Howard for 96a and 96b; Donald Insall and Associates for 62 and 88; Irvine Development Corporation for chapter 12 title-page; A. F. Kersting for chapter 8 title-page; Derek Latham and Partners for 26a and 26b; Lawrence and Wrightson for 44b and chapter 7 title-page; Polly Lyster for 28, 35a and 35b; London Docklands Development Corporation for 33; Manser Associates for 80, 81 and 82; Hugh Martin and Partners for 13; Peter McCurdy for 67 and 68; Merlin Photography for 23; Gordon Michell for chapter 5 title-page; Brian Middlehurst for 70, 71 and 72; James Mortimer (for the *Sunday Times Magazine*) for 19a and 19b; Music Hall Trust for 8; The National Trust for 49 and chapter 3 title-page; PSA Photographic Unit for 36; PTE for 101 and 102; David Pearce for 2, 3, 61 and 99; Ivo Peters for 41a; Pollard, Thomas and Edwards for 100; Renton, Howard, Wood, Levine Partnership for 90 and chapter 13 title-page; Anthony Richardson for 6, 74 and chapter 10 title-page; Royal Commission on the Historic Monuments of Britain for 1, 22, 47, 92a and chapter 11 title-page; Jerry Sampson for 86, 87a and 87b; SAVE Britain's Heritage for 5, 18, 29, 37, 48, 91a and 91b, 93, 97a and 97b, 98a

and 98b, 103 and chapter 6 title-page;
Southern Evening Echo for 63 and 64;
Alex Starkey (copyright *Country Life*) for
96a and 96b; Tate Gallery, Liverpool for
30 and 31; P. Q. Treloar for 27; David
Warner Ellis for 92b; Norman Whicheloe
for 24, 25 and 73; YRM Partnership Ltd
for 84b, 85 and chapter 4 title-page.

Chapter 1

After 1975: an Introduction

*New reflecting
old: Norman
Foster's Willis
Faber buiding,
Ipswich*

This book and the exhibition which it accompanies tell the story of the conservation and reuse of old buildings in Britain since 1975. Why that year? 1975 was European Architectural Heritage Year (EAHY); it can also be seen in retrospect that the mid-1970s was a time of fundamental change in attitudes about the treatment of what was just then coming to be called 'the heritage'. Interestingly, it was almost exactly a century since William Morris had founded the first national buildings conservation body, The Society for the Protection of Ancient Buildings.

EAHY was a success in that it caught the popular imagination and epitomized a general antipathy to the results of postwar planning and housing policies, or at least the most visible results – demolition, comprehensive redevelopment, and high-rise flats. Modern architecture as a whole tended to be condemned. The brief thrill of the new, Harold Wilson's 'white heat of technology', had rapidly given way to pain at the all-too-visible destruction of historic fabric and loss in environmental quality. EAHY showed a gentler way forward, namely preservation of historic buildings, conservation, and adaptive reuse of as many as possible redundant structures in our cities, towns, villages, and countryside.

There was something of a self-congratulatory air about the EAHY celebrations. The Countess of Dartmouth ably assembled the whole British establishment from the Archbishop of Canterbury, Prince Philip, and Henry Moore, through central and local government politicians and officials, bankers and builders, even journalists, at lavish receptions in St James's Palace and the Banqueting Hall, Whitehall. A group of the last category got together with a handful of younger historians, architects, and planners to point out that, while 1975 might well mark the turn of the tide, it also coincided with a climate of destruction exemplified by applications to demolish listed buildings at the rate of one a day.

1. Everton, Liverpool, in 1971; little more than St Chrysostom's church and a pub survive disastrous clearances

There had also recently been a shocking and influential exhibition, 'The Destruction of the Country House,' at the Victoria & Albert Museum. With the encouragement of Roy Strong, the V&A's director, John Harris and Marcus Binney, of the RIBA's Drawings Collection and *Country Life* respectively, mounted a visual polemic, a powerful trailer for the conservation group they then assembled which was shortly and immodestly to christen itself SAVE Britain's Heritage. Modern publicity methods were employed to awaken the country to the continuing loss of interesting and potentially useful buildings. Consciously manipulating the media in a

way quite foreign to the established and rather staid amenity societies, SAVE has issued some 400 press releases and about a hundred reports of various kinds; it has campaigned successfully to change legislation and shift policies of organizations such as British Rail and the CEGB. Most enterprisingly it has put together practical solutions for such massive problem buildings as Billingsgate Market, Battersea Power Station, All Souls' Church, Halifax, and Barlaston Hall, Staffordshire. SAVE's arguments and example have prompted others to tackle major cases like Liverpool Street Station, Smithfield Market and Little Britain, Temple Meads Station, Bristol,

and Central Station, Manchester.

SAVE has been more influential than any equivalent body since the early days of the SPAB, which was also launched on a wave of campaigning publicity, and its example, together with a generally favourable climate, has helped to enliven older societies who were used to working in a gentlemanly 'behind-the-scenes' way. Since 1975 the SPAB has increased membership, strengthened its technical capacity, and engaged in campaigns to conserve and reuse farm buildings, for example. Both the Georgian Group and the Victorian Society have also made their voices more audible in recent years, campaigning to preserve architecture such as

St Pancras Station and Georgian Bath; the latter is represented not only by its peaks such as the sacrosanct Circus and Royal Crescent, but also by contextual foothills like Walcot street. The charm of the nearly ordinary, though less easy to define than the quality of masterpieces, has become the focus of much conservation effort in recent years.

The Ancient Monuments Society, which was founded in Manchester in 1924 and had no connection with the other three national groups, eventually moved to London and was enclosed in the fold of the Joint Committee of the National Amenity Societies. This last, itself little more than a liaison mechanism, has spawned sub-committees, one of which, the Tax Group, has worked on recondite fiscal matters to the extent that it has even impressed the Treasury and secured more than one budget concession, particularly in connection with maintenance funds for outstanding country houses. Here again can be seen the hard-edged side of the conservation lobby, in a sphere where quiet efforts are usually the most effective.

The AMS itself has ranged over the whole field in recent years, untrammelled by the self imposed restrictions as to dates of buildings which SPAB, Georgians, and Vixoc – as it is known – have adopted in line with the interests inherent in their titles. The AMS is, however, run from a Wren church tower together with the related Friends of Friendless Churches group, and has specialized above all in ecclesiastical buildings. Such a stress very naturally reflects the personal interests of those whose largely voluntary efforts keep these remarkably small societies going; in the case of the FFC and the AMS, Ivor Bulmer Thomas, lately a member of the Church of England Synod. It also reflects another lively issue of recent times: the future of ecclesiastical buildings. Of some 16,500 Anglican churches, 1,147 have been declared redundant since 1968, but less than a quarter have been demolished. This represents efforts not so much of the Church or its Com-

missioners as those charitable societies who have often had to argue fiercely at diocesan level with church authorities. The latter, with some justice, sometimes resent the amount of time they are required to devote to the disposal of 'disused plant'.

Since 1975, as suggested above, there has been a quickening pace in the protection and environmental improvement of whole areas, now that outstanding monuments are generally regarded as 'safe'. The late Lord Duncan Sandys not only steered the Civic Amenities Act through Parliament in 1967, but he also founded the Civic Trust as a pressure group in this field and as a co-ordinating body for the 1,000 or so local amenity groups throughout the country. Thus conservation areas were established nationally before 1975. So were the equally important town schemes, to which larger amounts of grant money are attached. They came into effect as a system to deal with the integrated repair of large groups of buildings such as the terraces of Bath. Despite their title, town schemes can also operate in parts of cities or even in villages. An EAHY initiative, the Architectural Heritage Fund, has been administered by the Civic Trust since its 1975 inception. The British habit of identifying a problem and setting up yet another mechanism to deal with it is nowhere better exemplified than in the field of conservation. These mechanisms nearly all work very well for those whom I have labelled 'grants entrepreneurs', people patient and enterprising enough to have mastered the subject.

Another highly practical Civic Trust initiative has involved the sending of a small team – one or two people with minimal back-up – for three years in the first instance to small towns with potential for environmental improvement but with no energetic catalyst, no grants entrepreneur indeed, to enthuse the inhabitants, marshall internal resources, and attract external ones. This initiative has proved highly successful at Wirksworth, Derbyshire, and is still in progress and in the balance at Calne in Wiltshire (see pp. 73–6). The projects, which now number about twenty, might be seen as minute and temporary urban development corporations, although with a bias towards historic building refurbishment as well as economic revitalization.

The government intends to spend £223 million in 1990–1 on nine UDCs, which are on a rather different scale, but interestingly enough an external initiative deriving from the same external perception, the inability to deal with urban decay in specific older, built-up areas. The projects' effectiveness depends to a great extent on the willingness of the council to co-operate in practice, whatever its theoretical reservations. The difficulty in focusing was not helped by the creation of larger local authorities in 1975, and although at Wirksworth the co-operation of both district and county was remarkably positive, at Calne it has been less so.

Yet another difference since 1975 may be seen in the source of funds, which in tune with the times are increasingly private in origin, for example from Sainsbury's family trusts. A decade or so ago central and local government were seen as almost the only means of large-scale change. Since 1979 not only has central government stepped back and obliged local authorities to do the same in many spheres of activity, while encouraging private and commercial interventions by corporate and personal tax reductions, but Whitehall has also radically altered its own planning and housing policies. At least until the late 1960s, 'slum clearance' meant decanting large numbers of residents from the centres of such major cities as Glasgow, Liverpool, Birmingham, and Newcastle to huge, often high-density, peripheral estates and from central areas of London beyond the green belt to new towns. Vacated sites were bulldozed and quite often left derelict for a decade as cutbacks in expenditure resulted from recurrent economic crises. Blighted districts tended

to be further depressed as a result of actual or proposed road-building. The downward spiralling effect on urban vitality of the removal of specific activities was greatly underestimated, just as the positive effect of increased confidence and of the 'conservation impact' of prominent refurbishment and reuse projects can be underestimated (as recent experience in Glasgow has demonstrated). Highway engineers are obstinate, and an area in Glasgow has only been released from 'road blight' in 1988.

Most inner-urban motorways were abandoned by 1975, although not all problems were thereby solved, and fine nineteenth-century terraces in west London remain unattractive because heavy traffic, once destined for the 'motorway box', still thunders past their doors. The early and mid-1970s saw a complete turnaround in housing provisions: financial inducements to demolish old stock and to build high rise (which was favoured in the housing cost yardsticks by subsidy weighting) was abandoned in favour of area rehabilitation via general improvement areas and housing action areas. Although the National Building Agency lingered on into the early 1980s trying to specify remedial works for the prefabricated concrete system-built housing it had encouraged local authorities to build a few years before, at least it was no longer recommending such building methods. The idea behind HAAs and GIAs was to let loose whole teams of local council staff to speed up their own authorities' procedures and to help landlords and tenants in rundown streets to take up grants for house repair and area improvement. There was considerable scope here, and the various housing improvement grants administered by local authorities have long been the largest single source of finance for refurbishment.

It is a little difficult to have faith in planning policies when they are so frequently turned on their heads. One year, car-parking under or adjacent to new central-area offices is a requirement, the next there are inducements to remove it. Encouragement of employers to move jobs out of cities, especially out of London, via the Location of Offices Bureau was reversed in the 1970s when grants to bring them back were started. By 1975 local planners and development control officers were only just becoming convinced of the damage wrought by their zoning policies. Where implemented, these had resulted in a kind of one-dimensional city: offices here, housing there, commerce somewhere else, and factories preferably not at all. All was determined by coloured areas on plans, and 'non-conforming uses' were strictly discouraged. Awful American experience chronicled by Jane Jacobs in *The Death and Life of Great American Cities*, published in 1962, was long ignored, although she had vividly documented how a rich and complicatedly overlain pattern of building uses – and activities even in the spaces between – was the very essence of a city.

Practical politics are influenced not so much by official policy, often a little behind informed opinion, as by ministerial inclination and also sensitivity to that opinion. Thus Peter Shore, the Labour secretary of state for the environment after 1974, was less sympathetic to conservation than had been a Tory before; it was partly that he was less interested in old buildings than Geoffrey Rippon had been. There is more scope for arbitrary ministerial decision-making in this field than almost any other. The minister can decide whether or not to 'call-in' a case for public inquiry. Then he can decide whether or not to confirm his inspector's decision at that inquiry. Rippon, for example, decided to list some 200 buildings in Covent Garden overnight in order to block redevelopment. Although his officials had not completed their inspections an architectural magazine had already proposed a list. Shore, on the other hand, could have decided to persuade the Treasury to accept Lord

2. Warehouses in 'the clink' area of Southwark, London; postwar planners were blind to this tough beauty as well as the re-use potential

Roseberry's offer of Mentmore and its contents at a low price in settlement of capital transfer tax (death duty was the older term). But he did not, although the difference between the (roughly) £2 million offered and the £3 million asked (both figures seemed to fluctuate) was argued about for over a year. In the end the government got the worst of every world, for the public argument forced the Treasury to purchase a handful of outstanding items for the same amount that was asked for house and contents. These were sold at auction for nearly £8 million.

The Mentmore case in 1977, though apparently a failure of SAVE's campaign, underlined the shift towards conservation as received opinion, popular cause, and official policy. The National Land Fund (see p. 31) was reconstituted as the National Heritage Memorial Fund to avoid just such a fiasco in future. Everyone, including the heritage lobby, was taken aback by the general outcry about the dispersal of French furniture and porcelain, some good paintings, and a lot of indifferent ones, in a nineteenth-century Elizabethan-style pile. Serious newspapers reported the arguments day by day and so, amazingly, did popular papers to a considerable extent. Letters to the *Mirror* and thundering editorials in the *Mail* as well as hundreds of column inches in *The Times* and the *Daily Telegraph* must be noticed by any government. Even an administration not overly concerned with such middle-class preoccupations – as everyone had always considered them – and also in straitened financial circumstances can hardly afford to ignore the conservation lobby. Another secretary of state, Michael Heseltine (who was not disposed to ignore the lobby anyway), described it as the most effective with which he had had to deal. It was, in any case, a quite inexpensive issue. Indeed it has been argued that any monies spent on 'the heritage' more than pay for themselves in terms of tourism, job creation, and other stimulae to the economy.

Grants by English Heritage for historic building repairs totalled under £20 million in 1986–7 (these are the grants formerly made by the DoE), income from all aspects of incoming foreign tourism was about £8 billion, and a similar sum was spent by British people on all forms of travel. About 1.4 million people are employed in the tourist industry. Although only a small proportion of all this tourism involves visits to examples of historic architecture, the number of these visits was recently estimated at 67 million a year. The point is that it is now widely recognized that benefits of this expenditure are massive. Most visitors to Britain do not come for the food or the climate.

Michael Heseltine was the first secretary for the environment to fully grasp such factors. He did not hesitate to lean on local authorities to grasp them too. Circulars directed them to make sure that alternative uses had been considered, that their change of use policies were flexible, and that a listed building had been genuinely offered for sale at a reasonable price before its demolition was entertained. He expanded grants for churches in use and increased assistance to the redundant Churches Fund to preserve the best examples which were taken out of use. He effectively doubled the number of listed buildings to an eventual figure for Britain of about half a million (still under 3 per cent of the total) by insisting on an accelerated re-survey, for which almost a hundred extra DoE staff were appointed. They were supplemented on an agency basis by county council staff and even private consultants.

He encouraged the Treasury to accept maintenance funds and tax concessions for houses and related parks designated as outstanding and for which trusts were established. He prompted acceptance in lieu of capital taxes of heritage properties and contents. He helped to generate a climate favourable to conservation and reuse by many executive decisions, and by public inquiry calls-in and verdicts.

He bullied local authorities into serving repairs notices and even, for the first time, did so himself.

In this survey of the many changes since 1975 a few debits should also be noted. Heseltine himself started the policy of occasional disposals from public ownership (the disastrous sale of Heveningham Hall, now in a sorry state, was one), and mooted the much-criticized permission to museums to sell unwanted items.

Nearly half of the 67 million visits to historic buildings in 1987 were to cathedrals or churches; this building type would appear to be the least affected by post-1975 changes. Always recognized as being special, deliberately designed to be architecturally dominant, church buildings retain mystique even in a secular age. Indeed, among the least sentimental have been certain dioceses, the Church Commissioners, and some Nonconformist authorities. Church leaders have become more hard-headed regarding redundancy. Excepting the Methodists' banning of dancing and alcohol consumption in former chapels, they have come to accept virtually any new use, including restaurants and night clubs which, however impious, are likely to be less damaging to internal structure than residential conversion. On the other hand, opinions about what is worth preserving have become more inclusive for church buildings, as they have for old buildings as a whole. SAVE has fought successfully for High Victorian examples such as All Souls' in Halifax and St John's in Reading. The Thirties Society, founded in 1979, has struggled for St Wilfrid's in Brighton just as it has done for Odeon and Gaumont cinemas in the suburbs. Losses of certain ecclesiastical buildings have been awful however. Mighty Nonconformist 'preaching halls', often classical in style and expressing the commercial enterprise and piety of northern industrialists, have been wantonly destroyed. Not only have congregations vanished more completely than is the case with the

Anglican and certainly with the Roman Catholic churches, but the values they represented have been out of favour, especially in the areas where they most frequently occur – the north of England, Scotland, and Wales. These also happen to be areas where there are fewer commercial enterprises with needs and resources for costly conversions to new uses. The Brunswick Methodist Church in Leeds was demolished despite Grade II* listing and despite there having been a scheme several years ago for office use. The unlisted Gothic Northgate End Unitarian Chapel at Halifax went in 1980. The once beautiful Square Chapel of 1774 in the same town is derelict and rapidly decaying. So is the splendid Upper Independent Chapel, Heckmondwike, West Yorkshire.

At the other end of the scale is the infinitely sad loss by attrition of decay and vandalism of even medieval country churches in East Anglia. Distribution of listed Anglican churches is heavily biased towards sparsely populated parts of the country. Norfolk has 724 of which 183 are Grade I. All these conditions were perceived by government more than a decade ago. State Aid for Churches, as it was called, was introduced in 1977, and is now on a generous scale. But progress has been slow partly because the Church of England has tended to cling to shreds of ecclesiastical exemption from the planning process. As an informal *quid pro quo* for financial assistance the church grudgingly acceded to the DoE's insistence on the secretary of state's right to call in cases for public inquiry, albeit of a non-statutory kind. All this was rightly seen by Anglicans as a gradual integration into the secular system. Churches are now listed as other buildings, not grades A, B, and C as before. Their exterior surroundings and appearance have long been subject to planning controls, and since 1986 substantial demolition of a listed church, or one in a conservation area, would be subject to listed-building consent.

In the case of cathedrals, which are among the world's greatest buildings, the Church of England has fought a reactionary battle for total autonomy. It is seldom realized that cathedral deans and chapters are quite free to demolish 'their' buildings at whim – a situation almost unique in Europe. In late 1988 Synod accepted a modified Cathedrals Advisory Measure, having earlier rejected one carefully prepared over ten years by a large working party representing all interests. This will ensure that any significant works will have the prior benefit of the best scholarly and technical advice. Cathedral authorities were reinforced in their opposition to 'interference' by the crude argument of financial independence. Almost all of them have access to either capital or running provisions on a scale only comparable with that of the second half of the nineteenth century. Since 1975 most of their coffers have been filled with multi-million pound appeals boosted by distinguished patrons, often royal. Ely Cathedral has been the first to introduce non-voluntary entry charges.

The result has often been excessive restorations and sometimes insensitive alterations. Hardly a decorated surface at Southwark has not been repainted and gilded, Westminster Abbey has been blessed with chandeliers and also much gilding, and Canterbury, Norwich, and Exeter have carried out much-criticized work. Wells was pressurized into adapting a conservative approach to the restoration of its matchless west-front sculptures after an intensive campaign by the SPAB and others, but Lincoln shows signs of ignoring that experience. Despite reluctance of deans and chapters to take outside advice and no reluctance to take outside money, the fact remains that:

In general, listed ecclesiastical buildings have suffered much less than listed secular buildings despite the limited state powers to prevent demolition of the former. In the 19 years to December 1987, 67 redundant churches were wholly demolished. This represents 0.55% of all listed Anglican churches compared with 0.75% of listed secular buildings for which listed building consent was granted (3,193 buildings) in just 13 years to December 1987. Thus a listed building is nearly twice as likely to be demolished as a listed church. (*English Heritage Monitor*, 1988)

Among several hundred non-listed churches which have been demolished, however, there have been losses because remaining parishioners opposed changes of use even to that of another Christian group, as at St John's, Reading. Here Anglicans were very nearly successful in denying transfer to the Polish community. They were only thwarted by the local authority, informally in league with SAVE, refusing permission for demolition of a boundary wall which prevented access for large machinery to the site.

Another institution long resentful of its responsibility for a large number of listed buildings in its charge, British Rail, has often managed to frustrate would-be purchasers and reusers by the simple expedient of years of bureaucratic delay in divesting itself of redundant stations. Even a handsome station, such as that at Monkswearmouth, will daunt a refurbisher after seven years of decay and vandalism. BR wanted no truck with nostalgia. Resolutely determined to turn its back on the romance of steam, of *The Railway Children* ethos, of the fretwork valances on its platform canopies, it saw the only way forward as a ruthless, if largely symbolic, adoption of modernism. So, in 1958, BR was only too delighted when the prime minister, Harold Macmillan, refused to be swayed by the public outcry at the demolition of Euston Station and in particular the wilful, because quite unnecessary, removal of Hardwick's great classical arch. Even the £25,000 required to store the stones for possible re-erection was refused because 'the nation must not be backward-looking'. Even into the 1980s British Rail was convinced that more people would pass through stainless-steel barriers than cast-iron ones, that more tickets would be sold from aluminium and glass booking offices than from Victorian linenfold-panelled ones. Even the director allegedly caring for the historic railway architecture celebrated in SAVE's 1978 exhibition was convinced that BR could only make money by turning its back on the past. Recently, however, the board has become proud of its heritage: the £50 million reconversion of the St Pancras Hotel to its original use is going forward, for example, and a Railway Heritage Trust has been established with initial BR funding of £1 million and continuing subventions.

Until about 1975 most shopowners, restauranteurs, and office managers shared the view that they could only operate efficiently in a slick modern-looking environment. It took the hugely successful refurbishment of Covent Garden into a major shopping, entertainment, and tourist centre to convince them otherwise. Now the richness and intricacy of an old building is seen as a positive asset; if you don't have it, you fake it. The newly roofed Prince's Square shopping centre in Glasgow is designed to look Victorian.

Unfortunately many fine interiors were swept away before the pendulum swung. If one wants to patronize a large bookshop of the quiet, carpeted and wooden-panelled variety with which London was well blessed until the 1960s one has to go to Rizzoli's on Fifth Avenue in New York. So it was with public houses. The breweries spent much of the 1960s and early 1970s destroying hardwood bars and settles, brass fittings, etched glazing, gilt lettering, and elaborate plaster ceilings. They have spent much of the 1980s putting them back in replica. Conservationists, it should be stressed, are no more in favour of the second process than the first.

Sadly it is not just a fashion for nostalgia – for which writers like Robert Hewison blame conservationists – nor public boredom with modern (or what in the 1950s and 1960s was often called 'contemporary') design, it is not even an instinctive subliminal identification with natural materials whose grain and texture wear and weather better than machine-made ones, which have led popular taste back towards tradition. Although these factors help, the main one is that, having seen the future, designers have found that it doesn't work. Even in new kitchens oak and teak are replacing formica laminates. There is a rising market in old cast-iron grates and panelled doors soon disappear from builders' skips.

The infelicitous and eclectic styling of much speculative housing, even the pitched and tiled roofs and panelled doors being added by the council to award-winning former LCC housing blocks in Islington, stem more from the 'failure of modernism' than from the preaching of atavists. Such a mood cannot persist over a long period. But it cannot be lightly dismissed either. It is not only that concrete buildings were repetitively and crudely designed and that they stain and leak and promote condensation and fungus growth. Nor is it only that open-plan, air-conditioned, fluorescent-lit

3. *Stag Place, Victoria, London; roads, slabs, towers and windswept spaces of the 1960s – crudely detailed and alien to the texture of the city. The arrowed block is being redeveloped. (Buckingham Palace top left)*

offices are loathed by their users who actually feel less energetic and less well in them than they did in older, more solidly built, more cellular premises where they can control their own heating and lighting and open the windows. Again it is all these factors up to a point, but above all it is the failure of an idea about society, an ideal about the perfectability of human nature that once everyone is provided with decent, standardized accom-modation they will live happily and peaceably in collective harmony. They don't, they urinate in the lifts. Nor is this sheer brutishness, it is an angry protest at the removal from the individual of the opportunity to modify his or her own environment. The public disappointment with the products of modern architecture, especially housing, is in many ways a sep-arate phenomenon from the heritage cult. Perhaps conservationists do deserve to be identified with some of the more unfor-tunate and, it is to be hoped, passing manifestations of a reactionary culture because they have often not scrupled to employ some of its arguments when seeking to 'save' a particular building.

A new argument for conservation which has come into its own since 1975 is that concerning the need to preserve buildings as documents of social history, as evidence of the way of life of those somewhat patronizingly labelled 'ordi-nary people'. Few would criticize this idea except perhaps those like Sir John Sum-merson who actually established modern conservation just before and after the Second World War. For them an old buil-ding's architectural quality was the main justification for preserving it – though they did grudgingly admit as another cri-terion 'historic interest'. This essentially covered places where some very great person was born, lived, or died, or where some crucial historic event occurred, but is, of course, almost infinitely flexible and also, unlike great architecture, capable of counterfeit. While not doubting the great-ness of Catherine Cookson as a writer it is surely reasonable to complain that the local authority, intent on establishing her home as a tourist attraction, refused to be put off by the fact that its predecessor had many years ago demolished it. They simply re-created it in a nearby and no doubt similar surviving terrace. So far this shrine is not listed. It is going to be ever more difficult to maintain separation between genuine conservation and heritage-industry concoctions such as Vindolanda or Wigan Pier, or even the more respectable open-air museums such as that at Singleton.

As so often, Americans have shown the way. Tamara Hareven and Randolph Langenbach, contributing to a symposium report in 1979,[1] wrote of a 'gain of status of objects from more recent past' as being symptomatic of 'the growing historic consciousness of the value of the workplace [which] represents a recent departure from an elitist approach not only to buildings but to the industrial heritage in general'. The only criterion they admit is 'the symbolic value of the building – the way of life and the sense of community it represents'. They regret the 1975 demolition of the Quarry Hill flats in Leeds, a massive 1930s precurser of postwar housing. The building was valuable simply because it represented a large chunk of a lot of people's lives, no matter what the quality of those lives. Its architectural innovation, for which there was a respectable argument, was beside the point. 'The challenge of conservation is to preserve the meaning of the way of life which buildings represent to those who have worked and lived in them, as well as the more abstract and formal qualities based on knowledge of architectural history'.

Interestingly these two authors criticize Covent Garden because 'the extent and quality of restoration has ... removed the visible effects of its use as a market'. By this they mean the 'wear and patina of age ... one associates with an historical market' which has been turned into 'an anachronistically elegant shopping centre'. The loose use of language begs a

great many questions, but their presumably deliberate use of Ruskin's phrase 'patina of age' brings us neatly back to the thinking which resulted in the birth of the SPAB in 1877. The beauty and the evidence of history found in worn and weathered stonework is a romantic concept. It has little to do with the adaptive reuse of old buildings which is based on economic realities and the pleasure many people seem to find in the recognition of familiar forms.

This chapter set out to show that many attitudes had changed since 1978, that motives for conservation are many and various, that disentangling them has its interest but that their coincidence at this time has made the movement to conserve almost irresistable. Having discussed those incentives that might loosely be described as sociological it would be incomplete if it ignored that one other determinent – politics. Margaret Thatcher was elected leader of the Conservative Party in 1975. Although she did not attain government until 1979, those intervening four years are unlikely to be seen as significant from any viewpoint as the decade which followed. There is no simple party political division in terms of support or otherwise for the retention of historic buildings. In other words Conservatives are by no means always conservationists (as Macmillan made clear in the case of the Euston Arch). There are conflicting instincts in both main parties on this topic. While public initiatives in this field, as in others, are more likely to come from a socialist direction, and grants, technical advice, and designation of large areas for various kinds of improvement might well be more forthcoming from a Labour-controlled council, the sort of person most active in conservation matters tends to be a middle-class Conservative. This very fact has caused 'hard Left' councils such as Greenwich in London to be suspicious of conservation as elitist.

Personal tastes appear to have played a considerable part at secretary-of-state level. Heseltine, Crossland, and Rippon were interventionist because interested in the subject, Shore was neither interventionist nor interested. Ridley is interested in architecture, but more passionate about reducing the role of government. It can be seen that an examination of political dogmas would be unprofitable. The fact is that the flood of conservation projects has continued to swell during the 1980s. Public provision has enabled major expenditure on country houses, and often their contents. Indeed the many millions expended on Belton, Kedleston, Canons Ashby, and Calke, not to mention a score or so of slightly less ambitious projects, would have been unthinkable at any other period. Nor has there been any vocal opposition to such expenditures – still modest in the scale of the public budget as a whole, of course. The reason must be that politicians have been persuaded that resources devoted to conservation are both popular and good value for money. When a 'think tank' such as the Policy Studies Institute published a report demonstrating that the arts, which for this purpose includes all that is broadly labelled 'the heritage', produce more income than the motor industry, it is unsurprising that there is general agreement on the matter.

Aspects of the national economy reflecting political realities are crucially important in providing opportunities for conservation and new uses. Prosperity, at least in the south of England, together with property and, indeed, retailing booms have led to a willingness to take on all sorts of imaginative conversions which would be unthinkable in a depressed economy or one in which capital was scarce. Things have also looked a great deal better for owners of country houses. Reductions in personal taxation as well as special provisions to avoid the dispersal of outstanding houses, collections, and estates on the deaths of owners, have all helped. Rises in world art prices have meant that the sale of one or two old masters can pay for a large amount of building work, while at the same time contributing to an endowment fund for future upkeep.

Tax concessions for charitable donations, while perhaps making little differences to the Gettys or even the Sainsburys of this world, have no doubt provided a major boost to the funds of scores of modest historic buildings preservation trusts and other conservation charities. On the other hand, higher tax concessions may reduce income to charities from covenants by up to £0.5 million per annum. It has been argued that restrictive government financing for agencies such as the Historic Buildings and Monuments Commission have barely kept pace with inflation. Such funds are, however, very small compared with housing and urban aid grants (see Chapter 3) totalling hundreds of millions. Since the climate of opinion is so favourable towards reuse of old buildings these funds are extremely important. Here, finally, we return to the crudities of party politics. All the major cities are almost always Labour-controlled. They have been and probably will be for some years facing a government with a radically different ideology. If, as Glasgow has shown (see Chapter 4), a city administration is willing to co-operate and even 'play the system' there is every chance of spectacular renewal. Glasgow has seized nearly all available inner-city aid, urban-development grants, housing-association subsidies, and historic-building support. It has even been able to suppress some of its distaste for private enterprise, especially as far as city-centre refurbishment goes. The repair of building fabric and associated environmental improvements has not only brought greatly increased economic and cultural activity, it has also attracted far more visitors and international recognition. Apparently even Glaswegians feel 'miles better'. Where other cities have turned their backs on available opportunities, their buildings and even their people continue to be depressed.

Chapter 2

The Legal framework

*Denton
almshouses,
Lincolnshire,
criminally
destroyed*

The law relating to historic buildings and ancient monuments centres on the idea of protection. The first national voluntary body in the field, the Society for the Protection of Ancient Buildings, was intent on protecting churches in particular from the sort of destructive alteration called restoration. Its foundation preceded any substantive legislation, though not efforts to achieve some. The first legislation, Sir John Lubbock's Ancient Monuments Act, 1882, was based on the novel idea that a landowner did not have a right to destroy remains of former settlements which happened to be on his property. The idea was formed a century or so ago that the state had a duty to identify and protect monuments and buildings which were of such quality or interest that their preservation was in the common good.

Words such as 'quality', 'interest', and 'protect' are capable of wide interpretation. A hundred years of legislation has continued to define them ever more inclusively, and now about half a million buildings as well as up to 60,000 monuments are thought to be of listable quality and interest. Protection has been broadened not only to include an obligation not to destroy, or materially alter (which always does include some destruction), but also to 'keep in good repair' + another idea which it is not too easy to define narrowly. Implied in that last obligation is a reciprocal one from that state to assist those with insufficient resources by assuming responsibility for the building or monument, partly by grant-aiding its repair or wholly by taking it into guardianship. Because the laws and measures for assistance (and technical guidance) have 'just growed' and because they are based for the most part on qualitative judgements, few of the responsibilities, especially those from the state to the individual in terms of financial help, are absolute. In fact a good deal of bluff is involved, for enforcement is difficult in many cases. The planning law may sensibly require reinstatement of a building, even a wall, illegally demolished. But

since reinstatement of a historic edifice is impossible, and only a facsimile may be created once the original is destroyed, this sanction is seldom enforced. It is also extremely difficult for courts to impose genuinely deterrent fines when the profit from the demolition of an inconveniently sited old building can run into millions of pounds. Not surprisingly, therefore, the system of laws and regulations in this area is complex. It is, however, generally effective.

The idea of stopping individuals destroying monuments of interest was long opposed because it conflicted with what was claimed as a basic right, that of property. An Englishman's home is his castle with which, presumably, he may do what he wants. Well, no. Castles were held 'during the monarch's pleasure' and since the monarch and the state were virtually interchangeable the state does have a right to interfere. Sir John Lubbock's Act, passed after a decade of argument, represented the thinnest end of the wedge, since an ancient monument, being unoccupied for the most part, was fairly far removed from the connotations of 'an Englishman's home'. In 1987, however, Lord Hertford was fined £10,000 for ploughing up valuable remains on his land.

As protection gradually became more comprehensive, private houses, even of the humbler sort, predominated numerically. The first statutory list of buildings of special architectural or historic interest, started in 1944, comprised some 90,000 entries throughout Britain. The working hypothesis on which it was based was that any substantially complete pre-1714 building would be included, others depending on quality. A resurvey started in the late 1960s ground slowly on, being augmented by DoE 'spot-listing' of buildings drawn to its attention by local authorities of the opinion that the building was both threatened and of sufficient interest to merit protection. Criteria gradually became less exclusive, particularly after the founding of the Victorian Society in 1958 prompted the inclusion of far more nineteenth-century examples. Since that period had seen more construction than in all previous centuries combined, the number had greatly increased, totalling 367,000 by the end of 1985. Then a faster resurvey was commissioned by the secretary of state after publicity by SAVE and others of the calculation that at its then rate listing would be incomplete until at least 2020. Lists are now virtually complete, and will total under 600,000 entries in Britain as a whole, a large number but still less than 3 per cent of the nation's building stock. In June 1988 the total for England was 418,000, a reduction of some 20,000 because terraces and groups are now counted as one entry. There is an increasing amount of vernacular architecture now, mostly rural, which is quite natural since the country was predominantly agriculturally-based until the industrial revolution of the eighteenth century.

The series of compromises enabling the state to accept responsibility via ownership (and/or monuments guardianship) or grant-giving, is based on the concept 'outstanding'. It is a sensible way to avoid an 'open-ended' commitment, especially as 'outstanding' can be defined on an *ad hoc* basis. Almost half of annual construction expenditure of about £30 billion is spent on repairs and maintenance of existing structures. Assuming that 3 per cent are listed and that these cost twice as much to care for, requiring more careful work than other buildings, then something like £1 billion is spent per annum on listed buildings. The HBMC grant for this purpose is about 1 per cent of that sum. Most listed-building owners have an uneconomic obligation thrust upon them. Most accept it, though only for those living in favoured parts of the country does it attract a financial premium when selling.

District planning authorities can serve a BPN (building preservation notice) on a threatened secular building. Most of these are confirmed by the DoE before the end of the six-months' grace period. If not, under the provisions of the Town and Country Planning Acts of 1971, the owner may be compensated. Once the survey of an area is complete and formally confirmed by the secretary of state, a bound list of protected buildings is issued. The area covered may be for a district, or only part of one depending on how rich the area is in old buildings. These bound lists are sent to relevant district and local councils and sometimes central libraries. Complete sets are kept by the national amenity societies (SPAB, Georgian Group, Victorian Society, Ancient Monuments Society, and Council for British Archaeology). The Royal Commission on Historical Monuments is also a recipient, as is the Civic Trust Library. Loose additions are sent out from time to time. Modifications may occur if a new discovery requires the listing or up-grading of an already listed building, if destruction by fire for example, or illegal demolition of whole or part dictates delisting.

Owners affected are informed. There is not much they can do about listing, there being no formal appeal against it. List descriptions include addresses and a brief summary of the building's features, but non-mention does not mean non-protection. Interior fittings or external structures within the curtilage (that is, normally immediate grounds under the same ownership) are also protected if predating 1948, again whether mentioned or not.

A matter capable of causing confusion is the condition of a listed building; decay is no reason for delisting, nor even for giving consent for demolition. A would-be developer would only have to arrange a fire, flood, or other accident to achieve his ends. Demolition without consent is a criminal offence punishable by fine or even imprisonment – though the last has never been imposed. In 1981 a prosecution was successfully brought by the author, when secretary of the SPAB, against Sir Bruno Welby who had demolished seventeenth-century almshouses described by Pevsner as Artisan Mannerist in style and being among the most 'delightful in England'. Built in 1654 by an ancestor, they remained in a field near the parish church until Sir Bruno received from the local authority a notice of upgrading to Grade II* and a schedule of necessary repairs costing about £14,000. The decoratively carved, modestly sized masonry structure was derelict but capable of repair; many offers had been made to purchase, or even lease it. No doubt Sir Bruno, whose family had dominated the area for several centuries, felt that he was being persecuted by busybodies because an ancestor had been charitable to the local poor. Here the landowner still won in a sense; for apart from the inconvenience of being dubbed a criminal and having to pay a £1,000 fine and £2,000 costs, he saved himself £11,000. The condition of the building, it should be noted, was no bar to a demolition refusal or even a listing upgrading. On the other hand the fact that the owner had ignored grant aid, almost certainly payable for Grade II* building, as well as offers to buy the property exacerbated the offence.

A loophole in the law allows someone caught 'in the act' of 'carrying out unauthorized works to a listed building' to escape arrest. An injunction has to be served. There are three gradings to listing: I, II*, and II in England and Wales; in Scotland A, B, and C. Of the first grade – that is, 'buildings of outstanding interest' – there are only about 5,000; Grade II* buildings are 'particularly important' and number about 20,000; while Grade II buildings, the vast majority, are of 'special interest'.

Anglican churches in use are informally included in the lists, perhaps a subtle sign that their partial exemption from controls is an ephemeral condition. Assorted ingredients of a historic environment also protected include gravestones, bollards, cobbles, early lamp-posts, garden and other boundary walls of importance, sun-

4. The Welby Almshouses, Denton, Lincolnshire, among 'the most delightful in England', said Pevsner; listed Grade II, built 1653, and criminally demolished by the same family in 1981 to save £14,000 repairs*

dials, statues, and about 1,000 of Sir Gilbert Scott's red telephone boxes. To critics of the large and heterogeneous list, Mr Heseltine used to point out that 'protection', especially of the Grade II variety, did not guarantee inviolability, merely that when plans were made there should be a presumption of preservation.

Actual age is rightly significant, since there are far obviously fewer surviving medieval buildings than later ones. There has long been a 'thirty year rule' in Scotland, which was introduced in England in 1987, and recent buildings are now listed. Certainly early modern-movement designs, that is, those by *emigré* architects from Nazi Germany such as Gropius, or their handful of British followers, are rare and eminently listable. So are those by such disparate but gifted interwar engineers and architects as Sir Owen Williams or Sir Edwin Lutyens. So now are outstanding 1950s, even 1960s, buildings as disparate as Sir Albert Richardson's stripped-down classical Bracken House (Grade II*) and Sir Leslie Martin's Royal Festival Hall (Grade I). These decisions were undisputed, but recent efforts to obtain listing for Erno Goldfinger's interesting but unpopular Alexander Fleming House, at the apalling Elephant and Castle roundabout, a nadir of postwar planning and architecture, were unsuccessful.

Another recent initiative has been the publication of a *Register of Parks and Gardens of Special Historic Interest* in England by the HBMC. It is advisory, with no legal powers, and is chiefly intended to 'deter destruction by ignorance'. Practical and philosophical objections to the system which 'freezes' buildings at a particular point in their history have weight. The result is to value alterations and additions of the past that have made the building the thing now protected, but to allow no more. To attempt to fossilize gardens at a moment in time would be absurd.

A little-known provision of recent times is that of 'non-listability'. At the

same time as seeking planning approval, a would-be developer (or anyone else) can apply for a certificate of immunity from listing which is valid for five years, sufficient time for him to complete the development. It was regarded as somewhat unfair for a BPN, leading to spot-listing, to be slapped unexpectedly on a building on a site for which a detailed redevelopment scheme had been designed and negotiated, possibly expensively and exhaustively over several years. But, as Matthew Saunders points out, 'as many as half the buildings drawn to the attention of the Department under this procedure have been listed – so it is certainly double edged'.[2]

Under the Ancient Monuments and Archaeological Areas Act (1979), which came into effect in 1981, an owner wishing to alter or destroy a scheduled monument must apply for Scheduled Monument Consent from the DoE. Since legislation on ancient monuments preceded that for historic buildings confusion tended to arise in the case of those major historic buildings which were both scheduled and listed – half a century ago it was commonplace to refer to old buildings as 'monuments'. The monuments procedure, older and formerly less restrictive, had precedence. Now scheduling is generally used for the protection of archaeological sites, and buildings have been descheduled in many cases, so there is less overlap.

The number of scheduled sites, some 13,000, is small, a surprising fact considering the many hundreds of ancient settlements and burial sites, barrows in Dorset, and stone rings and village remains on Dartmoor which have been destroyed in recent years. A current resurvey will include about 60,000 sites.

The government is wary about accepting the open-ended commitment of 'guardianship'. HBMC is itself responsible for the maintenance of about 400 monuments and public access to them. For some years before the Commission came into being in April 1984 there was a backlog of structures agreed to be of guardianship quality which the DoE felt unable to take over because of shortage of funds. Such was the case with the vast medieval barn at Boxley Abbey in Kent; now it would probably be listed rather than scheduled anyway.

A radical widening of the protection concept was evolved by Duncan Sandys and incorporated in his Civic Amenities Act of 1967, namely that of the 'conservation area'. This involves the idea that charm and even historic interest in a group of buildings, perhaps as much as a whole village, may be identified even though few if any of them are listable. Also that the cumulative effect of their interrelation, the homogeneity of scale, style, date, and social origin, may be worthy of protection, which will also imply attempts to retain the setting in terms of 'streetscape' and landscape – that is, railings, paving, trees, and such like. The group may simply be pretty or, in a city, impressive. In any case designation is the prerogative of district councils, although the DoE could, exceptionally, cancel an order. There are now over 6,000 conservation areas. Historic centres of cities such as Bath, York, and Chichester and much of the City of London are so protected, as in Hampstead Garden Suburb (which does not seem to preclude its bisection by a main road) and the workers' village of Silver End in Essex (see p. 117), built in the 1920s and 1930s by Messrs Crittall.

Controls are limited, grants even more so. In fact conservation-area declaration is not without its element of bluff. Small structures (under 115 cu. metres) may be added or demolished under the general 'permitted development' provisions favoured by the present government to reduce bureaucracy. This is not helpful to a conservation area, the character of which often derives from the sum of small parts. Demolition as such requires 'conservation area consent' however – apart from redundant Anglican churches. Permission may well be forthcoming if an acceptable design for a replacement is submitted at the same time, technically an irrelevance in the case of a listed building.

If the character of a conservation area derives from uniformity of external finish and detailing, these may need to be controlled under the provisions of an 'Article 4 direction', permission for which the local authority may obtain from the DoE. Such is the case at Silver End. Control is exercised over major landscape alterations, tree-lopping for example. An Article 4 direction suspends permitted development rights under the 'general development order' of 1980 which allowed the construction of domestic extensions, conservatories, and garages, for example, not exceeding 15 per cent of the existing floor area of the dwelling (except in the case of listed buildings of course).

Applications to demolish 'in whole or in part', to extend or alter so as to affect the character of a listed building materially – inside or outside – must be made to the local planning authority. Neighbours must be alerted to the proposals by the display for twenty-one days of a notice on site and by an advertisement in the local paper. Local authorities may be influenced in their decision by objections from individuals or amenity groups. Five

5. Barlaston Hall, Staffs, a red brick Palladian design of the 1750s by Sir Robert Taylor. Damaged by coal mining, neglected by the owners, fought over at public inquiry and during protracted compensation discussions, this large villa is being repaired and converted to housing by a SAVE sponsored trust with notable English Heritage support

voluntary organizations, as well as the Royal Commission on Historical Monuments, must be consulted 'and their views taken into account'. These views, reported to the planning committee at the time of decision, can be significant if the applicant appeals against refusal and the secretary of state decides to 'call in' the application for public inquiry. The six organizations are those already listed, namely SPAB, GG, Vixoc, AMS, CBA, and RCHM, the last named having the opportunity to record the building before any agreed works commence. In Scotland the statutory consultees are the Scottish Civic Trust and the Scottish Architectural Heritage Society. These bodies may make representations, usually against consent but occasionally in favour if they consider an imaginative series of proposals may not be appreciated by a local committee of council. Normally a site visit will have helped them to reach a decision, but quite frequently a perusal of the papers is enough, for quite a lot of applications are 'benign' in that they may involve the removal of a pre-fabricated garage, for example, which is bound to improve the setting of an old building.

English Heritage (HBMC) also has to be informed if the building concerned in an application is Grade I or II*, or has

been grant-aided by central government. If the local authority is minded to grant consent, the HBMC has again to be informed. Whereas the local authority should normally determine cases within two months, the department can take three times as long. This also applies when an applicant appeals to the secretary of state against a local authority decision.

An inquiry is frequently conducted in a day or two, but contentious and complicated issues such as those concerning motorways, nuclear power stations, or even prominent buildings such as those proposed for demolition on the Mansion House Square site, can take months and cost a fortune. The last is because most participants find it impossible to resist briefing the most distinguished lawyers available although legal representation is not in fact necessary. The department issues a guidance leaflet on inquiry procedure. Inquiries are heard by inspectors appointed by the secretary of state, usually former architects, planners, or others from related professions. They usually favour an orderly although informal process; but with lawyers opposing each other a courtroom atmosphere is inevitable.

The inspector reports to the secretary of state after some weeks or months, depending on the complexity of matters at issue. The minister can and sometimes does come to a decision contrary to that recommended by his appointee.

Decisions remain valid for five years. Implementation may be conditional on planning approval being obtained for a replacement building. On too many occasions in the past permission for demolition has reluctantly been given after a hard-fought case and then the site has remained empty for years, albeit more valuable being vacant. If consent is refused, or is granted with conditions, the landowner may serve a 'purchase notice' on the local authority, claiming that the land has 'become incapable of reasonably beneficial use' in its existing state. The DoE is again the arbitrator.

For many years local councils unsympathetic to all but outstanding conservation cases (and that was the majority of councils before about 1975) made enthusiastic use of 'dangerous structures notices' (DSNs) to get rid of inconveniently sited old buildings. Council-owned, council-neglected, then council-condemned was all too frequently the fate of listed structures impeding redevelopment. A building does not need to be neglected for many years before grounds can be discovered for declaring it unsafe, or at the very least unfit for habitation. A classic case occurred in 1977 in Exeter where the city council condemned and destroyed seventeenth- and eighteenth-century listed houses in Magdalen Street, containing particularly rare plasterwork, which it had originally bought (and then neglected) in connection with what even the local newspaper called 'megalomaniac' traffic schemes.

In 1980 a High Court decision involving 57–62 High Street, Stroud, a handsome row of seventeenth-century stone buildings which local conservationists had long sought to save from a vandalistic council, made it clear that local authorities should try to ensure that danger is removed by methods other than demolition. Even after that some local authorities hardly leaned over backwards in their efforts to prop up and repair, rather than pull down precarious structures. Such was the case with the part-medieval Bull Inn at Burford after a fire. That caused a furore because local and national conservation societies were almost as quick to get architects and engineers to the site as the council got its surveyors. The former, of course, recommended much less drastic action than was enforced by the council. The Bull incidentally exposed another unfortunate fact of life too, namely the acute difficulty in commissioning established local professionals who are willing to risk alienating determined council officers. In 1986 the Housing and Planning Act removed the right to demolish after the serving of a DSN unless listed building consent was also obtained. Local authorities also have positive powers to help preserve listed buildings. Under section 101 of the 1971 Town and Country Planning Act (section 97 of the Scottish Act) urgent work can be carried out on neglected listed buildings or those in conservation areas provided that they are unoccupied, and in 1986 the provisions were extended to unoccupied parts of occupied structures. Such technical modifications of legislation can be of considerable effect. The cost of such repairs, which should be the minimum necessary, can be recovered from owners, subject to their means being adequate. Under section 115 of the 1971 Act repairs notices may be served whether or not the listed building is occupied. But this notice merely specifies necessary works, and enforcement in the event of non-compliance can only be secured by the threat of compulsory purchase. Under section 114 (104 in Scotland) the secretary of state confirms the compulsory purchase and, if he is convinced that neglect was deliberate, can specify a low price. Naturally these procedures are rarely applied since councils are not eager to be the owners of decayed listed buildings, but in 1988 a compulsory purchase order was confirmed for Sir John Soane's last house, the Grade II* Pell Wall Hall, Shropshire, *c.* 1822.

The secretary of state has power to serve a repairs notice himself but has done so only once, in the case of the Grade I Barlaston Hall in Staffordshire. He can also compulsorily purchase, but has never done so. In 1988 Nicholas Ridley, through the agency of HBMC, served a £90,000 repairs notice on Revesby Abbey, Lincolnshire, a Grade I house of the 1840s.

Although it is customary to discuss laws in absolute terms, they are simply means to ends which are subject to modification as policies evolve, and can also fall into disuse or be interpreted more or less strictly depending on local or national objectives. It has been suggested here that

provisions regarding dangerous structures were sometimes used to speed developments which councils saw as being in the broader public interest. So it has been with 'changes of use' for which it was necessary to apply for planning permission according to the original 1947 Act and the 1971 and later revisions. This is still the case, but local authorities, following guidance from the DoE, are now far more likely to approve such applications where a new future for a listed building is in the balance. Presumption is now in favour of permission being granted, unless excessive development in the countryside, or excessive traffic, for example, is thought likely.

It is a matter of priorities. In the postwar period the priority was enforcement of zoning of uses as indicated on official plans, more recently the priority has been to avoid loss of old rural buildings or, indeed, large redundant industrial structures in inner cities. The pendulum swings; now that hardly a single disused and unconverted barn can be bought in southern England for less than £100,000 there is pressure from local residents being priced out of the housing market for permissions to be less readily granted again. Perhaps other uses such as light industrial, information technology, educational or tourist conversions will find more favour. Certainly the supply of redundant farm buildings in parts of the country other than the south-east is likely to remain plentiful, despite the reduction in farm labour in Britain to below 3 per cent of the population, the lowest figure in Europe. The processes of agricultural mechanization and the amalgamation of holdings may have run their course, but there is now pressure to reduce production.

The emphasis of controls should now be to try and ensure appropriate and skilful conversions so that a fine timber-framed barn, for example, should retain something of its 'barn-ness' even though it has become something else. Otherwise there is no point in 'saving' it. To legislate for taste, which is inclined to change, has always been difficult, and the North Yorkshire National Park Authority has now put a ban on the conversion of barns.

Chapter 3

Paying
for
conservation

*Kedleston Hall,
Derbyshire: the
National Heritage
Memorial Fund
has preserved this
Robert Adam
masterpiece*

There is a new breed of 'conservation entrepreneur' skilled at assembling money as well as arguments. That money may come from many directions; increasingly as adaptive reuse of redundant buildings has become both popular and profitable funds from what is called 'the City' – that is, banks, insurance companies, and pension funds – have been made available. But this chapter will concentrate on the considerable variety of grants which can with luck and skill be dug out of the public purse. A basic requirement, apart from a house in bad structural repair and/or lacking basic services, is an exceptional building, or group of buildings. Usually that means they have Grade I or II* listing, as although English Heritage grants have gone to other buildings for which a case of 'outstanding interest' has been made, they are very few. If agreed to be grant-worthy they are normally upgraded. The vast majority of the country's almost half-million Grade IIs will receive no historic buildings grant. But they may if they happen to be in one of the 6,000 or so conservation areas, the 200-plus town schemes, the twenty-three programme towns, the twenty-eight Civic Trust regeneration project towns, are under the wing of a Historic Buildings Preservation Trust, are eligible for an Architectural Heritage Fund grant, or are in one of the local authority areas which give discretionary grants or loans towards the repair of historic buildings.

A single building, especially if sited in a run-down urban area, may be eligible for several different grants. In fact those responsible for repairing and reusing a major structure such as the Royal Agricultural Hall or Billingsgate Market in London, a city neighbourhood such as Canning in Liverpool, the Victorian textile area of Calderdale, a whole town such as Wirksworth, or a village like Saltaire, will find themselves putting together a complex public/private package of finance. Before 1975 'planning gain', whereby a developer could refurbish a

historic building as part of a bargain with a local authority which included valuable planning permission, was rather more likely to be negotiated than today. Both before and since then housing corporation finance might play a role. More recently building societies, especially the Abbey National, have seen it as part of their responsibility to help in particular run-down areas. There might even be a tourist board grant.

Not only does the grants entrepreneur need to know his way round all the multifarious sources, he also needs to have finely tuned public-affairs antennae. Conservation impact and political expediency are close allies. The £7 million of 'pump-priming' finance to drain the Albert Dock, carry out major exterior repairs, and overcome the city council's inertia seemed only a distant hope until a 'minister for Merseyside' was appointed following the Toxteth riots. Thereafter the public/private package, a particular feature of the 1980s, fell into place.

Aware of the multitude of possible sources of finance for the repair of historic buildings, English Heritage published a *Directory of Public Sources of Grants for the Repair and Conversion of Historic Buildings* in 1988. The following is a summary of the functions of these and other grant-giving bodies.

Historic Buildings and Monuments Commission for England

This gives English Heritage grants, equivalent ones being given by the secretaries of state on the advice of the Historic Buildings Councils for Scotland, Wales, and Northern Ireland. HBMC was set up under the National Heritage Act 1983, and assumed the roles of the Historic Buildings Council and of the Ancient Monuments Board in England on 1 April

1984. The Scottish and Welsh HBCs and AMSs function as before under the 1953 Act. 'English Heritage', to use HBMC's popular title, is intended to be 'an independent body devoted to the conservation and presentation of England's inheritance of ancient monuments and historic buildings'.[3] The commission is a curious hybrid: it has taken over some of the DoE's responsibilities, for example the care of some 400 monuments (but not the Royal Palaces and the Tower of London), it advises the DoE on some of the secretary of state's statutory powers including listing, scheduling, and calling-in for public inquiry, and, most particularly, it offers grants. To an extent it is 'independent'; it can for example object to local-authority decisions and it can argue its case at public inquiries, yet its income is largely derived from government grant-in-aid.

That grant was £62.5 million in 1986–7 out of a total of £66.5 million; the rest came from admission charges to properties, sales, and members' subscriptions. An increase over the previous year's income was allowed in order to cover the assumption of former GLC responsibilities, the care of Osborne House and, in the sum of £2 million, from the government's urban programme, the Merseyside special scheme. In approximate terms expenditure was divided as follows: nearly £31 million 'operational costs' (including salaries of the 1,445 employees), £19 million historic-buildings grants taken up (£21.4 million was offered), and £8 million on works to monuments in care, the balance being grants to owners of ancient monuments and the ex-GLC expenditure, the Osborne House and Merseyside programmes, rescue archaeology and management agreements for monuments.

Monuments

In 1986–7 fifty-three grants totalling £1.3 million were offered to monuments under section 24 of the Ancient Monuments and Archaeological Areas Act of 1979. The standard rate of grant is 40 per cent. In 1985–6 the largest were £117,000 to the Berwick ramparts, Northumberland, and £98,000 to the Ballast Pound, in Cornwall. As Britain's estimated 60,000 ancient monuments are, by definition, inappropriate subjects for conversion to new uses, there need be no further discussion on that topic. Regarding archaeology, it might be of interest to note the greatly increased figure in 1986–7 for rescue projects, the pace of redevelopment in the City of London and elsewhere having provided a record number of once-and-for-all opportunities to discover Roman, Saxon, and medieval remains.

Historic Building Repair Grants were divided as follows: £9.1 million for secular buildings of outstanding interest; £5.3 million for places of worship in use; £2.6 million for town schemes; £4.2 million for conservation areas; £0.2 million for conservation of contents and acquisitions.

Outstanding historic buildings

These are covered by the National Heritage Act, 1983, Section 3A and last year attracted 245 offers of grant totalling £9.1 million, the average grant being £34,000. Applicants can be private, public, or corporate, and should normally have owned the building for four years although this 'new purchase' rule was eased in April 1988. They may have to supply details of their finances. They must not have started the work in question, and the essence of allowable work will consist of structural repairs, but survey costs and consultants fees are allowable.

As has been stated the buildings will normally have been designated Grade I or II*. There must be some form of public access; this means, according to the ETB's *English Heritage Monitor,* that they are open to the public for a minimum of twenty-eight days a year (56 per cent), that they are open by appointment (27 per cent), or that they are open by reason of their function as hotels or theatres, market buildings, etc. (16 per cent).

The largest single grant in 1986–7 was £1 million for Calke Abbey, followed by £368,000 for the Palace Theatre in London (which has been bought and refurbished by Andrew Lloyd Webber), £250,000 for Dunston Staithes, the largest waterside coal wharf ever built on the Tyne, £215,000 for the library of Lincolns Inn, £200,000 for Tottenham House, Savernake, £200,000 for Ugbrooke Park, Devon, £143,000 for Christchurch, Cosway Street, London, £143,000 for Cawood Castle, Selby, £140,000 for Crowcombe Court, Somerset, and £131,000 for Dyrham Park, Avon. That list is instructive in that the traditional historic-building type, the major country house, still dominates, that new uses barely figure, and that the most skilled assemblers of grants are, not unnaturally, those such as the National Trust who have a lot of practice. HBMC is far from unimaginative in its offers – from cottages to railway stations, engineering structures

6. *Cable Street, London, 1978, an early project financed from one of the most capacious pockets – that of the Housing Corporation*

7. *Chepstow Castle, Monmouthshire, an outstanding monument in the care of 'Welsh Historic Monuments' (Cadw). Like its equivalent English Heritage Cadw feels the need to 'interpret' such buildings to visitors*

to windmills. The one-off owner and repairer of a historic building often needs guidance around the maze of provisions.

One of these is that if a building is quickly sold repayment can be demanded although it seldom is. The fact is that this provision is essentially designed to discourage profiteers looking for a quick turnaround of their investment. Unfortunately it has discouraged some very scrupulous and appropriate recipients for applying. The owner of the splendid and eccentric late-Elizabethan Chastleton House in Oxfordshire long resisted applying, despite encouragement from the former HBC, for this very reason. Another condition capable of variation, albeit rarely, is the limitation of grant to 40 per cent of 'allowable works' (25 per cent for local authorities). In cases of outstanding merit or dire need more can be paid, if only by the construction of a 'grants package' as in the case for Canning Street, Liverpool, where occupiers or landlords have been grant-aided to the extent of 85 per cent.

State aid for churches in use

This has been available to church buildings other than cathedrals for ten years and is increasingly seen, as for example in HBMC's annual report, as the ecclesiastical side of the outstanding historic buildings grant system. In 1986–7 403 grants were given totalling £5.3 million (a marked increase over the previous year's £4.4 million). Nearly one-third of the value of grants was concentrated in London, Suffolk, and Norfolk. The biggest grant was £150,000 for St James's Southwark, followed by £132,500 for the Roman Catholic Church of the Annunciation, Woodchester, Gloucestershire, £120,000 for St Mary, Brome, Suffolk, £90,500 for St Cuthbert, Kensington, and £74,000 for All Saints, Kilham, Humb-

erside. The average size of grant at £11,600 was much smaller than for secular buildings. Forty per cent of allowable works was again standard, and again, by definition, these grants are inappropriate for conversions to new uses, which can receive grants as 'secular buildings'.

Town scheme grants

There were 1,559 town scheme grants in 1986–7, also an increase over previous years. Grants are offered for individual buildings, but since the essence of this idea, as enshrined in section 10B of the 1972 Town and Country Planning Act is to upgrade groups of buildings, the more relevant figure is the 200-odd current schemes. Grants, which are administered by local authorities, are for structural repairs, usually external. The average grant from HBMC in 1986–7 was £1,552, and of the £2.6 million allocated to the scheme only £1.8 million was taken up. Expenditure always lags behind grant offers. The central-government grant is equalled by another 25 per cent of eligible costs from the local authority (either county or district) with 50 per cent coming from the owner, so a certain amount of co-ordination is required to get the average £6,210 contract under way. All the current town schemes are in conservation areas. One of the earliest and most ambitious town schemes was that set up in 1979 to preserve Georgian Edinburgh's 'New Town', which was granted £250,000 that year. Scottish public provision in many conservation fields is much more generous than English equivalents, grants varying between 60 and 85 per cent of comprehensive repair costs. In 1986–7 the largest English grants were £145,486 for Spitalfields, London, £117,500 for Bath, £106,000 for Shrewsbury, £104,700 for Cheltenham, £103,180 for Brighton and £89,835 for Canterbury.

Conservation areas

Of the 6,000-odd conservation areas about one-third have received grants under section 10 of the 1972 Act. Both outstanding groups of buildings in conservation areas and work contributing to the enhancement of the appearance of the area may be grant-assisted. Eligible works are much less limited than under section 10A and can, indeed, be complementary. For example costs of repairs as well as of conversions are allowed. The reinstatement of traditional materials intrinsic to the local character – which is after all most of the point of a conservation area – may be grant-aided. In the usual case they are more expensive than modern alternatives. Thus in 1987 the Ryders Wynd in Richmond, North Yorkshire, was recobbled with a £75,000 grant. Stone roof tiles were put back in Barnack in Cambridgeshire and Barnard Castle in Durham with help through block grants from local authorities.

In 1986–7 544 grants were offered, actual expenditure was £4.4 million. The biggest contributions tended to go to inner-city areas with social as well as repair problems: Liverpool (£346,550), Bristol (£215,440), Lambeth (£121,850), Norwich (£103,400), Newcastle (£100,000), Gloucester (£100,000), Kings Lynn (£100,000), Bradford (£90,100), Leeds (£76,970), and Halifax (£72,000).

Some £2 million of the section 10 budget was allocated to twenty-three 'programme towns'. Included in this 'special need' category was Maryport, once a coal port, Regency Cheltenham and the nineteenth-century textile area of Calderdale. Combining these section 10 grants with urban programme grants English Heritage spent some £1.1 million in the Canning conservation area in Liverpool 8 in 1986–7, some grants being as high as 85 per cent of works. As Michael Pearce calculates in *Conservation, a Credit Account*, published by SAVE, these section-10 grants are an indirect means whereby the largest proportion of Grade II buildings, perhaps 55,000, or 15 per cent of the total, are likely to find themselves eligible for grants. Otherwise the only other hope for 'non-outstanding buildings' is from local authorities which, under the Local Authorities (Historic Buildings) Act of 1962, spent some £9 million in England on grants or loans in 1986–7. The Greater London Council, no longer in existence at that date, had been comparatively generous, as was its successor section at English Heritage, offering 193 grants costing £2.5 million. The highest local-authority spenders are Hampshire, Birmingham, Norwich, Bristol, Kent, Chester, Cheltenham, Bath, Wolverhampton and Brighton. But local-authority grants are discretionary and really are a matter of luck: some councils give none (see the SAVE 1988 Survey).

National Heritage Memorial Fund

This government agency is responsible for the largest grants, although a comparatively small number of them. Re-established in 1980, and run independently of government by trustees, it steps in where circumstances are leading to a national asset beng at risk. Following the Mentmore fiasco (see p. 126), an important debate in the House of Lords and a select committee report, the dismembered corpse of the National Land Fund was exhumed in April 1980. Conceived by Hugh Dalton after the Second World War and then endowed with some £50 million proceeds from the sale of military surplus materials, the Land Fund had been intended to buy beauty spots and buildings as a memorial to the war dead. It was inactive for some years, perhaps partly because its founding minister had meanwhile been disgraced, and also because postwar Britain, building for a progressive future as symbolized by the

1951 Festival on London's south bank, did not care to look back to history. And the postwar building boom had barely shown signs of threatening the country-side. The fund was plundered of most of its assets in 1952 by Enoch Powell, then a junior Treasury minister. Only £12.4 million remained to go to the NHMF in 1980.

The remit of the reconstituted fund has been broad and, under the lively chair-manship of Lord Charteris, quick-footed, as is appropriate for its purpose. It closed the 1982–3 financial year with more than £26 million, having spent or promised £10 million for specific projects. Its balances fluctuate rapidly as needs arise. In 1985 it received a special grant of £25 million to 'save' Kedleston, Weston, and Nostell Priory. £3 million was originally allocated for the year 1987–8, and in December 1987 there was an additional 'top-up' grant of £20 million. In the event, spend-ing in the year up to March 1988 was £9.5 million compared with £37.7 million the previous year.

Recipients of grants, always for a specific pressing need, are usually organ-izations like the National Trust, building preservation trusts, and museums. 'Grants' are referred to but in fact NHMF can also provide loans or endow-ments as the case requires. So fund donations have helped to buy a Scottish peat bog, to lift the *Mary Rose* and restore the bells of Durham Cathdral, to repair Captain Scott's *Discovery*, to buy the Grand Theatre, Blackpool, and also to buy the Manchester Spanish and Por-tuguese synagogue for conversion to a Jewish museum. In 1987–8 Memorial Fund historic building grants have included £170,000 for Temple Cressing medieval complex in Essex, £125,000 towards the Ironbridge Gorge Museum, £43,220 for Brighton's west pier, £33,250 for Clevedon's pier (which has had a total of £637,000) and Temple Meads Station, Bristol, which received £21,750.

Architectural Heritage Fund

A quite distinct source of finance but one capable of confusion with that discussed above is the Architectural Heritage Fund. Growing out of European Architectural Heritage Year 1975, it is now a non-profit-making company registered as a charity having been run from the first by the Civic Trust. Essentially the AHF consists of a revolving fund providing low-interest loans to ease the cash flow of local building preservation trusts. Loans are usually quickly repaid, often in as little as two years. Of £6.4 million lent in support of 144 projects up to March 1988, £4.4 million had been repaid.

The buildings assisted by the AHF are usually of modest scale and have recently included the restoration of a sixteenth-century manor house in north Yorkshire and a seventeenth-century house in Chip-penham, Wiltshire, repair and conversion of the north range of college buildings at Ely Cathedral, and the conversion into maisonettes of a nineteenth-century stable block in Prestwich, Greater Man-chester. The heritage centre in Wirks-worth and Marden House, Calne, have also been assisted (see p. 67 and p. 73).

Other public schemes

After exhausting the catalogue of 'heri-tage' grants in general – and apart from those mentioned there are a dozen or so private charitable trusts although it should be noted that they cannot assist private houses[4] – it is worth exploring those many government schemes the object of which is job creation, housing provision and economic regeneration in general but an important side effect of which is often building refurbishment. Funds available for these purposes are of an altogether different scale to those available specifically for historic-building repairs. One such source which should be approached with great caution is the subsidizing of labour under various manpower services schemes. Work on historic fabric requires skill and delicacy especially in the case of churches, for example, where funds are likely to be so short that any assistance is welcomed. Sometimes untrained labour paid for by the Manpower Services Commission (MSC), supervised with insufficient care, has done more harm than good. The first matter to settle is that of skilled and virtually constant supervision. The greatest difficulty may well be in finding the suitably qualified foreman or clerk of works, although this can be grant-aided. An early example of the less than totally successful employment of MSC people was at St Pancras Station in London. A GLC stone-cleaning programme resulted in erosion of soft sandstone bands by 'run-off' from the harder and more acid areas of limestone with excessive use of water-cleaning methods. On the other hand, the MSC's community programme is ideal for environmental improvements. In 1987 the National Trust had 314 schemes in operation, mainly for estate work, and 3,900 people put in about 540,000 man-days. As from May 1986 the programme has provision for 230,000 places each year for the long-term unemployed.

Grants are also available, in particular places, from tourist boards, the Sports Council, the Countryside Commission, and the Council for Small Industries in Rural Areas (COSIRA). COSIRA assists conversion of redundant buildings in villages and towns with less than 10,000 population in its 'priority areas', which are chiefly in northern, western, and eastern counties. The Countryside Commission grant-aids the conversion of disused rural buildings where recreational purposes are appropriate, for example country parks.

The English Tourist Board, as might be expected, assists the conversion of structures for the provision of tourist attractions and facilities. 'Presentational purposes' are the board's priority, rather than the actual repair of historic building fabric. But recent examples include the conversion of Llantony Warehouse, Gloucester Docks, to the National Waterways Museum with a £120,000 grant, the refurbishment of the seventeenth-century Flitwick Manor, a hotel in Bedfordshire (£36,000 grant), and the restoration of Newcastle's Theatre Royal (£178,000 grant).

The Sports Council encourages the reuse of buildings for sports, which may be particularly suitable for large structures, especially churches or chapels, where subdivision is undesirable. There are no set criteria for grants, and approaches are best made through the council's regional offices.

All the foregoing sources of finance pale into insignificance when compared with monies from long-established Housing Act provisions and more recently from the DoE-administered urban programme. The aim of attracting private finance by the injection of sizeable, but still smaller, sums of grant to get regeneration schemes in run-down inner-city areas off the ground has been very successful. Indeed urban development grants can be immensely generous

8. Wilton's Music Hall, London, still incomplete after ten years of struggle and expenditure of some £700,000 by the GLC, LDDC, and English Heritage. A trust was on the point of securing a lease at the time of the abolition of the GLC

despite the requirement that applications have to be channelled through local authorities. The Business Design Centre in Islington, for example, managed to attract a UDG of £2.85 million – a great deal for a single project. In 1986 the DoE introduced 'urban regeneration grants' which were paid direct to the private sector. A total of 314 schemes have been approved under UDG and URG with £191 million in public money bringing in £777 million in private investment. The DoE's 'Action for Cities' office claims 33,437 jobs and 8,852 homes as the product of the urban programme up to August 1988, with 1,533 acres of land reclaimed in the process. Two recent conversion schemes in Nottingham are described in Chapter 4.

In March 1988 a new system of 'city grants' was announced to replace UDGs and URGs, intended to simplify procedures with quicker decisions direct from the department. In the ensuing six months five city grant schemes have been approved with £5.2 million of grant securing £14 million of private investment. Now all applications are direct to the DoE or the Scottish or Welsh offices.

The government's housing programme is on a larger scale still. Although a decreasing proportion of funds for new building is being channelled through the local authorities, councils do administer the 'home improvement grant' system. There are four different types: 'Intermediate grants' for basic amenities such as inside toilet, bath, sink, handbasin, and hot/cold water; 'repair grants' for necessary structural work on walls, roof, or foundations of houses built before 1919; 'improvement grants' for major works, especially the creation of new dwellings by conversion; and 'special grants' which go to landlords to assist in upgrading houses in multi-occupation. Naturally there are conditions and variations influenced by rateable values and allowable expenses, and these are modified from time to time and also depend on locality. Grants are higher in London and where

9. Agricultural Hall, Islington, a success in most terms. Despite dereliction, government inner city grants, together with private finance. have transformed this apparent lost cause

a building is listed. Information should be sought from local authorities.

Housing grants are funded by the DoE or the Scottish or Welsh Offices, as are most sources mentioned above, directly or indirectly, apart from the local-authority discretionary grants or loans under the 1962 Act. There is one supra-national source, however, which has so far not been fully exploited, namely the European Community. In 1987 and 1988 an EC fund for conservation of architectural heritage made £1 million available. Two UK projects assisted were at Whitchurch Silk Mill, Hampshire, and at Cressing Temple, Witham, where the Essex County Council has bought the 20-acre site of the Knights Templar containing several medieval buildings including two fine barns.

Building preservation trusts

There are many routes for the grants entrepreneur to explore. One, presuming his prime motive is charitable rather than directed towards profit – both perfectly respectable motives for repairing and reusing old buildings – is the establishment of a building preservation trust (BPT). Historically, however, these owe most to support from local authorities, both in original funding and even in secondment of staff. As Matthew Saunders points out[5] some trusts predate the Second World War, notably in Bath (founded 1934), Blackheath (1938), and the Cambridgeshire Cottage Improvement Society (1938 with SPAB support) but growth in numbers was spectacular following the availability of loans from the Architectural Heritage Fund in 1976. Loans from the fund seldom cover more than half of the cost of any single project and charities have proved valuable supporters, especially the Pilgrim, Carnegie, Monument, Dulverton, Manifold, Rowntree, and Chase charitable trusts.

There are some sixty BPTs, covering anything from a building type to a county – or, since 1985, the nation – the British Building Preservation Trust was set up then. They usually operate on the revolving principle: having bought and repaired a building, they then sell it on with covenants to try and ensure long-term protection. There is a lack of enthusiasm on the part of local councils who find themselves with long-term responsibility for 'problem buildings' in decay. The reason for this situation is usually redundancy of council premises, but local authorities can find themselves unwilling owners as a result of the service of, and non-compliance with, repairs notices. Compulsory purchase for abandoned road or clearance schemes was a frequent cause in the past. In such cases the existence of a BPT willing to take on a listed building of interest may be a godsend. Indeed an owner has been known to unload a burdensome building not only free of charge but with a capital sum. Such was the case with Ladybellgate House, which was conveyed to Gloucester Historic Buildings Ltd, a creation of the local civic trust, by the Post Office along with a £50,000 dowry. In divesting itself of responsibility for Liverpool Road Station, Manchester – the earliest railway building in the world, now a museum – British Rail also donated £250,000.

It would be unrealistic to ignore the effect of campaigns mounted by local conservationists, with or without support from SAVE Britain's Heritage or another national body, in persuading public owners of unused historic properties of the wisdom of making them over to trusts. Local newspaper stories – better still, national rows – can embarrass public utilities into the advantages of generosity.

Chapter 4
Inner-city
Renewal

*St Pancras
Station Hotel,
Scott's grand
stair, soon to
be used by
hotel guests
once again*

Introduction

Throughout the 1960s accounts of decay and depopulation of the downtowns of American cities filtered across the Atlantic. Twin effects of almost universal car ownership in the United States rendered inner areas congested and polluted and outer suburbs accessible, so encouraging at least the middle classes to migrate outwards. City blocks became either the run-down, lawless, and vandalized ghetto for the underprivileged or else the more profitable and easily policed parking lot. Shopping and leisure facilities followed commuters out of town. Such public-planning interventions as there were, usually city or federal clearance and low-income housing projects based on simplistic zoning policies, produced vast single-use, single-class, uniformly designed precincts which, as Jane Jacobs pointed out in her influential book *The Death and Life of Great American Cities* achieved none of the rich, many-layered mix of people and functions which not only characterizes but actually defines the traditional 'city'.

This experience was known and largely ignored by British planners. At the beginning of the 1960s Colin Buchanan had published a report, *Traffic in Towns,* proposing segregation of people and cars, not uninfluenced by Le Corbusier's 'ville radieuse' and other published ideagrams, but in towns it was the cars which were to inherit the earth and pedestrians who were to move on upper-level walkways and decks. Such ideas, together with the 'zoning away' of admittedly often noisome factories and workshops and the subsidized relocation of employment and subsidized 'slum' clearance and relocation of housing, effectively destroyed many inner cities by attacking both the fabric and the economic base at once. By another awful concatenation of circumstances redevelopment coincided with a period of building austerity and architectural ineptitude. The large-scale and shoddy redevelopment of inner Liverpool, Glasgow, Newcastle, and Birmingham, inspired by public idealism and later aided – but not much in those places – by private speculation, produced the less-than-inspired results we know. Many buildings may individually have been inexpensive, but total investment was huge. To it should be added the costs, both direct and indirect, of locating industry in the regions. It was not that the great northern and midland cities were 'starved of investment', as is sometimes claimed, rather that they had too much public expenditure which was inadequately directed. London and the south-east, which were specifically discriminated against, especially in terms of industrial expansion and infrastructure investment on such items as motorways, suffered proportionately less in the long run.

London and especially the financial quarter, the City, have not been spared the effects of the operation of two other negative factors. The first was an aesthetic and, indeed, almost ideological antipathy to things Victorian which included most of the fabric of inner cities. Thus for a decade or more the Corporation had an official policy of extending the high-level pedestrian walkways of the Barbican and London Wall throughout the City. The planners were quite unabashed at the effect this would have on the stone-built Victorian and Edwardian commercial palazzi which lined most streets. The second is a somewhat contrary effect to most of those described above, namely the tendency of successful cities to renew themselves too quickly. Thus long before bombing obliterated segments of the City, nineteenth-century entrepreneurs had swept away all but a few fragments of late-seventeenth and eighteenth-century buildings. The chief exceptions were those in ecclesiastical hands, an example being the wonderful Deanery of St Paul's which, incredibly, seemed to be in some danger in the early 1980s until more or less sensitively converted to offices.

In vibrant cities neglect even for quite

extended periods is a better preserver than the alternative – redevelopment. In London's docklands, however, the result of a fairly free planning rein and few aesthetic controls, apart from those over listed buildings, has not been quite an architectural triumph, but it has certainly led to much vitality in terms of both new buildings and many acceptable warehouse and other conversions. Thus the government has multiplied the number of such development corporation areas and also established rather smaller planning enterprise zones within existing local authority areas. The justification is the oft-argued blighting effect of long, complicated, expensive, and unpredictable planning processes.

Whatever is liberalized it is important that conservation-area and listed-building controls are excluded. The London Docklands Development Corporation has been reasonably effective in this respect. It is able to be generous in grant terms for at least some of the comparatively modest total of listed buildings in its large area. The City of London has generally been unsuccessful, especially in the conservation areas which, in a latterday change of policy, it declared over much of its territory and which, in less than a decade, have in many cases been so transformed as to be no longer appropriately designated.

It may well be argued that 'inner-city renewal' is usually taken to refer to revival of derelict areas, not the over-development of prosperous ones. But both result in the loss of historic fabric, one more irrevocably than the other. One condition can also follow the other with dizzying rapidity, such as the London Docks and even parts of inner Glasgow. The speed with which Brave New World postwar redevelopment proved not only disastrous but ephemeral has been a shock to many. Again two apparently disparate factors add up to the same results – inadequate buildings from the 1950s and 1960s giving way to better quality new ones. On London Wall the motive for

redevelopment might be booming commerce, on Liverpool and Glasgow's fringes it might be near-destitution in the high-rise housing estates. In one case shoddy glass towers are being replaced with better-built and infinitely better-serviced post-modern blocks, in the other shoddy concrete towers give way to little brick boxes with gardens. Both replacements return to more traditional patterns of ground-level circulation and both tend to employ period architectural motifs to endow the new structures with a comforting sense of historic continuity of the very kind the last generation was trying to escape. Those stylistic topics are discussed elsewhere.

Birmingham may be taken as an example of a city illustrating most of the factors discussed while being at neither extreme in terms of prosperity or destitution. Formerly-fashionable planning concepts wrought as much damage to Birmingham's central area as that of any other city. The loss was chiefly of the 'splendid and bold business premises in such places as New Hall Street' which were the product of the second generation of industrial wealth, according to the current principal development officer who remarked in an article in *The Times* that cities 'renew themselves too quickly'.[6] Only in places like Bath, he continued, where decline follows a period of fashion and prosperity, do old buildings survive for the couple of centuries necessary for them to be admired sufficiently for preservation.

Birmingham's stone-built commercial centre was largely demolished in the 1960s in favour of developments like the Bull Ring, which resemble planners' models built on a giant scale. Developers knew that if they submitted proposals which kept very much to the sort of building envelopes on plans drawn up by the authorities, they were likely to receive planning permission. Hardly ever has a city renewed itself more quickly than Birmingham at present, and the 'new' centre is itself being redeveloped. So are many less well known shopping 'precincts' of the 1960s. Infamous Arndale and other crudely detailed covered malls are giving way to ever more lavish indoor shopping centres some of which, like the famous Metro-Centre at Newcastle, are posing a threat to the viability of the city centre itself because of the attraction of easy access and parking.

Sadly there is no valid way of recreating the canyon-like streets of the City of London which were destroyed in compliance with postwar highway engineers' minimum 32-feet road-width rules. That historic buildings should be destroyed for the sake of drivers' convenience will amaze future generations. Not a great deal can be done to recapture the solid grandeur of the Birmingham merchant city, but the corporation is now determined to protect other once despised parts of the urban area. The best of 1930s suburbia, 150 houses in Hall Green, typical of the half-timbered arcadia which doubled the city's population between the wars, has been declared a conservation area.

The revival of the worst of inner city centres requires a major input of government funds. Urban initiatives from the Home Office, Department of Trade and Industry, and the Departments of the Environment and Transport have recently been co-ordinated as part of a more directed campaign. Discussion of such infrastructure and 'pump-priming' expenditure is best exemplified on the ground in such cities as Glasgow and even Liverpool. That is the subject of the following case studies.

Glasgow

In 1977 a conference lugubriously entitld 'Save Our Cities' dealt in depressing terms with the 'inner-cities crisis' – to use the phrase of one of the participants, Reg Freeson, Minister of Housing. Others there were described as 'leading specialists and administrators in environmental,

housing, health, population, transport and urban affairs together with economists, architects, politicians, bankers, and, especially, representatives of the media'. Very much a seventies collection – apart from the bankers and media,but then the *Sunday Times* was a sponsor. The others were from just the sort of disciplines which had created the 'crisis'. The official account of the proceedings spoke of firms, 'particularly perhaps in Glasgow', which had been casualties of changing postwar industry. But most of them had been 'planned out of existence' – condemned as 'non-conforming', refused permission to expand or diversify, or swept away wholesale in the slum-clearance programmes. In Liverpool it was calculated that 80 per cent of the available jobs in the redevelopment areas were lost. The conference report[7] carried Peter Wilsher's despairing question 'Can we actually tame the monster that we have created?'

'The realities' the report added,

in many inner areas are vacant (and over-priced) land, dereliction and vandalism, the abandonment of neighbouring premises, traffic snarls and the prospect of endless wrangling with the local authority if you surmount these obstacles and wish to expand, diversify, acquire the site next door as a loading bay and so on. And as Peter Shore admitted in his Manchester speech of September 1976 '. . . governments have only limited powers to create and above all to locate investment.'

A little over a decade later the mood is different. In some cities at least the monster has been tamed. Notable among these is Glasgow. Ironically it is the remains of the Victorian city, now refurbished and much admired, which the planners of a couple of decades ago were determined to destroy in order to drag Glasgow into the twentieth century. In the 1970s British Rail demolished St Enoch's palatial station and hotel, and developers swept away the even grander YMCA building, a multi-storey stone chateau on Bothwell Street. More poignant still is the imminent loss of the Eagle Building, also on Bothwell Street, a design of 1854 by Alexander Kirkland who, having built a suspension bridge and many city buildings, went to work in Chicago where he was equally influential. The elegantly arcaded two-storey Bothwell Street building was to be preserved in an early 1980s redevelopment which foundered in bankruptcy when work was well under way. The facade, now exposed on both sides, is doomed. Another fine terrace was lost last year in even more farcical circumstances. Eldon Street was long defended by conservationists against the expansive ambitions of neighbouring Queen's College. The institution succeeded in getting the terrace removed just before the Minister for the Environment vetoed expansion and even suggested that the college itself might be closed.

The threats to 'Greek' Thompson's forceful neo-classical churches are a longer tale. One, the Queen's Park church, was bomb-damaged and demolished shortly afterwards. Another, the Caledonia Road church, was bought by the city council, caught fire, and was left as a shell. Every effort to find a new use was thwarted by the threat of major road proposals which blighted the area until very recently. The third, St Vincent's, is also city-owned but remains in use for worship.

The fact remains that, while there are still disappointments for conservationists in Glasgow, the inner city is rapidly transforming itself as a result of the co-operative efforts of both public and private sectors. In the 1970s 'hardly a week passed without reports of shipyard closures, layoffs or disputes, and large parts of central Glasgow looked as if they had just been bombed'.[8] Now we are several urban initiatives later – and it is instructive to recall that the East End project had already been started by the Scottish Development Agency at the time of the 1977 conference, so it is no overnight phenomenon.

Remaining tenements, having been condemned as unimprovable in the 1960s by all authorities and neglected for many years since, are now nearly all refurbished. Warehouses and other nineteenth-century commercial buildings in the glamorously renamed 'Merchant City' part of the centre have been transformed into new offices and inner-area housing. Exciting new shopping precincts have grown out of the St Enoch's Station site, Briggait, the old fish market, and in the Saltire and Prince's Square developments. The newer GEAR (Glasgow Eastern Area Renewal) project will build on the East End initiative and perhaps begin to give hope to the awful postwar housing ghettos of Easterhouse and Pollock on the eastern fringe. There has even been a revival of private house-building within the city, for, to quote the Chamber of Commerce chairman: 'We have a sensible Labour Council here ... they have to throw a few sops to the loony left ... but ... it is possible to work with them'.

A wealth generator largely missing from London docklands and quite unexpectedly potent in Glasgow in recent years is the arts. A century ago it would have caused no surprise if one spoke of the city in connection with music, painting, or architecture, but in the postwar period it might have been regarded as a little eccentric. Endless delays in the building of a major concert hall, even of a gallery to house the Burrell Collection, are evidence of the city authority's failure to think of itself with any confidence as a cultural metropolis. The increase in visitors to the city from 700,000 in 1982 to 2.5 million in 1987 can in part be attributed to the popularity of the Burrell Gallery, built at last in a delightful parkland setting after forty years of procrastination. Apart from the attractiveness of the building design, which provides landscape as a backdrop for many of the works, there is a personality about the collection of one man with particular enthusiasms which makes it more accessible than many institutional galleries.

Glasgow University has opened its own gallery, the Hunterian Museum, and an art gallery has opened in Kelvingrove. There is also the spectacular 'People's Palace' museum of workaday life and culture, housed in a newly refurbished building on Glasgow Green onto which a large winter garden has been added. With abundant foliage under a spectacular glass roof this building, like so much recent Glasgow architecture, is determined to be light and cheerful and, while not turning its back on the past, to eschew the gloomier aspects. In this museum are roomlike re-creations of the tenement 'single-ends' which even the elderly who moved out of such accommodation only a few years ago are glad to see. Old settings, recently regarded as evidence of deprivation, acquire the gloss of nostalgia in a remarkably short time. The children of those who thankfully threw away copper kettles, wooden mangles, and plate racks are buying them back from antique fairs.

A proud feature of Glasgow's resurgence is its famous college of art. Famous, that is, as the best example of the architecture of Charles Rennie Mackintosh, but now doubly so for the achievement of the young painters of the 'Glasgow School'. The elegant refurbishment of Mackintosh's Willow Tea Room, in danger of demolition some years ago, is but one of many late-nineteenth-century buildings reused for recreation.

The North Rotunda riverside restaurant is another, and so is the handsome Briggait shopping centre, for the shopping there is of the non-serious, Covent Garden variety. Unfortunately it looks liable to fail; such a place needs to be in a vibrant and attractive quarter of a city, but this former fish market is on a riverside site where surrounding developments have been delayed.

In fact the river-bank areas of Glasgow have been among the last to receive attention, perhaps because they are so dauntingly extensive – Clydebank stretches for 30 miles from the east side of the city westwards to Port Glasgow. Barely a start has been made on the renewal and reuse of the old dockland warehouses. Progress in the former heavy-industrial eastern hinterland, perhaps the most depressingly derelict of all of the nineteenth-century areas, has been isolated but effective. The GEAR programme was criticized at first for concentrating on landscaping, but it was soon realized that, far from being extravagant and frivolous (words also applied to the 1988 Garden Festival, but more justly because that was temporary) this environmental upgrading could alter people's perceptions of an area. Now several listed buildings have been repaired, advance factories built, and Templetons' locally famous carpet factory converted into Templetons Business Centre. Even the cynical are taking notice.

Just as decline of the commercial centre led to a spiralling down (the removal of the fruit market from the East End had a knock-on effect on related businesses and nearby economic activity was blighted by road plans), when key buildings and their environs are brought back into use and up-graded this revival also builds upon itself. There was resistance at first to the conversion of the Merchant City's nineteenth-century warehouses into flats, but these now change hands at £80,000, a high price in Scotland. And more recently rehabilitated blocks have seen demand for commercial space on lower floors. Put at its simplest the argument favours going in and *doing something* about derelict land and decaying buildings of interest and that something should be visually prominent.

Glasgow, almost miraculously after the decades of mistakes, destruction, and blight, remains one of the most complete and impressive Victorian cities. Among the more recent conversions with 'conservation impact' is the Albion Building, a late-Victorian warehouse, unlisted but within the Merchant City part of the central conservation area. The building was vacated in the mid-1970s in line with a general exodus of warehousing and commerce from what was seen at the time as an outmoded and obsolete part of the city. Having lain empty for some years, it became the first of the Merchant City warehouses to be converted for residential use.

Again in the Merchant City, 110 Brunswick Street has recently undergone conversion to housing, with offices on the ground floor, as part of the Ingram Square development. Not far away, 113–23 Candleriggs has survived that death sentence which local authorities were only too willing to execute until recent years – a dangerous-building declaration. Late Georgian, this building had the notable feature of a turnpike – a spiral stair in a rear tower. It is now successfully converted into town flats in line with Glasgow's excellent current policy of encouraging the repopulation of the inner city.

The oddly named Babbity Bowster – it refers to a traditional Scottish dance – occupies the restored and partly rebuilt remains of a merchant's town house designed by Robert Adam. The building was originally to be part of a large housing development which in the event proceeded no further. It very much followed the general pattern of decline in the Merchant City, ending up as a local fruit and vegetable shop in the 1970s, almost unrecognizable without its top storey and pediment. A few years ago the potential of even the remaining stump was seen by two brothers with a keen interest in the performing arts. With the help of architect Nicholas Groves-Raines they set about restoring the building for use as cafe, restaurant, and pension. Spontaneous musical performances by well-known musicians are very much part of the character of the establishment and the building has come to exemplify the spirit of revival throughout the Merchant City. Most of Glasgow's churches, with only a handful of exceptions, are nineteenth century in origin. Postwar replanning of the city shifted entire communities,

making many places of worship redundant. In Scotland, however, there is no equivalent of the Redundant Churches Fund in England; and there has been a widespread prejudice against converting church buildings for secular use.

Despite these problems there have been a number of successes of which the best known is, perhaps, the conversion of James Adam's Tron Church into the Tron Theatre. Others include Trinity Church, Claremont Street, now the Sir Henry Wood rehearsal and recording studios for the Scottish National Orchestra. The Elgin Place Congregational Church has been converted into a suc-

10. 'Babbity Bowster' (named after a dance) in Glasgow's Merchant City; a fragment of a planned square by Robert Adam, now a bar, restaurant, and small hotel

11. Trinity College of Divinity, Glasgow, another landmark – exuberantly and awkwardly dominating part of the skyline. Abandoned by the church in the early 1970s, now converted for a variety of uses

12. Tron Theatre in a converted Glasgow church of great townscape quality

Charles Wilson as a College of for the Church of Scotland, and the crowning feature of the park area as well as being a major Glasgow landmark for miles around. Abandoned by the church, it lay empty for years while a number of schemes for reuse came and went. Finally Trinity College was converted for a variety of functions including homes, offices, and a television studio.

Physical changes in Glasgow have been more than matched by changes in social attitudes; visitors with preconceptions of a gloomy and rather poverty-stricken place can easily be taken aback by conspicuous and very fashion-conscious consumption by a large section of the younger population. Among the many lavish shopping precincts, restaurant and entertainment complexes, and beauty, hair and fashion salons, perhaps Prince's Square is the present highlight. Created at a cost of £20 million by the imaginative roofing-over of a little square surrounded by the facades of eighteenth- and nineteenth-century professional and commercial chambers, it is Victorian in the spirit of its glass and metalwork, but modern in detailing and servicing. Escalators give access to various levels. Among novel features is a food court on an upper deck. This reused merchants' court exemplifies Glasgow's new exuberance rather than a meticulous historic-building-repair approach: interiors behind the stone facades are all new.

These are among notable successes. There nonetheless remain huge problems in dealing with the effects of Glasgow's postwar history, namely the dereliction of miles of Clydebank and the appalling condition of life in vast twenty-year-old housing estates such as Pollock and Easterhouse. A joint study is being prepared (in late 1988) by the Clyde Project Group comprising Glasgow District Council, Strathclyde Regional Council, the Scottish Development Agency, and Clyde Port Authority – the sort of combination which, despite expectations perhaps, has been effective here in recent years. For

cessful restaurant/dance and 'function' complex under the name of 'The Cardinal Folly'. Rather similarly the John Street Church is now used as a wine bar and restaurant on the ground floor, although the future of its upper hall has yet to be decided. St George's-in-the-Fields has been converted into flats and St Andrew's-by-the-Green is now the office headquarters for a housing association specializing in the adult homeless. The poignancy of the dereliction of the most dominant buildings was long illustrated by Trinity College. This superb composition was built from 1855 onwards by the speedy improvement of major public housing projects there can be less optimism, simply because of the huge sums involved in achieving much with such intrinsically unattractive buildings designed according to a gospel of functionalism and performing worse than almost any building type in the history of world architecture.

Liverpool 8

One of the nineteenth century's leading ports and industrial cities, Liverpool's decline in the last thirty years has been sad and remarkable. The reasons are easy to find – a decline in shipping, especially of American trade and in heavy industry, a failure to adapt to new methods and technologies, and too much investment. By the last is meant an excess of redevelopment especially of housing and roads involving relocation of both people and industry with consequent loss of employment. The old fabric in central areas, fine Georgian terraces as well as bold Victorian warehousing, offices, and commercial buildings, much of it near the river, was neglected. Small-scale terrace housing was simply swept away, massive dock buildings abandoned. The net result of these and other postwar trends has meant a population loss from about 750,000 to not much more than 500,000.

Much of the new housing, vast estates including considerable high-rise and industrialized, system-built blocks, was on the periphery at places like Kirby. So Scott's marvellous Anglican cathedral towered over a near wasteland.

What is now the Canning Conservation Area in Liverpool 8 was a partial exception; English Heritage describes it as 'the most extensive and probably the finest area of late Georgian housing in the North'. Built in the 1830s from land leased from the corporation, the three-storey terrace houses were intended for merchants and shipowners. As the century progressed it became fashionable

13. Prince's Square shopping centre, Glasgow; not exactly a conservation project – façades of demolished professional chambers form a backdrop for one of the city's most sparkling developments

for such families to seek more spacious homes. So the area's prosperity was quite brief, and from the 1850s the more prosperous citizens moved to substantial villas in the leafier suburbs of Prince's and Sefton Parks. A century of slow decline accelerated after the Second World War. Listing in 1970 achieved little and even the availability of DoE conservation grants from 1976 made slight impression; few of them were taken up. However it was noticed after the riots of 1981 that, while damage had occurred in Upper Parliament Street, which is part of the conservation area, those houses which had been recently repaired were left undis-

New financial arrangements resulted in direct offers of high rates of grant aid for whole terraces. But actual building work had to be initiated before residents felt sufficiently encouraged to participate. Long years in a neglected and squalid environment create lethargy and scepticism regarding official efforts at improvement. Government invited the Liverpool Housing Trust, whose ownership was extensive, to act as managing agents for a rehabilitation scheme. Wimpey Construction was similarly encouraged in relation to another group of properties. Three smaller schemes, in Mornington Crescent and Huskisson Street, were also initiated. In every case English Heritage monitored the quality of work, having required the appointment of approved architects.

The first scheme to be completed comprised five late-Georgian houses in Mornington Crescent facing the cathedral, two of which were owned by a surveyor who was appointed agent. All owners participated and work was finished in September 1985. Next was the much larger project managed by the Liverpool Housing Trust which owned most of the eighty-two properties joining the scheme. Eight of the eleven non-participants were in houses owned by the city council. Funding came from the housing corporation; Merseyside Task Force assisted negotiations with private owners helped by a special recruit from the Abbey National Building Society. A two-year on-site contract included some interior improvements – not always a feature of these English Heritage schemes. Work was completed in January 1987.

Wimpey's scheme involved forty-eight properties out of a possible seventy-two, though some of those participating were 'latecomers' who had seen restoration work carried out on neighbours' houses. About half of them were owner-occupiers and half housing association tenants. The city council excluded its own eight properties. Many of the houses, said English Heritage, had received little attention

turbed. Following 1981 and the increased attention of central government to dereliction in central Liverpool, there was concern at slow progress in the renovation of the Canning area. The city council did virtually nothing to the sprinkling of properties in its ownership and was not helpful to the housing associations wishing to buy and restore houses. Conditions in parts were appalling; English Heritage itself describes narrow alleys behind properties as 'rat-infested rubbish dumps, often the territory of prostitutes and dangerous for local people'. As the government policy for the revitalization of inner Liverpool evolved, conservation came to play a larger role.

14 (a) and (b). Liverpool 8, a special housing renovation project initiated by the government in the face of council intransigence. Now these properties, mostly housing-association owned, are a beacon in the area since the 1830s. Work on rear façades, news buildings, and boundary walls was recommended, as well as on street frontages. Building work was divided into three phases carried out between 1985 and 1988.

A small scheme involving two listed houses in Huskisson Street owned by the Rodney Housing Association was completed by January 1987 and about a year later several unlisted properties in equally bad condition and contributing to the cohesive character of the street were added. By December 1986 English Heritage could report that twelve terraces and six mews buildings had been restored and that 'a major conservation impact had been made'. This impact was not simply that improvements had been seen to be done and this had encouraged others to join in, but that thorough and probably long-lasting renovation had been achieved. Much local interest was shown in the quality of work, since there had been disillusion with quick facelifts which had proved of only temporary benefit, whereas it was possible to credit claims that these houses would be fit for another fifty years – provided that they were routinely maintained.

Local people were rightly impressed with better detailing and superior materials than those they had become accustomed to in recent times. Lead was used in a traditional manner to ensure good weatherproofing, for example. Better proportioned sash windows and doors also contributed to a feeling of quality which has, perhaps, been a contributing factor to the low incidence of thefts during the contracts and vandalism afterwards.

It remains to improve the overall environment, which is important if tenants in particular are to feel committed to the area. Only in one case was it possible to improve both sides of a street. More important are the problems posed by inadequate refuse collection services and the continued dumping of rubbish which is thereby encouraged. These

factors dull the 'conservation impact' obviously considered important by English Heritage.

Nonetheless the whole approach – a thorough up-grading of housing, including such vital threshold features as porticoes, steps, and railings, the improvement of lighting, and visible supervision of back areas by the insertion of railed panels in previously solid walls – has boosted confidence among residents. Follow-up moves have included the conversion of a number of abandoned and ruined buildings, the smartening up of local pubs, and the appearance of flower pots on balconies. In such a situation gap-filling is also significant. Local contractors have been encouraged by the general feeling of rejuvenation to propose new housing on vacant sites. After all, once the appearance of the area had improved, Canning has much going for it including good access to the city centre and a potentially very attractive character. English Heritage is thinking of extending this successful special project to neighbouring areas of architectural and townscape merit, but with the virtual completion in 1988 of the works originally planned there is at least a pause. The scheme was admittedly 'special', but with such high rates of section 10 grant (85 per cent for owners, 75 per cent for commercial concerns and housing associations) further spectacular progress could be expected in Liverpool and similar areas. The cost was not massive; with 184 houses transformed at a public expenditure of £4.8 million (by 1988, perhaps £5.8 million when all bills are paid) there have been far more profligate initiatives.

Birmingham's Jewellery Quarter

This specialized and concentrated area of small-scale manufacturing to the north-west of the centre is an atypical conservation case. It is not especially ancient in origin, it has not produced outstanding architecture, and, despite the best efforts of the authorities, it continues in its former activity, albeit on a reduced scale. The quarter was still a pleasant suburban area in the early years of the reign of Victoria. A few industrial buildings were dotted about, but it was mostly villas and large gardens until about 1850. There were heavier trades developing nearby – electro-platers, brass founders, and die sinkers were establishing themselves a little to the north. A few houses had been taken over by jewellers and some workshops built but jewellery making is a small-scale activity and the gradual intensification was not too noticeable. A

15. Birmingham's Jewellery Quarter, the Argent Centre, a building of an architectural presence which shames the redeveloped parts intended in the 1960s for the whole quarter

workman would start in a room of his home, take over the house, move next door, erect a workshop behind. The historical seeds had been sown some time before. The Birmingham-born engineer Matthew Boulton had established a works at Soho, immediately north of the city, in 1764. Ten years later he was employing a thousand workmen making buttons and buckles, boxes, and trinkets in gold and silver and introducing silver-plating. He had succeeded in establishing a branch of the Assay Office in Newhall Street, and had joined with James Watt in improving coining machinery. Canals had improved transportation, and a gas supply for jewellers' blowpipes was available by 1840. Elkington invented electroplating in premises now used by the Science Museum. Compared with all this jewellery was an almost trivial concern in the 'City of 1,001 trades'. Nevertheless by 1861 7,500 people were engaged in it and the conversion of houses to workshops was well under way.

A depression of the 1880s was followed by consolidating initiatives such as the formation of a Jewellers Association and in 1890 by the setting up of a School of Jewellery and Silversmithing. By 1914 employment in the local industry had grown to 20,000. Support activities such as bullion and precious-stone dealing,

redevelopment. Extensive road widening and the gathering of 'non-industrial functions such as shops and pubs . . . into well defined groups' was to be facilitated by the city's acquisition of 28 acres. Years before this the manufacturers' association had espoused the idea that the replacement of 'the warren of workshops and houses' by parallel rows of flatted factories set among lawns would be beneficial. So there was a welcome for the 1954 report's findings that 'The new development will equally express the nature and scale of the industry, reflecting the contemporary design of the products and the outlook and thought of today'.

Fortunately only a part of this Utopia was realized. A significant part of the quarter, the Vyse estate which had been developed north of Warstone Lane in about 1850, was acquired by the city in 1963. A triangular site between Vyse Street, Warstone Lane, and Hockley Street was redeveloped as the first phase of concentrating the industry 'in about a third of the present area'. The upheaval no doubt contributed to the fact that the industry which had employed 8,000 people in 900 firms in 1965, just before the redevelopment of the 'Hockley Centre' got under way, had been reduced to 4,000 people in 600 firms by 1985. It will be noticed that the average size of firm had been reduced. It is a volatile industry, with a high rate of business formation. As recently as 1985 it was observed that 'the run down state of many of the premises allows firms to come and go fairly regularly'. The trade ebbs and flows, hectic activity and expansion being followed by contraction. Not surprisingly there is much 'putting out' of work to sub-contractors. With the average new firm only lasting 2.8 years the leasing of space in flatted factories is impractical. A recent study of the area by Clive Gilbert concluded that the quarter had to remain 'more or less in its present state to enable a continuation of these practices'.

An extremely delicate balance must be struck between 'leaving well enough

16 (a) and (b). St Paul's Square at the heart of the Jewellery Quarter, before and after refurbishment

tool supplying, and packaging, had also benefited. But the typical unit of production remained the artisan workshop or, at most, the small factory. The Second World War and the austerity following it hit the industry hard. But by 1948 it was reported that, while lower-quality manufacturing on the fringe of the area was in decline, makers of jewellery in the centre of the quarter were showing signs of expansion again. Only a few years later, when Birmingham was dominated by the city engineer, surveyor and planning officer Herbert Manzoni, a report recognized the 'sluttish charm' of the old Jewellery Quarter and its unique atmosphere, but determined upon comprehensive alone' and the kind of interventions which local authorities find irresistible. In 1987 a report by consultants Segal Quince Wicksteed, commissioned by the city council, noted that since 1980–1 the council has provided a good deal of support both to environmental improvement in the Jewellery Quarter and directly to businesses in the industry. Under industrial improvement area and refurbishment schemes, grants and other assistance of over £4.5 million has helped upgrade over 300 buildings and led to additional private expenditure of over £6 million. Expansion has apparently gone hand in hand with 'increasing public interest in visiting the Jewellery Quarter' and the city has been considering how this 'potential as a visitor attraction might best be realised'.

In fact the same year, 1987, saw a great deal of realization. The first new housing in the area for a hundred years was accompanied by the opening of a wine bar and the conversion of one firm's premises to an advertising agency, the refurbishment of Anvic House as workshops, and the conversion of a warehouse in St Paul's Square into flats by a housing association. A further scheme of housing-association flats together with a church and a community centre was also started. The Jewellery Quarter clearly has a future, but does the jewellery industry? Quite remarkably, after 'structured discussions with approximately one hundred of the smaller firms', the consultants 'cannot report a consensus as to the City Council's future role'. There is a healthier scepticism than was evident a generation ago!

Nottingham's Lace Market

Unlike most other industrial cities Nottingham had a long pre-eighteenth-century history as a regional centre – who can forget the evil sheriff of Nottingham?

17. Nottingham Lace Market; in a city scarred by appalling 1960s redevelopments, which destroyed many historic buildings of early date, these substantial nineteenth-century merchants' warehouses survive to be revalued and reused with help from a reformed council

A leading medieval town, a fashionable early-eighteenth-century provincial capital it was, nevertheless, almost wholly transformed into a nineteenth-century industrial and commercial city.

There is evidence of a sixth-century settlement east of the present-day Lace Market area and four centuries later the burgh was actually centred on that area, defended by ditches and ramparts. The Normans built a castle on the crag to the west of the burgh and the town expanded to link the two until a fifteenth-century decline reduced the population to as little as 3,000 again. The future Lace Market site became derelict at that time and remained so for three centuries until it became the setting for elegant seventeenth- and eighteenth-century mansions, built mostly in brick instead of the timber framing of the medieval town.

The new prosperity was based on a booming textile industry, but for a long period the city fathers resisted boundary extensions, so the fivefold population increase during the eighteenth century resulted in a densely built up and very unhealthy environment. The corporation, whilst fiercely resisting enclosure of open fields, encouraged canal links which added to the industrial expansion. Framework knitting, especially of hosiery, gave way to machine-made lace in the second half of the nineteenth

century. In 1890 about 17,000 people ~~→ allowed~~ were employed in 500 lace factories, mostly in outlying quarters where development was at last permitted. The heart of the industry was centred on the Lace Market. Massive and ornate warehouses were replacing Georgian mansions, but with impressive centrally placed entrances they often resembled huge town houses. The Adams Building of 1855, by local architect T. C. Hine, was a prime example, though its character was somewhat that of a lofty chateau.

Nottingham's Heritage, an affectionate view of conservation in the city published in 1985 by the planning department, speaks of the Lace Market as:

a highly distinctive landscape, a fusion of the ancient street pattern with Victorian warehouses of enormous confidence and scale crowding in along the narrow medieval streets, and juxtaposed with the magnificent 15th century church of St Mary's, the 18th century town houses and elegant Shire Hall on High Pavement.

From under 30,000 in 1800 to 250,000 by 1900, the population of Nottingham continued to expand in the twentieth century; the Victorian centre remained substantially unaltered until the 1950s. *Nottingham's Heritage* itself criticizes its predecessors' plans as having

everything in common with other major provincial cities. The ethos of those times, in sharp contrast to that of today, encouraged wholesale redevelopment. 'Old' was synonymous with bad and 'new' with good. Perhaps the losses of pre-19th century buildings were worse in Nottingham than in other less historic industrial cities.

When a city published such wholesale indictments of the effects of its own former policies that very fact is of crucial significance. The report enumerates 'great destruction' from the construction in the 1950s and 1960s of its incomplete inner ring road Maid Marion Way, including the seventeenth-century Collins Almshouses. The Georgian scale of the streets

was lost, and apart from the odd church and isolated house the dual carriageway is 'flanked by office blocks of inhuman scale'. Another new road cutting off the centre from the Midland Station is described as rivalling Maid Marion Way for ugliness. The sorry tale continues:

Only a fragment of the Primary Highway Plan of the 1960s was built but the widening of Weekday Cross, Fletcher Gate and Barker Gate and further demolition elsewhere in the Lace Market seriously eroded the enclosure and townscape of this unique area.

The lace industry had gone into rapid decline after the First World War. Many of the proud warehouses were subdivided and let to small textile firms who were able to pay only minimal rents. Lack of maintenance had led to a very run down condition of the area by the 1960s. Official plans for comprehensive redevelopment and a network of new roads added to the blight. The story is all too familiar up to this point, but change in Nottingham comes at a brisk pace and in 1969 the Lace Market was designated one of the city's first conservation areas. Redevelopment plans were abandoned, key buildings were identified, and plans were made for the improvement of derelict sites, though funds were not available for this until 1973.

A central problem was in changing the general perception of the area. The fact of the council having changed its policies did not instantly mean that everyone suddenly felt positive about a run-down place that they had been taught to regard as a 'grim legacy of the past'. It took considerable time and effort to get renovation projects under way. Now three of the larger derelict sites have been developed as new housing, two by the council and one by a housing association. In such projects the designers have been encouraged to relate to the scale and detailing of adjoining commercial buildings while achieving a pleasant residential environment.

More than thirty once-derelict sites or

ARCHITECTURE LIBRARY

unmade car parks have been landscaped to improve their general appearance, but also to boost confidence. A corner site, disused for fifty years, has been made into a small park which won several awards. The crucial job was to secure rehabilitation of the major Lace Market buildings. Only significant grant aid would convince owners that these former palaces of commerce had a future as well as a past. In 1976 a town scheme was established jointly with the Department of the Environment and the county council. Among a number of early renovation schemes was the conversion of Gothic House on Barker Gate. A near-ruinous building was adapted and divided after repairs into office suites, with a restaurant, wine bar, and penthouse flats – much the same as has been happening more recently in Glasgow's Merchant City. Success with this and other projects encouraged the DoE to designate Nottingham a 'priority town' under section 10 of the 1972 Act. In 1979 the Lace Market was also designated an industrial improvement area, thereby extending the range of financial help available for building improvements.

Between 1976 and 1985 over 100 buildings had been renovated with grants totalling £500,000 and overall investment in the area had exceeded £3 million excluding new housing expenditure. The once condemned Lace market has been transformed into a lively, attractive, mixed-use quarter, an achievement recognized with a Europa Nostra award in 1983.

Billingsgate Market

This is the remarkable story of adaptation and reuse of a major riverside building condemned because of its unsavoury associations and because its owners, who also happened to be the local planning authority, were convinced that a vacant site was more valuable. The winner of the argument was once again Marcus Binney, encouraged by the success of Fisherman's

18. London's Billingsgate; the last and grandest building for a 1,000-year-old fish market has recently been the subject of a costly renovation for a high-tech banking headquarters

Wharf in San Francisco, but still more by the spectacular conversion into a shopping centre of the former Ghirardelli chocolate factory in that city. It is appropriate, therefore, that Billingsgate is to be the headquarters for Citicorp International Banking Ltd, an American company.

The first toll regulations for fishing vessels landing catches at Billingsgate, a wharf conveniently below London Bridge, date from 1016. Other produce was landed there over the centuries but fish predominated and the trade increased. There were no substantial buildings until 1850, but these quickly proved inadequate and were superseded by a large structure designed by Sir Horace Jones and opened in 1877. Here, as so often, the most emphatic architectural expression of a function was realized when its viability was questionable. The site near the heart of the City was wrong. As early as 1883 it was reported that 'the deficiencies of Billingsgate and its surrounds are a great scandal to London'.[9] It was not until 1977 that the corporation decided to close the market and move it to a new site on the Isle of Dogs. This was accomplished at a cost of £11 million in 1982. The fierce argument to prevent demolition had begun in 1980, and broke new conservation ground for

no one could claim the building to be of first-rate architectural or historic importance. The exterior has features of character and there are some fascinating spatial and constructional effects inside, but the century-old justification for the preservation of a building – that it be 'outstanding', itself a disputable quality – was not pursued. Pevsner's *London* (volume I) gives it short shrift, speaking of one of the chief motifs as 'typically weak early to mid-Victorian'. The associations of fish and foul language (Billingsgate porters were notorious) were not helpful. 'Architecturally, the glory of Billingsgate was its riverside site', said Marcus Binney, intent on reversing preconceptions and getting the authorities to look again. 'Billingsgate with its pavilions, mansard roofs, dormers and gilded dolphins had once struck an immensely festive note on the waterfront, and could do so again if only the wretched row of sheds ... on the river edge were removed ... there is the most spectacular view of the Thames in London' he claimed, pointing out that there are very few places on the north bank where people can sit and relax directly on the water's edge. No doubt councillors were surprised by the gathering fuss, and they were appalled when on 2 April 1982 Michael Heseltine spotlisted the market.

Billingsgate consists of a large, three- to four-storey square on plan; two parallel market halls occupy most of the area, separated by a double line of Doric iron columns constituting a two-storey central 'nave'. This last is largely glass-roofed, while the halls have impressive timber vaults with many dormers as well as sections of glass. Here and elsewhere were movable glass louvres for ventilation. In the Victorian way the three chief façades were fronted by classically designed blocks in yellow brick with stone dressings. Arcaded with roofs and windows described by Pevsner as 'Frenchy', the building is, nevertheless, dominated by a figure of Britannia on one central pediment, as well as by the dolphins and

weather vanes atop the end pavilions.

Even before the listing SAVE had risen to the challenge to produce practical proposals and had raised funds to commission a scheme of adaptive reuse of the market from Chrysallis Architects in association with Richard Rogers. Ove Arup were the engineers, and advice was taken from both a chartered and a quantity surveyor. The key to unlock the whole project was the opportunity for a new building on the adjoining lorry site. The corporation's application to demolish remained in suspension while discussions proceeded. A planning brief was issued broadly indicating retail uses in the market building and offices on the lorry park, much as suggested in SAVE's proposals. At the end of 1980 the City voted itself planning permission for such a mix. Tenders were invited in August 1981; SAVE's scheme, backed by developer Trevor Osborne of Speyhawk, offered £19.6 million, a notable example of conservationists putting money, even if not their own, where their mouths were. That bid was the runner-up apparently, the winning tender coming from S. & W. Berisford in association with the London and Edinburgh Investment Trust at £22 million.

A blue-glass-clad multi-storey office block designed by Covell Matthews was rapidly erected on the lorry-park site, and is occupied by bankers Midland Montagu. Work on the market-building conversion by the architects associated with SAVE's efforts, Richard Rogers of Pompidou and Lloyd's building fame, has proved more complex. Two basement floors of stunning brick vaulting as well as the earth beneath had been affected by half a century of deep freeze for the cold stores. Although groundheave and collapse of the building above as foretold in the national press was avoided, months of careful technical work was necessary, and most of the timber roof was replaced. Ownership was transferred in 1984 to Citicorp and, more importantly, all 120,000 sq. ft of the building will be in commercial office use. There will be no retail, nor indeed public access, except a right of way along the river bank. The double-height market place will be occupied by Citibank's trading floor equipped with the latest technology. Mezzanines over part of that space, as well as in the peripheral blocks and corner pavilions, will be offices. The vaulted basement will be occupied by two levels of offices as well as plant, storage, computer facilities, and a staff restaurant.

Citibank staff, many dismayed at first by what they thought was an expensive slum, are now thrilled at the headquarters of character they have acquired and converted for some £40 million. Binney's original vision of a sort of Covent Garden by the City riverbank has vanished, but a building of character will sparkle once again, the quayside will be a new public amenity. Billingsgate is a conservation victory, not quite a triumph.

Royal Victoria Patriotic Building, Wandsworth

A very different struggle was going on at the same time as the Billingsgate saga involving a building of similar date. The unlikely salvation of the Royal Victoria Patriotic Asylum resulted from dogged individual effort in the teeth of local-authority obscurantism.

The building was erected in 1857–9 to the design of Major Rhode Hawkins as a home for female orphans of the Crimean War. A flamboyant Gothic Revival style composition reminiscent of a Flemish town hall, it consists of three lofty storeys of brickwork, stone dressed, under a steep slate roof. Towers and turrets are liberally distributed. Its plan is symmetrical, with a central hall flanked on either side by courtyards one room deep approached off cloister-like corridors. As befits the institutional title rather than its function

19 (a) and (b). Royal Victoria Patriotic Building, Wandsworth, London; once an asylum for Crimean War orphans, it was then partly used as a school, neglected, and finally saved. The hall was gutted by fire started by vandals just before restoration began. Insurance monies allowed a more lavish standard here – the ceiling was replaced and restencilled with the original design by a small entrepreneur despite official obstruction

the architecture was designed chiefly for effect.

A childrens' home until the Second World War, though briefly a hospital during the First, after 1945 only the ground floor was used, and that partially as an Inner London Education Authority school. Viewed as a liability, especially in the light of its Grade II listing, the building was neglected and in 1978 abandoned. Incapable, despite their resources, of maintaining the Royal Victoria themselves, the ILEA and Wandsworth Council did not scruple to make the task as difficult as possible for a would-be private owner. Conditions imposed on purchasers were so oppressive that the ILEA's own surveyors were in agreement with an estate agent about the building's 'negative value'.

Eventually Paul Tutton, entrepreneur and restaurant owner, bought the property for £1, though the freehold was not transferred until he had spent £250,000 on fencing the site, arresting the dry rot, and repairing the roof. Conditions of sale specified low-cost housing, small workshops and studios at ground level, and

community use of the hall. Vehicle access was limited by a tortuous approach through a housing estate and all parking had to be on site. Arduous two-year negotiations overcame the GLC's objections to a limited sharing of means of escape between the mix of users the contract required, commercial and residential. Although the insertion into the plan of six extra fire-separated staircases was apparently insufficient, any additional ones would have involved external alterations which were, of course, opposed by another part of the GLC, that concerned with listed-building protection. During this period the developer was obliged to proceed with conversion work though at

20. St Pancras Chambers, London; Gilbert Scott's Gothic fantasy of a prestige hotel is to be reconverted to its original use in a £50 million refurbishment which includes a shopping centre in the vaults

the risk of not being allowed to use the building on completion.

Loan finance was unavailable since the Royal Victoria was considered to be of no value. Mr Tutton was forced to stage the work, not according to constructional logic, but to allow progressive sales of 99-year leases on flats and the letting of workshops to provide cash flow. This method of proceeding was unacceptable to contractors so he formed his own direct labour team of up to ten craftsmen and labourers. The disposal of the chapel, a detached building behind the main block, for conversion into offices for architects Davis & Bayne was a help. Remarkable flexibility was also required from Mr Tutton's own architect Giles Quarme of Dickinson Quarme & Associates.

Everything had to be done at minimum cost, in spite of the fact that the repair of a semi-derelict listed building, riddled with dry rot, into multiple uses, is considered one of the most labour-intensive operations possible. When work started in 1981, in advance of completion of ownership formalities (in a vain attempt to prevent further decay and vandalism), the little lead that remained on the roofs was stolen by the workmen brought in to repair it. Three kilometres of cast-iron guttering was blocked, broken, or missing, together with downpipes. Slated roofs were badly damaged as were most of the windows. That all this could be put right over a period of six years for £1.9 million is a real achievement, the cost for almost 80,000 sq. ft being as little as £25 per sq. ft. Some flats were sold as shells for owners to divide and fit out, and in fact prices obtained in the later stages were much higher than envisaged at the beginning; the property boom aided this project as it did many other conversions.

One element in the project was atypical. Shortly after the workmen caught stealing lead from the hall roof were dismissed that roof, indeed the hall itself, was gutted by fire. This being a week before the sale went through the ILEA's 'new for old' insurance policy applied. The £450,000 spent on the hall meant that standards there were a great deal more lavish than elsewhere. Stencilled decoration on the interior of the timber vaulted roof was carried out by Campbell Smith, the first-rate decorators founded by architect William Burges to work on Cardiff Castle about a century ago. This space now provides an attractive setting for dances and many other community activities.

The core of the scheme and the scope of the achievement was to provide eighteen workshops, thirty-one studio offices, and twenty-six flats in what had been a local authority 'white elephant'.

St Pancras Chambers

St Pancras Station is one of the world's great buildings, the best known Gothic Revival structure in Britain, the most successful of Sir Gilbert Scott's 800 designs, a symbol of Victorian achievement – of which the railway was a major component. It has long been a neglected, misused, and latterly mostly unused item in British Rail's property portfolio. A handful of works of architecture have assumed the status of unalterable national icons – St Paul's Cathedral, the Houses of Parliament (neither quite Victorian nor quite Gothic). A feature they share is having sprung from one mind, or at least one partnership; they haven't grown over the centuries like the medieval cathedrals – with the partial exception of Salisbury. St Pancras Station is perhaps a fraction short of being iconic, but it is possible to speak of it in the same breath as a cathedral. Though the irony there is that 'cathedral-like' is a term applied most commonly to Barlow's iron and glass roof over the passenger platforms. When it was built it was the world's largest, at 689 ft long with arches spanning its full 240 ft width, and constructed 20 ft above the level of Euston Road so that the tracks could cross the Regent's Canal. Cellars beneath provided a vast Burton beer warehouse. Thus St Pancras Station is two buildings, separate physically, in date, in authorship, and in materials. This separateness is shared with many industrial plants, such as the much-admired Hoover and Firestone buildings which consisted of prestigious fore-buildings and working sheds behind. To have a front and a back is against the canons of modernism, but these forms follow their functions admirably – except that the booking hall and hotel block to the south of the train shed need not have been so big, need not have been a fourteenth-century-style Gothic fairy palace. It can be argued, though, that the architect's task included the glamourizing of travel and the expression of the prestige of a

successful railway company. Scott's commanding design won the 1865 competition despite the fact that he had added two floors in excess of requirements and that his estimated cost far exceeded that of the other entrants. A financial crisis followed a bank failure, but the self-confident directors saw the project through to completion in 1872.

The polychromatic frontage of banded brick and sandstone is 565 ft long, with a 270-ft-high clock tower and a bulkier west tower of 250 ft as well as flèches, pinnacles, stepped gables, and dormers achieving a rooftop silhouette both romantic and imposing. The building is

21. Langham Hotel, London; like St Pancras a luxury hotel until about a half a century ago, then 'institutionalized'. Having escaped proposed demolition, it is also being reconverted to a hotel

lavishly ornamented in an eclectic High Gothic strain which in the interior is supplemented by Frederick Sang's frescoes. The most conspicuous features of the 250-bedroom hotel were the magnificently appointed curved dining room on the ground floor and an imperial staircase. It was also noted that in this 'most sumptuous and best conducted hotel in the empire' the mechanical services worked well. They included a ventilation system for the kitchens, a 'dust shaft' (rubbish chute), fire-fighting apparatus, speaking tubes, and an electric bell system. Smart and successful only until the end of the century, the hotel on the wrong side of town continued until 1935. The minimally

converted building was used for offices until recently, and now St Pancras is to be a luxury hotel once more.

In November 1988, Camden Council, which had been less than enthusiastic about the project and seemingly unconcerned about the fate of the Grade I listed masterpiece, grudgingly gave planning approval. The design by architects YRM for developers Speyhawk & McAlpine is expected to cost in the region of £50 million. Lord St John of Fawsley, chairman of the Royal Fine Art Commission, had protested in March 1988 about Camden delaying the 'great and imaginative scheme'. By holding out, the local authority has apparently secured 206 jobs in light industrial and warehousing premises at the rear of the site. This was at the risk of losing 1,500 jobs the developers claim will be created in the hotel and in the catering, retail, and leisure facilities to be constructed in the undercroft. Detailed planning and listed-building consents will probably be forthcoming more expeditiously.

There will be 127 bedrooms, among them some of the largest to be found in any British hotel – even though space must be found for the now essential *en suite* bathrooms. Historic fittings retained will include original ornate fireplaces in many rooms. In some of the more prominent areas, such as the guests' entrance, it will be necessary to restore Victorian detailing eroded by alterations over the years. The remarkable hammer-beam roof over the ticket hall will be reinstated, though the space beneath will be a brasserie. Serviced apartments, rather than hotel rooms or suites, will have the best views from the building's fourth and fifth floors. 'Club' facilities will occupy some of the finest spaces, including the long curved dining room, the expression of which on the façade is one of the design's most striking features. A Turkish bath will occupy the original kitchens and a night club the Victorian cellars.

The new retail element of 130,000 sq. ft – is there an unlimited demand for such centres? – will be approached via the dominant arch in the main façade, leading into a glazed winter garden. It will also be accessible from street level, or from the underground interchange. That is by no means the end of the facilities promised in the lower reaches of the complex – a museum, six small-screen cinemas, and a health club with swimming pool and squash courts will cater for the whole man, or woman. As for British Rail, it will get the modern, high-technology travel centre and booking office it has long craved in a new position within the station concourse. Thus the two parts of St Pancras will at last be divorced and the railway chiefs will be disassociated from a masterpiece of architectural grandeur so long an embarrassment to them.

The Royal Agricultural Hall, Islington

The 'Aggie' was built in 1861 for the Smithfield Club which had been holding agricultural and livestock exhibitions since 1798. The site on the London side of the village of Islington had long been a stockyard for cattle destined for Smithfield Market. Frederick Peck's impressive design, with an iron-arched roof spanning 130 ft and flanked by two towers, had similarities with St Pancras's great train shed built a couple of years later. Additional accommodation, including a music hall, was added so that eventually the buildings extended to nearly five acres. Besides cattle shows there were exhibitions such as the 1873 World's Fair, walking and bicycle races, concerts, circuses, and the forerunner of the Royal Tournament. In the 1890s Crufts Dog Show and a very early Motor Show were held at the Royal Agricultural Hall.

Closed in 1939, and used as a main post office parcels depot from 1943 to 1971, the hall, and particularly its subsidiary buildings fronting Upper Street, became progressively derelict and apparently destined for demolition. Had the GPO left a decade earlier no doubt destruction would have ensued; by the mid-1970s, however, an active local campaign for preservation was sufficiently in tune with official thinking for Islington Council to purchase the 'Aggie' in 1976. It was also listed then.

Exhaustive searches for new uses produced mostly entertainment or cultural schemes – a Disneyland Dickens was one idea. Even after 1981, when the buildings were purchased for conversion to a trade exhibitions centre, financial problems and planning complications

22. Business Design Centre, Islington, London; the Agricultural Hall was north London's exhibition centre for almost a century until falling on hard times during the last war. Here it is the site of a tram show in 1900

23. Business Design Centre; an individual entrepreneur with imagination but limited funds overcame local inertia and, indeed, opposition by councillors to any commercial solution

delayed a start on building work until early 1985. A successful shop-fitting entrepreneur, Sam Morris, eventually raised a total of over £10 million, but without help from clearing or merchant banks. The key to success was the largest-ever urban development grant of £2.85 million from the Department of the Environment. A second mortgage on his firm's offices and workshops, a £1 million loan guaranteed by Islington Council, assistance from Investors in Industry, and help from an American financier who retains a minority stake in the centre, supplied the remaining £7 million or so. Opened as an international business design centre in 1986, the hall provides

major exhibition space, 124 individual company showrooms, four restaurants, and a car park. Buildings separating the hall and Upper Street were demolished to allow access to a new main entrance.

A main construction task was the replacement of what remained of the extensive roof glazing with double-skinned plastic panels. Historically 'impure' this was necessitated by heat insulation and safety requirements. The only sizeable addition, an exuberantly arched entrance and foyer forebuilding, is roofed in double-skinned aluminium which raised some doubts at English Heritage. But generally EH and the Royal Fine Arts Commission were encouraging.

Islington councillors were ideologically divided, but those opposed to any profit-linked initiatives were narrowly defeated in the planning committee with the energetic help of the council leader, Margaret Hodge, a supporter throughout.

Mr Morris's company CIL, which runs the Business Design Centre, was determined to encompass all interior trades and products. All space could have been let to furniture companies and the present 90 per cent occupancy rate reached sooner. In mid-1988 an imaginative conversion of the hall into a 3,500-seat theatre saw the wheel turn full circle to the commerce and culture mix of a century earlier. After this successful experiment the Kirov Ballet Company are unlikely to be the last visitors to the hall. American Express, which had also supported Mr Morris's project at an early stage, sponsored the ballet, which is confirmation of a recent 'think-tank' report about the importance of the arts to the economy.

Chapter 5

Conservation in Towns

*Wirksworth,
Derbyshire,
contained by hills
on three sides*

Introduction

Thirty years ago an observer might justifiably have thought that town councils were intent on the destruction of their patrimony. They wanted to provide the best of roads, parking provision, shopping centres, and new housing as well as increasing rateable income and – just perhaps – their own importance in the process. They had been told by government and metropolitan authorities that 'improvements' would be achieved by redevelopment of centres in co-operation with property companies, of housing areas with ministry subsidies. Money was available for 'housing clearance', and most architects were only too willing to oblige with new designs, for they too believed that sweeping away narrow terraces was the way to free the underprivileged from the detritus of an oppressive past.

So it was that proud ancient cities, medium-sized towns now, like Gloucester and Worcester laid waste whole sixteenth- and seventeenth-century quarters, destroying medieval street patterns, burgage plots, and even remnants of ancient buildings. Smaller towns gave road works priority, Calne sacrificing one side of a high street to do so; Ely demolished a fine corn exchange so that the market place could be dominated by a new public lavatory and a chain supermarket; Exeter swept away splendid seventeenth-century merchants' houses as if vying with Bristol to disfigure itself. That city replaced an ancient harbour inlet in the town centre with municipal flower beds. Taunton surrounded itself with a record number of roundabouts. Ashford destroyed a lovely old market town so that it could have its roundabouts and multi-storey office buildings in the very centre. Salisbury struggled for years to get a major new shopping scheme as a replacement for its medieval core. So too Chesterfield was determined to get rid of its old market hall and square and replace them with modern facilities. These last

24. Trinity, Frome; surviving houses are repaired and the street admirably closed with new buildings of charm and diversity – even if their 'language' is alien

25. Trinity Area of Frome, Somerset; half of this seventeenth-century textile-manufacturing quarter was demolished as part of a total clearance planned in the 1960s. New houses on right

two towns were slow off the mark; the rising tide of conservation sentiment in the 1970s stopped the burghers doing their worst. It is touching how defeated councils are able to claim credit for popular results of refurbishments they fought tooth and nail against a decade earlier.

Even when opinion had changed and official policies had become avowedly conservationist, there were arguments about where to draw lines. So many buildings below the level of outstanding didn't look 'very old' and were often in a seedy condition which appeared to local authorities to justify 'unfit for habitation' or 'dangerous structure' notices. No matter that their blighted state was the result of years of threatened demolition for road building by that very council! So, even when Chesterfield Council abandoned redevelopment of its market, it took a lot of persuading to retain a semi-derelict public house in a prominent position. Pebbledashed without, hard-boarded within, it was some time before one of the most magnificent timber-framed buildings in the region came to light.

Even if buildings do not prove to be of outstanding intrinsic worth their 'townscape' value often merits retention. Perhaps in the 1930s the great circuses, crescents and squares of Bath were vulnerable, or would have been if it had shared the financial pressures that saw the destruction of London's Regent Street, the Adelphi, and historic houses in Piccadilly and St James's Square. A generation later the great buildings of Bath were 'safe', but not the lesser streets which provided the context and allowed a largely eighteenth-century town to be seen as a unity. Modestly two-storeyed but stone-built Georgian Walcott Street was long under threat. At first the city council seemed genuinely surprised that the nice people who started the Bath Preservation Trust and Civic Trust could get so cross. The idea that the foothills were almost as necessary as the mountain peaks took a long time to sink in.

Elsewhere in this book Duncan Sandys' 1967 Civic Amenities Act and the whole conservation-area approach is celebrated. The arguments about the detailed grain of streets and gardens, and the need to restrain garish shop fronts, huge areas of glass under masonry façades, the planning of 'defensible spaces' which are usually traditional and familiar ones – all these are well rehearsed arguments. The danger that has to be resisted now is complacency. Building and retailing booms – and conversely blight in centres affected by out-of-town developments – are twin threats. Too much prosperity can transform historic environments much more rapidly than gentle decay.

Frome

Moxley Jenner are thoroughly modern architects who have turned their skills to restoration and infill work in historic settings when the need has arisen. Trinity, a seventeenth-century suburb of Frome, Somerset, is the earliest area of industrial workers' housing to survive in Britain. Economic decline over the last hundred years resulted in the gradual degeneration of Trinity into a slum. In 1974 Mendip District Council included it in a conservation area. Moxley Jenner were commissioned to produce a study which recommended rehabitation and then, with the aid of a Historic Buildings Council grant, to carry it out. By including new building on infill sites as well as upgrading of standards of existing dwellings, provision in the area was a total of 76 houses and 33 flats, with 105 parking spaces.

The surge in prosperity after the Restoration resulted in virtually a new town being built alongside old Frome in the decades following 1680. Straight streets on a rectilinear grid were lined with stone-walled and probably stone-tiled houses of generous size and with long gardens. As early as 1750 those gardens were being developed with rows of smaller and less

sturdy dwellings. Although the last textile mill in Frome functioned until 1965, the industry had been in decline for a century and much of the area had declined into a slum. The addition of upper storeys as well as infill led to overcrowded conditions. Nineteenth-century reroofing in slate and replacement of windows and doors with, in many cases, ugly new stone surrounds, gave a generally Victorian appearance. Trinity's historic importance went unrecognized, and only a handful of buildings was listed.

Most houses were entered straight off the pavement and had no modern facilities such as bathrooms or proper kitchens, and quite a few were structurally substandard too (these being almost entirely later infills). When at the end of the 1950s Frome Borough Council decided on clearance and redevelopment – then a universally approved and government-supported policy – few objected. Not only are local authorities often wrong, they are also usually slow, and it is to the latter factor that we owe the existence of nearly half of Trinity today.

The first of three phases was demolished in 1960, including some of the earliest houses. In 1968, the new housing having been completed, the second phase started. Attitudes to history had begun to change and a small group of houses was preserved and converted to old people's dwellings. Nonetheless compulsory purchase for clearance of the third phase was doggedly pursued and, despite opposition to demolition from the Frome Civic Society from 1971 and the production by them of a viable rehabilitation plan in 1974, ministerial approval for the CPO was obtained in 1975.

What remains of Trinity was preserved not so much by the energetic 'Save Trinity' campaign as by the abolition of the council in the 1975 local government reorganization. The new district authority declared all of old Frome an outstanding conservation area. Still four years passed before rehabilitation work started on the basis of proposals in a study commissioned from Moxley Jenner in 1977. The council eventually decided to renovate all of the remaining houses itself and for its own tenants. This appeared to mean funding from the general housing allocation and an overriding emphasis on economy. Fortunately the DoE proved flexible by increasing the normal allocation and its Historic Buildings Council, especially in the person of its chairman, Jennifer Jenkins, was enthusiastic. Thus the five-year, £3.6 million scheme was assisted by a £337,000 historic buildings grant.

Even then there were hurdles in the form of regulations applicable to new housing which were often indiscriminately and destructively imposed on historic building work at this period. Frome suffered with other Somerset towns such as Yeovil and Taunton. Moxley Jenner were successful in agreeing with local officials that the conservation project would be meaningless unless it was recognized that such features as low ceilings and doorways, even steeply winding stairs, were intrinsic to the character of the buildings. In fact to replace old stairs with modern ones would have taken up so much space that many of the houses would have been unviable. As for lowering ground floors and raising roofs! – but it is too often forgotten how many old buildings have been condemned to destruction by such bureaucratic myopia. For years officials were unwilling to see that the middle classes will pay hundreds of thousands of pounds for the privilege of banging their heads on beams, so were unlikely to recognize that council tenants might also accept this part of their architectural heritage.

One of the planners' sticking points, a requirement that all family houses have gardens, helped to solve a problem. Most of the houses built in gardens were demolished, thereby ameliorating overshadowing. In some of the narrower streets and closes houses on one side had been permanently gloomy. Removal of the later and flimsier infill properties also made the required parking provision practicable. Thus, although 35 out of 145 houses were demolished, none were of seventeenth-century date. Parking was masked by locally typical high walls. A few gaps had to be filled to 'maintain the urban texture'.[10] This last is well described by the architect in his 'history of its development, decay and renewal'. Describing the 'very tight crowding of the houses', he continues: 'There were few gaps, and when there were, they were closed off by walls built well above eye level ... Though the stone walling is very similar to that found in a Cotswold town, and though there are similarities of scale and continuity of street frontages, Trinity is harder and tougher'.

Financially constrained, the architects employed great ingenuity in achieving modern standards by combining small houses into one and dividing very large ones into flats. The only quibble can be in terms of appearance: 'vacant sites were filled with modern houses or flats designed in sympathy with older neighbours'. Is this self-deluding? Inexpensive new buildings are going to differ essentially from old in that they are machine-made, or at least comprised few hand-crafted components. Gradidge's Surrey mansions, where the 'best' was specified and meant second-hand materials put together by craftsmen, is a world away. Everything is in straight lines unless, which is worst, it is deliberately faked. Nothing has settled with earth or structural movement. Everything is also too big – windows, doors, rooms with regulation ceilings. Architects know this, yet their own perspective sketches deny it, as is the case with one on the Frome report's cover. Given inevitable new–old disparities some of the deliberate choices of materials and the way they are detailed here seem rather perverse. Rendered blockwork instead of random rubble may be a matter of cost, but why choose horizontal casements in a street with nineteenth-century vertical sashes? No doubt because they survive on the older houses. But steeply pitched pantiled roofs surely don't survive anywhere, and mass-produced pantiles do look very mechanical. Where is the pattern for the deliberate irregularity of the quoins on lower windows? Most incriminating of all in this light-hearted indictment is the inclusion of that never-never-land vernacular of stone-arched walkways and pretty little cupolas with weather vanes atop which only existed in the pages of the *Architectural Review*. Architects designing in a semi-vernacular style should make sure it is local.

All that said, Trinity, Frome, is a great success. Views are satisfactorily terminated, visual interest is provided, and the new language is robustly handled. New buildings loom over old as little as possible, and the whole environment appears to be an attractive place to live.

Wirksworth

Wirksworth was once the third largest town in Derbyshire; the handsome mid-eighteenth-century town houses, inns, and other public buildings in the centre attest to a past of prosperity and pride. In Roman times lead had been extracted, and continued to be mined until 1827 by which time Wirksworth was also a thriving centre of local commerce and agriculture. Intensive limestone extraction took over from lead and resulted within little more than a generation in a rapid boom followed almost as rapidly in mid-century by a gathering decline. A large, new quarry near the town centre covered the whole place in a pall of dust which soon drove anyone who could afford to move to a neighbouring and more salubrious area.

So Wirksworth sank over the last century into obscurity and neglect, continuing to decline. When in 1978 the Civic Trust sought a depressed small town in an economically unfavoured part of the country which nevertheless had the potential for regeneration by means of vision and co-ordinated effort, here seemed to be somewhere crying out for such external help. Assisted by 'pump-priming' grants from local and central government unlocked by a small team sponsored by a private charity established by the Sainsbury family, Wirksworth has been brought back to a more confident life and appearance, with at least the chance of continuing prosperity.

The 'team' consisted of little more than an experienced architect/implementer with part-time clerical assistance and occasional voluntary help. The key task was to enthuse local people about the potential both of their town and themselves and then to bring together all possible resources to 'make things happen'. Wirksworth's location has fine natural qualities, a compact settlement of 6,000 people, 14 miles north of Derby, yet nestling in a valley at the head of the River Ecclesbourne and thus hemmed in on three sides by hills. The scarring of the landscape by disused quarries adds a stark impressiveness to the scene.

Let us return to the nineteenth-century history of the town, for this had shaped the place as it looked in 1978. As so often happens the biggest developments coincided with the onset of decline. By 1867 a railway linked Wirksworth to Derby and beyond. An ambitious town hall was started in 1870. In 1879 a tunnel was built below the town centre connecting the newly opened Dale quarry with the railway sidings. The entrepreneurial spirit responsible for the commerce and industry was expressing itself in major construction works while simultaneously throttling the town beneath polluting dust. The very speed of decline had the effect of preserving the hotels and public buildings unaltered. Grand town houses for merchants and business people were occupied by the less well-off and nothing was spent on their maintenance. Even the cramped workers' housing remained remarkably unchanged for a century. Of major buildings, only the mansion of the Hurt family, a handsome 1780s building, was lost in 1923. There was gradual decay of large buildings, either abandoned or occupied by people too poor to maintain them, but none of the continual redevelopment of more thriving communities.

If not quite fossilized, Wirksworth did have a rather hauntingly unaltered and rugged appearance: hill-enclosed, tight-knit, hard-edged, a townscape of stone, slate, and dark brickwork. There were few open spaces between narrow streets; even the market place was reduced in size as commerce withdrew. The town by no means lacked striking visual qualities –

encircled as it was by tree-topped hills, scarred by the 300-ft-deep grey limestone quarry walls – and only desultory twentieth-century suburban sprawl in the one possible direction, that of the river valley, diluted the intense urbanity of the place. Although mostly small-scale, Wirksworth is dominated by the towers of the town hall and the ancient parish church as well as by the bulk of a fine 1831 vicarage, Nonconformist chapels, and, on the outskirts, an impressive textile mill. This resonant architectural quality was important, for part of the secret of the exercise was to be able to attract 'heritage' conservation funds as well as to help towards job-creation.

It is fortunate that a matter of broad and early agreement among all participants in the Wirksworth project – pre-eminently the townspeople – was that while halting decay and brightening up the town was vital, 'prettying up' was to be eschewed. In fact one of the first practical suggestions, namely that an area of waste ground behind the town hall should be landscaped after being cleared up, was shelved because of typically thrifty local reticence.

Unemployment was not especially high, but only because more than half of the inhabitants left the town to work. So they did for most of their shopping, despite a decline in public transport – the railway had gone. There was a lower than national average car-ownership level. Down-at-heel shopping facilities added to sub-standard living conditions, and a generally decaying economy had long been matters of concern to both district and county councils which, incidentally, worked unusually well together and continued to do so after the start of the 1978 initiative. The 1970s had seen the declaration of both a conservation area and a GIA (a general improvement area for housing) encompassing much of the town. In late November 1978, the Civic Trust's consultant Gordon Mitchell moved in with a skilled mixture of ideas, diplomacy, and local ego-massaging. A public meeting attracted 450 people who approved the aims of the project: 1. to encourage increased pride in Wirksworth and a greater awareness of its attractive qualities; 2. to enable more people to live in and make better use of the older properties, thereby taking care of them; 3. to encourage provision of more jobs; 4. to stimulate greater investment in shops; 5. to develop the town's visitor potential.

The Civic Trust made it clear that the financial resources it alone could bring were 'peanuts', but that it expected to draw in help from every quarter. The commitment of an influential district councillor and a major local employer were regarded at the meeting as a good start. The project's aims were tackled at once. A study by landscape architect Mary Mitchell was commissioned at the same time as a survey by Alan Hedges of townspeople's views on Wirksworth's essential character, shortcomings, and hopes, but a start on public relations did not await survey results. The civic society was encouraged to publish wall charts and a town trail, and to undertake practical improvements to, for example, street lighting, a bus shelter, and tidying up the churchyard, monuments, and lych-gate. Trees were planted too.

Results breed enthusiasm; the society's membership doubled in three years. The four schools co-operated in an environmental study and mounted an exhibition. A Wirksworth Heritage Education Group was set up to press for the comprehensive to be made a community school so that all could share its facilities. The town council, a body with very limited powers and resources after urban district council status was removed in 1975, agreed to devote one-sixth of its annual budget to a project scheme and to co-operate with the other local authorities to create a community information centre at the entrance to the enlarged central library. Finally, in terms of public relations, it was agreed that newsletters would be delivered to every household.

At the core of the project had to be the upgrading of the physical environment. Following the report of the landscape architect into the setting of Wirksworth, a massive extension of the conservation area was agreed which included the slopes of the hills on three sides. Central and local government were persuaded to fund a town scheme; the Historic Buildings Council, advising the DoE, set aside £30,000 a year towards conservation projects. Casting the net wide the Abbey National Building Society agreed not only to favour mortgage applications for properties in the conservation area but also to fund a demonstration house to show how improvements could be carried out in an environmentally sensitive way. The rehabilitation of two particularly problematic buildings was investigated on the principle mentioned elsewhere in this book of the 'conservation impact' to be achieved by the transformation of prominent buildings *pour encourager les autres*.

Continuing the theme of encouraging by example, the Derbyshire Historic Buildings Trust, one of the country's most resourceful rescuers of 'hopeless cases', was encouraged to take on responsibility for four key building-repair projects. They later chose Wirksworth as the location for their office headquarters. In the third aim, the area of jobs, the project could be less directly creative but building work itself is labour-intensive and there is also the positive effect on potential employers of a more positive 'feel'. Near the end of the first three years of Civic Trust involvement it was estimated that an extra £350,000 had been spent on construction. The county council, together with the development commission, was induced to fund the rehabilitation of a central group of buildings to provide office accommodation, all of which was quickly let. A redundant clinic was also converted to offices for COSIRA and the Derbyshire Community Council. On the outskirts of the town COSIRA built five advance factory units for start-up firms.

Improvement of shopping, the fourth aim, was notably successful, though to an observer the range of new outlets seems a touch genteel for this rugged town. New shops included a bookshop, a toyshop, a restaurant, a delicatessen, an art gallery, and a 'specialist shop for the sale of lingerie made in the town'. The combination of newsletter publicity and a brightening up of existing units had some effect too. But the general impulse to the town's activity helped to support a richer variety of shopping.

Development of the tourist potential, not unhelpful for shopping of course, took place both within the town and in its surroundings. A new reservoir two miles south-west of Wirksworth was recognized as offering a whole range of leisure and sporting opportunities: windsurfing, camping and caravaning, canoeing, fishing, public boating, underwater swimming, and, in the environs, walking, riding, and cycling. To attract more visitors the civic society bought and raised funds to adapt a near derelict building as a heritage centre complete with a cafe, bookshop, and other information facilities as well as craftsmanship demonstrations. Perhaps most imaginative of all, and most germane to the history of the town, was the proposed establishment of a national stone quarry centre on a site having six worked-out limestone quarries.

A project like that undertaken at Wirksworth, while it concentrates on town improvement where it is established, has the larger purpose of being an example to other places. This one has proved inspirational. A town apparently in a downward spiral of decay was persuaded to see itself in a more positive light; if outsiders see potential in a place then inhabitants are encouraged to overcome scepticism – especially if there are financial inducements, however modest. By its nature this kind of exercise cannot be repeated everywhere, and central government agencies, or even county councils, can hardly be persuaded that everywhere is 'special'.

26 (a) and (b). 1–3 Greenhill, Wirksworth; an ambitious seventeenth-century house in the centre was a ruin, but with just enough evidence for a sensitive reconstruction by architects Derek Latham & Partners. Development Commission and Derbyshire County Council grants helped the Derbyshire Historic Buildings Trust meet the £185,000 cost

The idea is that if a small town which has lost its former quarrying, marketing, and textile enterprises during a century of neglect, during which time it has become a dispirited dormitory for neighbouring centres, can be revived, then so can other problem areas.

A successful partnership of all possible organizations both within a town and outside it is only possible at this personal scale in a small place. A city district – less separate, compact, stable, and homogeneous – would be less amenable. The kind of co-operation of successive local authorities, even of different political parties at county and district level, seen at Wirksworth, can seldom be achieved. In a sense this is why more forceful externally imposed agencies such as development corporations have been seen as necessary. Where the less disruptive intrusion on a temporary basis – usually three years in the growing number of regeneration projects – of a 'team' consisting essentially of one or two experts supported by several national organizations playing low-profile supporting roles, can do the job, it is an ideal solution. It requires a near miracle to achieve the sort of co-operation between local authorities and businessmen, central government, civic societies, schools, and a building society which Gordon Michell accomplished in this obscure Derbyshire town. It can be repeated elsewhere and, if some practical lessons from the Wirksworth experience are learned, even a little more expeditiously.

Now the Wirksworth project is over ten years old. The Civic Trust and Gordon Michell withdrew after three years. He was replaced by Barry Joyce, the county council's conservation officer, seconded to spend half his time in Wirksworth. During Joyce's time the Heritage Centre got fully under way and several practical schemes such as the resurfacing of the market place were implemented. After a further three years Lesley Law took over and, among other things, saw the full establishment of the project as a town

development trust with charitable status. Thus the town council's insistence that it should be the body assuming responsibility for continuing initiatives was made effective.

Calne

Like many another small country town, Calne in Wiltshire, with a population of about 10,000, has suffered at the hands of local authority 'planners' in the past twenty-odd years. In the 1975 edition of the relevant *Buildings of England*[11] Sir Nikolaus Pevsner starts his description of

27. *Calne, Wiltshire, a successor to Wirksworth in being the subject of a special project to galvanize local regeneration efforts*

the town: 'The hub of Calne is without any doubt Harris's Bacon Factory, founded about 1770. The nice two-storeyed office building of stone, Tudor, with Baroque motifs is dated 1901. It was originally the Capital and Counties Bank.' Towering over all was the 'big utilitarian', five-storey main building, of the 1920s, 1930s, and 1950s. Pevsner had more ire to vent: 'Calne to the west of the factory has been ruthlessly gutted by the widening of the A4 in the 1960s, a point-less exercise since the M4 has now taken away the traffic.'

A story typical of the period, but there is more . . . : 'to the south the short Castle Street leads to Castle House, once an interesting building, now sadly altered'. He adds a footnote: 'A deplorable story. It was acquired in 1961 by the Borough Council, who were not allowed to demol-ish it, but left it to decay. It was then damaged by fire. It has now been con-verted to old people's dwellings by gutting the C18 part, and replacing the C17 parts by a new wing.'

Not known in 1973 was the authority's next achievement, namely the demolition of the town's 'hub'. Even in 1986 the Calne project established by English Heritage and the county and district councils was worried about 'the state of Council-owned properties in Church Street'.

Harris's bacon and sausage factory was closed down and demolished in 1983. The dominant employer, it had been the town's economic as well as visual hub. A vigorous attempt to convert the sub-stantial buildings to new uses would, if at all successful, have been of great social benefit. Evidently a vast 'hole' in the middle of the town was preferred. The district council, having done its best to destroy the ancient centre in recent decades, seems lately to have turned its back on it. A modern shopping develop-ment has been sited away from existing shops and must be a counter-attraction. As it is the huge vacant site in the centre has had predictable effects on surrounding streets, parts of which became semi-derelict.

In 1985 the North Wiltshire District Council produced central-area-development proposals which appalled a public meeting influenced by an active civic society. Everyone was understandably wary of an authority responsible for the banal Phelps Parade, an 'example of how not to design a shopping street in an historic town' as *The Architect's Journal* put it. The council bowed to immediate pressure, but seemed slow to adjust to public opinion.

The Calne project was based on the pioneering success at Wirksworth, but its progress has been comparatively halting. Local attitudes were different. At Wirksworth there had been a certain hopelessness despite quite positive local-authority initiatives. The Civic and Monument Trusts team had taken over 'the hearts and minds' of everyone involved with a mixture of charm, confidence, and a little money. There was willing co-operation.

Attitudes in the Wiltshire town were not so uniform. Calne, like Wirksworth, had lost its own local authority in 1975, but the district council, based in Chippenham, had no intention of ceding any effective authority even temporarily. It helped set up 'The Calne Development Working Party', but it almost seems that the aim was to smother rather than stimulate local initiatives. 'Instead of cutting through red tape it just adds to it', said Gordon Michell, two years into the project. Much time and energy was diverted into long discussions with the district about designs for a major central-area redevelopment on a council-owned site, 'The Wharf', beside the 'canalized' River Marden.

This exemplifies a difficult and classic problem: just what architectural language is appropriate for new housing in a historic context? Calne was essentially made in the seventeenth and eighteenth centuries of a mixture of ashlar and random rubble, together with a little brick and some rendered façades in both early and later versions of vernacular Georgian. There could be no argument that the scale had to be respected, and both the council scheme and the project's modified version did that. The buildings were all to be of two and three storeys. They both also tried to pick up the characteristic mixture of pitched roofs and gable ends, together with the irregular street fronts where heights and detailing of each house differ.

Here already we enter the area of the contrived, which either has to be done with a sense of self-conscious fun – as at Woodham Ferrers or even Richmond Riverside – or not at all. If one has gone so far as at the end of the twentieth century to build with the scale and materials of a past age, there is a case to be made for going the whole hog and designing pastiche. Laymen usually enjoy the results and do not understand why architects, having abandoned the idea of being up-to-date, insist on their 'integrity' which demands that there are hints 'of our own age'.

The district council's designers did this in the crassest possible manner by adorning the top floor of their blocks with metal panels in red-brown, so achieving in some way 'a building of the eighties'. The project's alternative was more sensitive, especially in its massing and in allowing views between the blocks to neighbouring streets.

Both related only loosely to Calne. The official design with its unholy mixture of real Bath stone and fake random rubble was rather less convincing than the average spec housing scheme. The project's timid version at least managed windows nearer the vertical Georgian proportions of the rest of the town.

The Wharf controversy was a diversion. If the project team's version had gone ahead at least no harm would have been done. What else was achieved in the first two years of the three-year initiative? The *Calne Project Second Annual Report* speaks cheerfully of 'Active involvement, in one way or another, of townspeople of all ages'. Fund raising and the clearing up of 400 yards of the silted-up Wiltshire and Bath canal were mentioned. Architect Mary Maxwell, 'after many frustrating delays', converted a derelict former outbuilding of the meat factory into a community centre called Marden House. The team secured charity funds and also a two-year loan at low interest from the Architectural Heritage Fund for the centre. It supported the Wiltshire Historic Buildings Trust in taking over key neglected council-owned buildings in Church Street. Run-down residential accommodation over central area shops is a recurrent concern in town centres; success in tackling it in Calne could be a useful example. A town scheme, intended to give these and other initiatives a boost, were agreed by both county and district but not launched until year three.

The local civic society has been active in landscape improvements in both a housing and an industrial estate. Traffic problems have been studied by consultants Colin Buchanan and Partners and, indeed, by the county council's director of planning and highways who was prevailed upon to visit Calne. The objective is to exclude through traffic. The consultants foresee a growth in local traffic by 36 per cent over fifteen years. Proposals to ease flow in the centre, especially in Curzon Street and Wood Street, by extending an existing route called 'the Pippin' were unanimously rejected by the project's executive committee 'on account of the environmental damage'. Everyone wanted a relief road on the north side of the town.

There were a number of minor initiatives but much of the first two years' energies were expended in preventing the worst happening. That task was made no easier by the fact that the Calne Working Party's meetings had been 'somewhat intermittent', a frustrating aspect for Michell who was seeking 'action, swift decisions and dynamism' as he said in his second annual report. In the third year much seemed to improve, and the council modified its Wharf scheme satisfactorily. It is being constructed of natural sandstone, Welsh slates and clay roofing tiles, and the panels at the top of the three-storey flats are to be rendered.

The Bank site, part of Harris's original factory, will provide temporary parking for seventy cars to replace space lost on the Wharf. A brief for a shopping development on the Bank site itself is being prepared jointly by the council and the project team – with a sense of urgency now. When all is said and done the main problem remains the 'hole in the centre'. Road proposals in 1988 from the county surveyor, opposed by all local groups, continue to frustrate long-term planning.

Despite this the project thrives, in ever greater heart. If its financing is anything to go by it continues to enjoy support from all the authorities who contributed so readily at its initiation in June 1986. The three local authorities jointly contribute 50 per cent (£20,000) annually and are joined by English Heritage which contributed 25 per cent (£10,000) a year. The £10,000 the trust has to find for itself has not been a serious problem, such is local enthusiasm. All these authorities, together with the main business and voluntary organizations of the town, who constitute the executive committee, have asked Gordon Michell to continue leading the project after the first three-year term expires in June 1989.

Chapter 6
Industrial
Monuments

Albert Terrace
Saltaire

Introduction

Fascination for, and study of, the buildings and machinery of industrial production and processing, although of comparatively recent origin, is intense and all-inclusive. Remains of the manufacturing and extracting processes dominated much of the Midlands and north of Britain until a decade or two ago and yet were totally absent from most of the south, east, and west of England. That these monuments of the late eighteenth to early twentieth centuries should be regarded as part of the national heritage and so worthy of conservation is an idea far removed from traditional concepts of preservation, concentrating as they do on beautiful and ancient churches and castles, together with the architectural grandeur of country houses and the picturesqueness of cottages. The nineteenth-century workers' terraced house with its outside lavatory, its tin bath in front of the kitchen range which provided whatever there was in the way of hot water, heating, and cooking facilities, is a museum attraction only decades after it was the way of life for the majority of the population.

Now it is almost inconceivable that St Pancras Station with Scott's spectacular Gothic forebuilding to Barlow's mighty train shed were considered for demolition in the 1960s. Now St Pancras is listed Grade I as would be Hardwick's monumental neo-classical Euston Station up the road which was demolished. Other termini went too, among them London's Broad Street and Glasgow's St Enoch's. British rail felt it had a mission to free itself from its glorious past.

Attitudes after the Second World War to relics of Britain's nineteenth-century worldwide industrial predominance were mixed: a certain pride in the skills and courage of the engineers – Stephenson, Brunel, Telford – a post-imperial guilt allied to a desire to remove symbols of class oppression such as the northern textile mills and the rows of workers'

housing nearby. There was also a smugness that, having excelled before, all that was needed to do so again was to avoid nostalgia and start again with a clean slate. As has been suggested in the first chapter, all this was neatly expressed in a rather puritanical, egalitarian modernism. Not only was the exuberantly carved and coloured Victorian ornament, together with its frequent religious symbolism and imperial snobbery, loathed and its manifest pride and wealth resented, but the utilitarian engineering structures which had underpinned it were swept away with relief too.

Everything had to be thought out afresh – housing, schools, hospitals, and factories – and often replaced on a more modest scale which would allegedly be more economical. Of course the flimsiness of the new buildings led to huge unbudgeted costs later. While the scale was modest in terms of architectural rhetoric, institutional buildings were to have none of that florid, oversized grandeur of the Victorians. However in the sheer repetition of standard units in public housing and some other building types the actual size was immense. So innumerable large buildings which could have been adapted to new uses were destroyed and replaced, on the one hand, while on the other there was felt to be a need for 'economic realism'. So the world's most intensive railway network was savagely cut back 'to save money', at the same time as stations were unnecessarily rebuilt for reasons (as far as one can make out) of image.

Now all has changed. Conservation has a second arm, so to speak – that is, a wish to study, enjoy, and preserve structures and machines, indeed even artifacts, for their own sake. Both the guilt about nineteenth-century history and the remaining fear of its oppression have been purged.

Conservation also has a third arm of course – adaptive reuse. Some of the structures discussed in the following pages will have no use once their original function has ceased; neither the Tyneside coal wharves, nor the railway viaducts suggest viable conversion. Their interest will be as tourist attractions. Old railway hotels, dockland warehouses, textile mills, even pumping stations and breweries not only lend themselves to conversion, they also present society with choices between residential, commercial, retail, office or workshop, and studio uses, depending on location. Vast complexes like the Albert Docks in Liverpool allow most of those possibilities to be explored simultaneously, together with museums, leisure facilities, restaurants and bars, and a TV studio! Such richness of opportunity behoves planners and decision-makers to make appropriate judgements about reuse which take account of historical and aesthetic factors as well as practical and financial matters. Clearly the most important, rare, and beautiful monuments require the most sensitive approach. That is a universal touchstone in conservation and should be safeguarded by official protection, listing and grant-giving policies. The second requirement is that all such structures, whatever their intrinsic rarity or other quality, should be converted in a manner which makes it possible not only to identify the original use, but also to experience empathetically something of the quality of life and environment which formerly prevailed. A warehouse should retain some of its rugged 'warehouseness'. Several good examples could be quoted, such as the New Concordia Wharf, now in effect a block of flats and by no means unaltered in the process of so becoming, yet the recipient of three major awards. The additions are 'in character', indeed are difficult to detect at a superficial glance, and there have been sufficient crucial retentions, of cranes for example, to make some of the building's history and purpose readable.

Stroud textile mills

The Gloucestershire town of Stroud represents several of this book's strands: pre-Industrial-Revolution manufacturing buildings (here as at Frome there was an important seventeenth- and eighteenth-century textile industry, the remains of which have been little appreciated until recently), represent an area where the local authorities came late to conservation policies, but where now they are especially active. In the 1970s, when an active group of local conservationists fought fiercely to preserve seventeenth-century stone-built houses in the High Street, the council was to say the least unsympathetic. Now Stroud District Council has joined with others in tackling a far larger problem, that of the derelict textile mills in and around the town and its surrounding valleys. As a splendid example the council has taken over one of the largest, Ebley Mill, for conversion to offices for its own use.

The town of Stroud is situated at the convergence of five valleys and has been a centre of industrial activity since the late Middle Ages. By the sixteenth century the manufacture of woollen cloth had become well established and in 1824 there were over 150 mills, the majority producing military cloth such as the world-renowned Stroudwater Scarlet, used for uniforms. The industry has been in decline since the mid-nineteenth century, but many buildings survive, some in good condition, complete with water wheels and machinery. There are also mill owners' houses, weavers' cottages, a canal system, and many examples of railway architecture, including a goods shed by Brunel. All this is described in a 1988 report by Mike Goodenough on behalf of the 'Stroud Valleys Project'.

That study also reminds us of the steep valleys with fast flowing streams, of access provided by a network of footpaths, canal towpaths and a new cycle trail, all of which make this part of the 'Cotswold Area of Outstanding Natural Beauty' an obvious tourist destination. Yet it is largely unknown. Whatever the outcome of publicity efforts, the need remains to repair and, where possible, convert the mills and other woollen-

industry buildings. Some have been demolished, some cheaply reused for small industrial units. But both rents and maintenance standards have been low. In many cases only the lower floors are occupied, and two of the largest mills have been entirely empty. At the same time there has been increasing pressure for new development, partly perhaps because of the decay of the old buildings and the neglected rubbish-strewn state of the land around them.

A new conservation attitude encouraged by the successful restoration of a number of important listed buildings in Stroud, and their return to viable commercial use, stimulated the district council to com-

mission a report from consultants URBED. This was published in 1986 with the up-beat title *Making the Most of Stroud's Industrial Heritage*. Meetings and seminars culminated in the formation of a working party with representatives from the district and county councils, the Countryside Commission, the Stroud Civic Society, and various local associations and trusts. Among destinations for fact-finding visits were Wirksworth and Calne.

Unsurprisingly, the project's general aims coincided to a considerable extent with those in Wirksworth, for example: to encourage local pride and awareness; to protect and enhance the built and natural environment; to encourage owners to care for old properties and promote new uses especially for redundant industrial buildings; to encourage tourism by the sensitive development of the area's recreational potential; and, finally, to provide job opportunities through the above activities.

The Stroud Valleys Project sees its role chiefly as an enabling one, 'offering advice and expertise to the private sector and acting as a catalyst for voluntary organisations and Manpower Services Commission agencies'. It will help to feed in public resources to private or community-based initiatives. A recently created Industrial Heritage conservation area runs the length of the Stroud, Chalford, and Nailsworth valleys. The project's trust, an independent charity, is concentrating its efforts for the first three years on two demonstration areas within the overall conservation area, at Chalford and Wallbridge. Following a launch donation of £3,000, the district council allocated core funding of £20,000 for the financial year 1988–9.

Saltaire

Titus Salt – 'perhaps the most outstanding representative in Bradford of that class whose activities transformed the economy, the social structure, the politics, the administration of this country between about 1830 and 1860'[12] – arrived in the town in 1822. His father gave up farming during the agricultural depression after the Napoleonic wars and became a wool merchant. Titus, aged 19, followed him and became a worsted-stuff manufacturer on his own account in 1829. By 1850 Salt was Bradford's richest man and the city's biggest employer, with five mills and many outworkers; he had commercial links with both Europe and America. His innovative use of exotic fibres, alpaca for example, was recognized at the Great Exhibition of 1851. A committed Congregationalist churchman,

28. Ebley Mill, Stroud, Gloucestershire, typical though among the later in date of the textile buildings in and around the town and surrounding valleys which had become largely derelict. The council has converted this building for its own offices

social reformer, and philanthropist, an MP from 1859 to 1861, he was created a baronet in 1869.

Titus Salt was still in his 40s when in about 1850 he conceived the idea of building the separate self-contained community which became Saltaire. He was not the first to build houses, chapels, and schools for workers: Arkwright at Cromford, the Strutts at Belper, Ackroyd at Copley had all preceded him on a smaller scale. He may have been encouraged by such examples, but the impetus had chiefly come from a recognition of the appalling conditions in Bradford which had doubled in population in the 1840s to 104,000. Slum conditions seemed to be worst for those working at home. Air was foul with smoke, water polluted with excrement, the world's textile capital famed for violence and promiscuity. Worker unrest had been focused by the Chartist movement in 1848.

Salt, as industrialist, mayor, and magistrate, was able to combine conscience and self-interest in typical Victorian vein by concentrating wool-combing and other processes in a new factory – outworking was increasingly inefficient in a rapidly industrializing industry – at the centre of a model village. 'Work, health, education and moral instruction for all who wanted it, and reasonable provision for a sensible use of leisure' were regarded as 'basic necessities of a decent life'. Saltaire had no beershops or public houses.

Three miles from Bradford on the edge of the Yorkshire moors, Saltaire extends over almost 50 acres beside the River Aire. The plan is rectilinear, the building material is mostly stone from local quarries, and the architects were the regionally dominant firm of Lockwood & Mawson. Besides housing, the buildings essentially comprised two churches, a railway station (closed in 1965), a school, public baths and wash-houses, a gasworks, almshouses, a park, and 'the finest mill in Europe' covering 10 acres and eventually employing over 3,000 people. In the works dining room 600 took breakfast and 700 dinner every day. A hospital and an instutute were also added to the remarkable public provision.

This most ambitious of model villages was widely influential; Krupps at Essen, Cadbury at Bourneville, and Lever at Port Sunlight as well as several American experiments were indebted to it. The Salt family connection ended in 1893; the housing was sold off separately in 1933. Latterday attempts to preserve a unity in the character of the place depend on the designation of the village as a conservation area. Guidance leaflets on such features as windows and doors are issued. In recent years Saltaire has come into its own as a tourist attraction for Bradford, that city having destroyed most of its fine Victorian centre in the 1960s. At Saltaire it is still possible to imagine the mill workers' way of life.

Taking 1871 as a date still in Titus Salt's lifetime when his creation was thriving, the village had a population of 4,400. Most of them lived in two-storey cottages with two bedrooms, a living room, a kitchen, and a pantry. Accommodation, as well as services such as drainage and water supply, was superior to normal standards of the period. The two-bedroomed house cost £120 to build, the three-bedroomed version with front garden cost £220. There were also three-storey houses for managers. Each house had a backyard and within it sanitation in the form of a privy. Economic rents of 2/4d to 7/6d a week were charged. At the almshouses, incidentally the buildings together with the churches which were most elaborately decorated, there were no rents. Indeed a couple living there received a weekly pension of 10s (50p). For visitors there is a very satisfying comprehensibility about Saltaire, almost as if it were a model village in both senses. It is small enough for most views to be closed by the rugged hillsides, and natural and man-made features – river, canal, former railway, give it shape. The massive Italianate mill, the formal park, the Con-

29. Saltaire, near Bradford. Titus Salt removed plant and workers from the overcrowded, unhealthy city to a planned model industrial village. The vast mill is still largely empty despite efforts to find new uses since production ceased

gregational church are on one side of the railway line and the neat houses on the other – together with a few shops with the school facing the adult education institute, the social facilities of which were to be an uplifting alternative to a pub. It is now an open-air museum of early Victorian philanthropic capitalism. Cobbled streets discourage cars, but the temptation to bring back gas lamps, mill girls, or even trams seems to have been resisted.

There remains the problem of the mill, which is in fact a tremendous complex of buildings based on the original combing and weaving sheds of 1853, the latter with 1,200 looms making 30,000 yards of cloth a day, to which was added the New Mill of 1868 on the other side of the canal. The chimney of that second group, being designed as a Venetian campanile, provides one of the landmarks of Saltaire.

Closed for textile production by the then owners Illingworth Morris, new uses were needed. A major initiative by SAVE culminated in April 1986 in a seminar, 'Crisis at Saltaire', chaired by Dame Margaret Weston, former director of the Science Museum. The chief result of this was an agreement by the owners to sell the whole vast group of buildings for a reasonable sum. The purchaser, Jonathan Silver, was a successful clothier who had assisted Ernest Hall in the conversion of Dean Clough Mill at Halifax into a business centre. Silver has established an art gallery and has been endeavouring to set up a museum based on the possible transfer of the Victoria & Albert Museum's Indian collection to Saltaire. He also envisages a specialized shopping centre, in which venture he has secured the interest of Joseph, the high fashion retailer, and for which he has planning permission. As yet it has to be admitted that many of these Grade II buildings await a new function.

30. Liverpool's Albert Dock of the 1840s; Jesse Hartley's monumental and inventively constructed warehouses were nearly lost, but now constitute an economic focus and huge visitor attraction

Liverpool's Albert Dock

The Albert Dock is listed Grade I, is among better known buildings in England, and is a centre of entertainment and culture as well as a source of pride and a landmark of hope on Liverpool's once thriving waterfront. The old dock buildings house the Tate Gallery of the North, a maritime museum, various commercial and residential uses, and a large number of shops, bars, and restaurants. One of the city's major attractions, this group of buildings, like that great tourist draw in London, Covent Garden, came

31. Albert Docks; also the setting for James Stirling's Tate Gallery of the North

near to demolition in the late 1960s. Both these projects are huge popular successes; naturally they are also subject to the barbs of fastidious critics.

For the latter the Albert Dock epitomizes what writers in *Architectural Review*, for example, see as the 'theme park' aspect of conservation. For them these complexes, in the cause of their salvation, have been both gentrified and vulgarized. In any case they are no longer redolent of the sweat of the horny-handed sons of toil which conveys such a delicious *frisson* to the aesthete.

Peter Buchanan,[13] accepting that 'this conversion is part of the triumphant regeneration of the area', regrets

31. Albert Docks; also the setting for James Stirling's Tate Gallery of the North

the distortion and destruction of history. At least when derelict and threatened with destruction, the Albert Dock was not just powerfully poetic in its solidly stoic and noble forelornness but still stirred the imagination to cram it with ships and goods from around the world, with bustling activity and sweaty toil.

Buchanan complains because the Albert Dock is now 'prettified and touristed', and part of a theme park that 'all of Britain is rapidly becoming'. These arguments, deriving from a standpoint of artistic modernism and, in the case of Robert Hewison,[14] of technological progress, have to be faced by those committed to conservation and reuse (where appropriate) because they comprise the inevitable intellectual backlash which the very success of the historic buildings protection movement generated.

Nostalgia there undoubtedly is; inevitably the restaurants and bars pick up the maritime theme. It is all too nautical for another critic, Waldemar Januszczak, who complains of the new museum's setting being 'Captain Pugwash country ... the gallery must compete with the jaunty sea-faring mood that is being cultivated around it in the theme dock (the pizzas in the café opposite have names like The Trafalgar and Bosun's Surprise)'.[15] Mr Januszczak finds the location *arriviste*, 'a very insistent ambience.... Ferries chug across the Mersey. The air smells strongly of the briny.' He dislikes the look of 'heirlooms in perfect stages of (useless) preservation, capstans, tall ships, lock gates, lifting gear, cranes, pulleys'.

Such etiolated tastes are repelled by popular architecture and its attendant kitsch which are rapidly making the Albert Dock the biggest tourist attraction in the kingdom with nearly three million claimed now and five million expected when the complex is complete in a few years time. It is important not to allow recent history to be rewritten by implication. Liverpool-born, -bred, and -educated architect James Stirling may well be quoted as recalling 'the perfect piazza of water', and it is also important to recall that the planning authority, having entertained the idea of demolition, seemed prepared to go along in the 1970s with the developers' scheme to fill and then asphalt over the dock basin, which is indeed the historic and visual *raison d'etre* of the whole vast quadrangle of warehouses. Perhaps the latterday critics would have preferred a car park, so much more redolent of Mr Buchanan's 'grim, gritty reality'. Less 'briny' too was the six metre thickness of Mersey mud silting up the dock until the current rescue project got under way during Michael Heseltine's

reign as 'Minister for Merseyside'. He it was who made these the largest group of Grade I buildings in the country so, at SAVE's prompting, seeing off Mr Zisman's asphalting and speculative office scheme. He it was who, having created the Merseyside Development Corporation (MDC) to sidestep the nihilist city council, encouraged MDC to invest the first £7 million dredging the basin and repairing the exterior of the buildings. He it was who helped to sponsor the tall-ships race with the Albert Dock as its finishing point in 1984, thus wonderfully concentrating the minds of all the parties involved in the task of achieving some kind of vibrancy at the docks by August of that year.

Ministers can only seize opportunities presented to them, agree essential pump-priming, enthuse, try and remove obstacles; the actual work is carried out over months and years by those involved. Chief among these has been Michael Franklin, of architects Franklin Stafford and Leonard Eppel of Arrowcroft Group, a development company whom Franklin persuaded that the Albert Dock could work. Mr Eppel could only ignore the unanimous opinion in the property world that Liverpool should be avoided at all costs and a vast derelict dock complex above all, on the strength of the major financial input at early stages by the newly formed MDC. The whole development when completed is likely to have cost £100–120 million of which the public sector will have contributed about 20 per cent, but in the early days the proportions were reversed, that is 80/20 public/private – a splendid example of pump-priming to get a major 'conservation impact' scheme under way. There were no other grants, the Treasury regarding the development corporation's input as subsuming all others. Even the proposed English Heritage contribution towards the rebuilding of a missing clock tower from block E was suspended.

Commercial faith has proved justified: in a few years time there will be thriving occupation of most of the total of 1.25 million sq. ft. In approximate terms this will divide into: 300,000 sq. ft for offices, 250,000 sq. ft residential, 200,000 sq. ft for a five-star (Loews) hotel, 250,000 sq. ft for museums, and 220,000 sq. ft for quayside facilities, mostly shops. There is a Granada TV news studio in the former dock traffic office and a certain amount of as yet unallocated basement. The 27-acre site will also include about 1,000 car spaces. All of the prime space having been committed, other London-based property companies are looking at nearby warehouses including Albert Waterfront, already being converted to more retail space.

Jesse Hartley (1780–1860) was chief engineer to the Liverpool Docks from 1824 until his death. This was a period of great expansion, yet the goods unloaded at the various docks constructed by Hartley and others up to 1836 were stored in cotton, coffee, tobacco, sugar, and rum warehouses in the commercial town centre. London's West India Docks built at the turn of the century had shown the advantage of warehouses alongside the wharf for direct unloading. But it was the noble St Katherine's Dock, constructed in 1827–9 by architect Philip Hardwick, which provided the model for the Albert Dock and later examples. It is thought that the brilliant engineer from Liverpool may have assisted Hardwick at London's St Katherine's, and certainly the architect contributed to the design of the five-storey brick, iron, and granite warehouses ranged round this, the largest enclosed basin of its time, beside the Mersey. Hardwick was also responsible for the separate dock traffic office on a corner of the site, with its columned portico and string courses rendering it a little less austere than the rest of the Albert buildings. Often characterized as being in the English 'Functional Tradition', the warehouse façades convey what Pevsner called 'sheer punch' unequalled in the 'early commercial architecture of Europe'. Almost plain brick walls sit on

massive Doric columns of iron at quay level on the dock basin side. At irregular, but happily rhythmic intervals the colonnade is interrupted by two-storey, nearly half-round arches which accommodated unloading cranes. Above the arches are recessed gantries which again counterpoint the regular rhythm of the segmentally arched windows. It is a composition both masculine and elegant, achieving the function-based appearance of inevitability so sought after by early modernists.

Built between 1841 and 1846, opened by Prince Albert, and so clearly recognized as a national achievement, the docks were outmoded by the increasing size of ships by the end of the century. By 1920 almost empty, they were used by the navy during the Second World War and returned to partial use in 1945 before final closure in 1972. Destruction was averted by protracted discussion of various reuse schemes including one for a vast 'Aquarius city' of 11 million sq. ft which involved filling the basin, as did the slightly more modest World Centre proposed by Gerald Zisman and abandoned in 1981 when Michael Heseltine ruled against the filling of the dock after a public inquiry. Sadly a scheme to house the Liverpool Polytechnic in the Albert Dock had also foundered in 1976, this time because funds were inadequate.

New hope came as a result of a lightning survey of 6 million sq. ft of derelict space by the pre-designation team prior to the establishment of the Merseyside Development Corporation in March 1981. Part of that team had been London architects Franklin Stafford, whose interest continued as consultants to Arrowcroft, introduced in 1982 and thereafter responsible for nearly three-quarters of the project. Together with MDC's overall co-ordinating architects, Holford Associates, acting for the corporation as owners of the complex, they have determined the infrastructure, external repairs, and treatment of the docks themselves. Brock Carmichael have designed the Maritime

Museum and James Stirling, Michael Wilford Associates have been architects via the PSA for the Tate. They have made so attractive a place that visitors already total nearly 3 million a year. Bluff was used along the way: shops, restaurants, and bars were rushed into being by Summer 1984 to create a lively quay-level environment among the arcades facing the basin. The brickwork above was sandblasted clean (perhaps a little over-enthusiastically), rusted cast-iron windows were replaced in replica aluminium versions, and everything looked attractive and humming for the arrival of the tall ships. But behind all the upper windows was dereliction despite the bright lights temporarily installed to suggest otherwise.

The most serious structural problems had occurred in the thicknesss of the walls. In his determination to avoid risk of fire no timber was used in the dockyard construction; Hartley had made lavish use of a network of wrought iron flats and bars to reinforce the brickwork. Expansion caused by the rusted iron had actually lifted the walls several inches in height resulting in stress cracks and bulges. All this iron work was removed, and necessary repairs carried out and fissures filled with an injected grout of epoxy and polyester. This work, together with repair of cast-iron beams, the dismantling of the stone parapet destabilized by the wall movements, replacement – most of the stone was sound – and associated making-good, cost nearly £3 million. A common approach to the restoration of the Albert Dock was accepted by all architects involved apart from Stirling and Wilford. This was that new work on all façades facing in towards the basin should be as faithful to the original and as unobtrusive as changes of use and modern regulations would allow. The brickwork was cleaned and the corner of the block destroyed by a wartime bomb faithfully rebuilt. Windows were replaced in replica, albeit in a different metal. A necessary mezzanine floor, constructed,

ironically in wood, to provide additional office and retail space and to render the height behind the arcade less daunting, has been set well back behind the massive columns, as has the plainly detailed entirely glazed external wall to shops and their grand-level uses. No neon lighting or obtrusive lettering is visible from the quayside, apart from that attached to the Tate. The wharfage paraphernalia – winches, bollards, chains, cranes, rings, and pulleys – is considered to provide ample visual interest. Indeed the limited amount of developers' interior landscaping introduced has been widely disapproved as flimsily unnecessary in this robust context.

Some notable concessions have been made to requirements and prejudices of investing institutions, both public and private. The exterior elevations, that is those facing the Mersey and its mud flats, which are generally not viewed at close quarters, have modern clear and undivided glazing to save money and improve lighting levels in admittedly deep interiors. Less understandable is the destruction of most of Jesse Hartley's remarkable intuitively engineered roof. The shallowly arched structure consisting of iron plates, barely half an inch thick, held itself up contrary to apparent logic, or the local-authority engineer's ability to calculate how it did so, or the polytechnic's strain gauge experiments, for 140 years. An apparently flimsy, very fine and elegant series of 'bow-string trusses', allegedly inspired by the structure of an upturned boat, do not support the arched roof, merely stiffen and tie it, contrary to many published descriptions. Certainly the very early and primitive galvanizing of the wrought iron had failed to prevent corrosion and leaking in a few places and certainly in heat-insulating terms the metal actually had a negative value. Unquestionably an insulating and weatherproofing exterior sandwich and membrane was necessary and in the small areas retained at the insistence of the present writer when SPAB secretary, this has been applied. But most of the roof structure – with the exception of a typical bay and early prototype variant which are in the Science Museum – has been destroyed because the bureaucrats could not understand it and the developers and their bankers could not afford to hang around for many more months of wrangling.

Interior character has been retained in many parts however: granite paving and brick-arched ceilings have been exposed where possible, together with areas of original tiled flooring and, above all, the slim interior cast-iron columns which are such a feature of the Tate's galleries for example.

A very remarkable aspect is the unexpected demand for very expensive housing by Liverpool standards. In a city with vacant property and where modest flats can be bought very cheaply, no agent was interested in handling Arrowcraft's first phase of thirty-six flats offered at what were regarded as virtually London prices. Within two hours of the sale office on site being opened, and with no advertising, all units were sold on long leases at between £50,000 for one-bedroomed apartments and £110,000 for three-bedroomed. There is a waiting list for the second phase, in which nearly twice as many dwellings will include some twenty penthouses at £200,000. They are in block C, and the adjoining block B is now intended for a hotel of the highest international class. It will be interesting to see how that succeeds.

Undoubtedly there was high prestige in a gallery for exhibitions of modern art of the finest quality designed by an architect of international standing. James Stirling's Staatsgalerie in Stuttgart is greatly admired, and his extension to the Tate in London is also distinguished. Here, working within a Grade I listed building, he has been even more constrained than at the Clore on Millbank. Neither Stirling's authoritatively plastic inventiveness nor his ability to quote period references in ensembles which are both entirely serious and characteristically his own could be given rein. Indeed he and his partner Michael Wilford consciously restrained their contribution to 'making the most direct response to the existing organisation of the building and to making decisive alterations only where strictly necessary'. This first phase occupies most of the end four bays of block C and some of a narrower link block. It is, nonetheless, a spacious building of seven floors including basement and mezzanine. The basic provision, besides reception, bookshop, restaurant, and staff and office facilities, with necessary plant, storage, and cloakroom spaces, is in the form of long, near white, indirectly lit galleries. These rooms are punctuated vertically by the original cast-iron columns and horizontally by large air-conditioning and lighting ducts slung beneath Hartley's brick vaulted ceilings. Of course there are the typical touches of fiercely coloured metal doors, partitions and pipes in strategic places. These have met the usual criticism from some quarters, but a modern art gallery is the right place for a little visual *élan* and the Albert Dock is quite tough enough as a context for the odd nonconformist touch.

It had been a bold move of the government's Property Services Agency, acting on behalf of the Tate's trustees, to appoint James Stirling to prepare a feasibility study for this conversion and, by implication, to execute it. In fact there proved to be no very serious problems; the building was in good condition and the chief expense over what might have been expected arose from the Tate's determination to have air-conditioning. The total cost is expected to be about £10 million. The first phase of £6.5 million was raised by £1.5 million in private donations and £500,000 from the Arts Minister, that is, from the Office of Arts and Libraries budget, which were added to the MDC grant of £4.5 million.

With an area of 1,700 sq. m, the Tate of the North is already as big as London's Hayward gallery; its projected completed size of 4,000 sq. m would mean that it was 50 per cent the size of the Millbank Tate. There attendance exceeds 1.5 million people per annum, and the Albert Dock gallery's target for the moment is 500,000. There will be one major exhibition each year and several minor ones, as well as opportunities to show more of the Tate's permanent collection of paintings and sculpture, three-quarters of which has been in store. Apart from studios and workshops for artists, a full student-education and teacher-training programme is planned. Fifty new jobs have been created.

London's docklands

The origin of London's docks was in the quays or hithes of Roman or Saxon times, mostly in the vicinity of what is now Lower Thames Street. Only smaller vessels tied up above London Bridge in medieval times; chief mooring places were at the Tower, Billingsgate, Puddle Dock at Wapping and Southwark on the south bank. Increases in both traffic and smuggling in the sixteenth century prompted Queen Elizabeth to establish a limited number of 'legal quays' where duties were collected. They proved inadequate, especially as the wool and cloth trades expanded. Congestion reached an appalling level in the later eighteenth century as the empire grew and the Industrial Revolution burgeoned, but the first enclosed dock, the West India, was not opened until 1802. Here, safe from tides and with secure warehousing alongside, was a sound basis for organized mercantile trade. Further and larger docks developed rapidly as London expanded eastwards and became for a century and a half the world's largest port: the London and the East India in 1805, the Surrey in 1807, St Katherine's (which covered 10 acres) in 1827, and so through the Millwall and Royal Victoria Docks to the Royal Group covering 245 acres. The last was opened in 1921.

Much of the teeming, polluted, and unhealthy life of the capital was centred in a number of riverside boroughs which now have a grittily romantic ring: Wapping, Limehouse, Bermondsey, Rotherhithe, Poplar, Millwall – there was indeed a line of windmills on the western edge of the Isle of Dogs. East London became the 'enterprise zone' of the capital in the nineteenth century as *Docklands Heritage* points out: 'with shipbuilding, engineering, chemicals, furniture and clothing manufacture, brewing and other industries'. Remarkably, despite massive bombing in the Second World War, recovery afterwards was dramatic, and the port handled over 50 million tons in 1959. Progress was illusory; a combination of 'advances' in planning and resistance to advances in technology destroyed the port. Vast London County Council housing estates did not help; 'the socially rigid formulae of the Brave New World redevelopment contributed to the catastrophic collapse of the East London economy' says the London Dockland Development Corporation book. Policies of removal for 'non-conforming' industries made local people ever more dependent on dock employment at the very time when new cargo-handling requirements were leading to closures and development of the Tilbury dock system down river. Vast areas of riverside were simply abandoned and, needless to say, no attention was paid to remaining seventeenth- and eighteenth-century houses and churches, let alone cliffs of nineteenth-century warehouses, during the period of postwar redevelopment nor the subsequent collapse. Here we shall concentrate on the fate of a number of surviving bonded warehouses, some of which are listed Grade I. But first a word about money and jobs. The LDDC report for the year to March 1988 speaks of £4.4 billion of private investment since 1981 (ten times the government grant), of over 11,000 additional jobs, of over 5 million square feet of commercial and industrial floor space completed and nearly 6 million square feet under construction, nearly 8,000 homes completed and over 6,000 under construction.

Tobacco Dock

Much of the London and St Katherine's docks have gone, splendid four-storey brick blocks on rusticated and decorated stone plinths, but a non-typical survival, the New Tobacco Warehouse, remains largely intact. Little known until recently, it is 'one of the greatest of all monuments to the daring and inspired eccentricity of dock engineers'.[16] Built in 1811–14 by David Asher Alexander, architect and surveyor to Trinity House, and engineer John Rennie, it consists of the misleadingly named Skin Floor, a vast single storey, top-lit store, and sales area for imported sheep skins, over a vaulted basement which is one of the wonders of London. Tobacco had given way to wool in 1860 at ground level, and the vaults were always used for wines and spirits. Then in 1968 the last ship sailed from London Dock. There began nearly twenty years of silence, decay, small-scale demolition and finally the alarms and excursions centring on News International's 'Fortress Wapping' built alongside. But as early as 1979 two entrepreneurs, Brian Jackson and Laurie Cohen, had recognized not only the fascination of Tobacco Dock, but also its potential. In that year they established Tobacco Dock Developments. LDDC, itself set up the following year, was supportive of ideas for refurbishment, but it was not until 1983 that the current architect Terry Farrell, and engineer Ove Arup, got to work.

What they found above ground were six warehouse bays totalling 80,000 sq. ft in area. The structure comprises a series of parallel roofs with timber queen-post trusses with continuous glazing at the apex. The trusses are suported at 54-ft centres on striking and very early cast-iron columns, formed of bifurcated stan-

chions resting on a stone base; they support a timber bolster below the continuous roof gutters. The most remarkable feature of this 176-year-old kit of parts, which has recently been dismantled and reassembled, are the raking prop supports to alternate trusses bent to follow compression forces. Below all this and extending far beyond it are the remaining four acres of vaulting, once part of a 20-acre system. There are beautifully chamfered granite columns under brick groins, the structural integrity of which has been necessarily disrupted in the creation of eight large openings, or courts, between the two floors to create London's new 'shopping village'. Now the two contrasting levels will be seen at once.

The Tobacco Dock centre comprises 160,000 sq. ft of lettable accommodation for retailers and restauranteurs, three times the size of Covent Garden. The architects for the £20 million scheme have adopted an approach which recognizes the chief quality here to be an engineering one. Large sections dismantled and re-erected include a whole bay on the west side which has been moved to the east to preserve it. Interventions are frankly modern, so new staircases, shopfronts, and such features as the reinforced concrete beam around the floor openings do not pretend to be nineteenth-century.

32 (a) and (b) (overleaf). Tobacco Dock, London; only four acres of these Piranesian vaults survive, those under the lightweight and top-lit structure of the 'Skin Floor' have been incorporated in a shopping centre three times the size of Covent Garden

There was a particular problem in the conversion of a customs warehouse on two isolated floors to an interlinked multi-use complex with over fifty tenants hoping to attract hoards of visitors. This was in satisfying the fire officers' requirement for one hour's fire resistance for the delicate cast iron columns and timber trusses. In many conversions the reluctant answer has been to encase cast iron in other materials. Here Terry Farrell even resisted the use of intumescent paint in its usual thick, mastic-like form which would have blurred the sections. A thin film of intumescent coating, carefully monitored and maintained, was agreed upon.

Timber decay was also a major headache, exacerbated by the removal of lead gutters in the 1960s. Here again the radical replacement of 80 per cent, as at Billingsgate Market, was avoided by on-site repairs. Contractor Harry Neal's thirty in-house carpenters claim to have evolved sixty or seventy types of repair, most of which meant scarfing in new timber to replace areas of rotten wood; but sometimes difficult access resulted in mortice-and-tenon joints, even butt joints using steel plates, and joints employing flitch plates and concealed split-end sheer plates. There is little attempt to hide such work, since it is all in the worthy cause of retaining as much original fabric as possible, not only for the sort of historical reasons espoused for over a century by the SPAB, but also because it is almost impossible to obtain new timbers in the sections and lengths required to replace whole members.

New Concordia Wharf, Bermondsey

London, St Katherine's, and Albert Dock in Liverpool are all examples of enclosed docks. In 1853 the Customs Consolidation Act allowed a different type of warehouse, on the river's edge, no longer behind high walls. New Concordia at St Saviour's Dock, Bermondsey, is an imposing example of multistorey 'Engineers Classical'. Built for North American grain in the 1880s, a little east of Tower Bridge on the south bank, St Saviour's Dock was closed with the rest of the inner London docks in the 1960s. Nothing had been done with the building though it had been in the hands of major developers for some years when Andrew Wadsworth, aged 22, came to London from Manchester in 1979 and looked for a home. Amazingly he succeeded by the end of 1980 in persuading Town & City Properties to sell him the 120,000 sq. ft build-

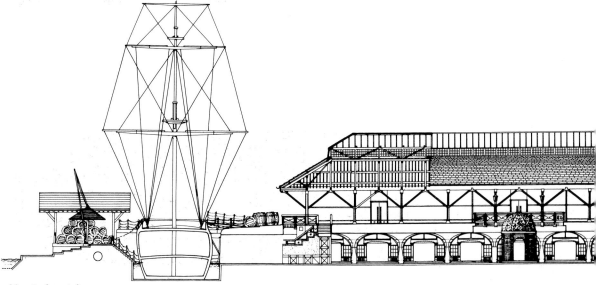

ing. In April 1981 Southwark Council granted planning consent for the mixed-use scheme he sought. By the end of that year architects Pollard Thomas Edwards had been appointed to join Alan Baxter and Associates, who were already the engineers. New Concordia was listed Grade II in early 1982, the recently established LDDC granted listed-building consent shortly thereafter, and all was ready for one of the first, cleanest, and most successful of the large warehouse conversions.

At a cost of about £3 million some sixty flats, twenty-four studio workshops, 3,000 sq. ft of offices, a large restaurant, communal spaces, and basement car park were created. One of Wadsworth's decisions was that nearly all the space should be let on long leases in shell form so that tenants could fit out interiors in a large variety of ways.

The building is not unaltered, the chief additions being a new and largely glass-clad sixth floor and metal balconies across the vertical rows of grain-loading doors, but the essential 'warehouseness' has been retained. Two cranes are still attached to the river elevation. The original metal windows have been replaced in careful replica, albeit of plastic. The splendidly quixotic approach is exemplified by the restoration of the tall brick column of a chimney beside the street-

33. Butler's Wharf, London Docks, in process of conversion; beside it the picturesque Anchor Brewery and Boilerhouse have also been converted to housing and leisure uses

facing entrance to the courtyard from which most of the accommodation is reached. This was condemned as a dangerous structure in 1979 and was only just saved from demolition by the new owner; it was subsequently restored with the aid of a generous Historic Buildings Council grant.

Butler's Wharf and Courage Brewhouse

New Concordia was completed in May 1984, although Andrew Wadsworth had to wait a year or two to occupy his own apartment, a conversion by Piers Gough of the other vertical feature, the former water tower. The 'conservation impact'

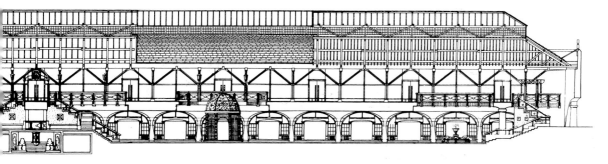

of this scheme was obvious even before completion; barely five years later hardly a warehouse on London's river remains without actual or planned conversion to new uses. By mid-1984 a consortium including developer/designers Conran Roche had purchased the Butler's Wharf group to the west of New Concordia. The two ends of this vast riverside block have now been developed, largely for commercial users. Just to the east of New Concordia, in a little gap between it and the now also converted Reed's Wharf, is the colourful new China Wharf (see p. 178), designed for Wadsworth by Piers Gough of CZWG. More ambitiously, in 1984 Wadsworth bought the 4.75-acre

34 (a) and (b). London's New Concordia Wharf before and after conversion into flats. A pacemaking scheme by young entrepreneur Andrew Wadsworth, the building's quality is retained despite modifications

former Courage Brewery site beyond Butlers Wharf and adjacent to Tower Bridge. 'Because he believes that it is "irresponsible" to hold a site for long periods he has sold off some of this site, choosing the purchasers and contractually determining the use, design and completion date of their works.'[17]

The Courage group of buildings is no cliff-like warehouse, rather an older, richer, more varied species of architecture consisting of the brick and white timber, many-gabled Anchor Brewhouse built by John Courage in 1787 at one end and the dramatically centre-chimneyed Victorian boilerhouse block at the other. Bill Thomas of Pollard Thomas Edwards, the

partner in charge of the site, drew up a master plan in 1984 which included the demolition of the newer buildings between and behind those mentioned. There is a wide variety of uses including new housing, offices, workshops, retail premises, and leisure facilities. The old riverbank blocks have been converted into some sixty-five residential shells. The first phase, consisting largely of the boilerhouse, was divided into thirty-five units in 1985. Included was a spectacular high-level penthouse sold for £2.25 million. The second phase of thirty-odd flats in the Brewhouse, finished in 1988, was something of a traditional historical buildings job, complete with new cast lead

35 (a) and (b). Gloucester Docks; sturdy 1830s warehouses not far from the cathedral in this historic city which was also an inland port. Recently converted to office, commercial and museum use

work on the handsome cupola.

These developments represent the last riverside opportunities in this part of docklands, and attention is shifting inland towards the much bigger Jacob's Island project.

Gloucester docks

Sturdy and handsome brick warehouses around Gloucester's dock basins have unexpectedly provided the central area room for expansion which that thriving city needs. Local planners and specu-

36. Chatham's
Historic
Dockyard's still
operative ropery
may be Britain's
longest interior at
1,140 feet.
Timber decay
was repaired by
PSA at same time
as reroofing was
carried out.

lators dealt harshly with the ancient town centre in the 1960s, but did not get around to the redevelopment of the unique Victorian inland port nearby. Twenty-three listed buildings in an outstanding conservation area remain substantially as built because, although the port only recently reached the end of its useful life, it never boomed to the extent that major internal expansion or change was demanded. The result, as the city's own publicity leaflet stated in 1983, is 'a 9.6 hectares site containing 27,000 sq metres of vacant historic buildings, still by and large in good condition and awaiting an injection of new life'. Ideally poised to take advantage of the economic upturn, Gloucester docks are by no means vacant now.

Gloucester was a major city of medieval England, its cathedral a place for royal burials and a coronation – of Henry II in 1216. The Romans had been the first to develop a port on the River Severn. This fell into disuse until the later Middle Ages and it was not until the reign of Elizabeth I that letters patent granted formal port status and established a custom house.

Large-scale nineteenth-century developments included the cutting of a canal in 1827 from the lower estuary to the town, by passing some of the hazards of the river – silting, shifting sand bars, and the famous tidal flow of the Severn Bore. At the same time the impressive Main Basin was constructed. It was lined by nine of the fourteen historic warehouses. A row of them along the east side are six-storey, with gable ends toward the water and retaining their old names – Herbert, Kimberley, Phillpotts, Vinings, and Double Reynolds. At the southern end the flank wall of the older Biddles Warehouse and to the north of the Main Basin is the North, or 'Telford', Warehouse, dating from the time the great engineer was in charge of the canal's construction. To the west and separated by a lock is the Lock or Jennings Guildings Warehouse, now in use as an antiques centre. East of the Main Basin the Victoria Docks were opened in 1849; more wharves were needed to cope with the corn trade boom following the repeal of the Corn Laws.

Though all with light red brick walls and slate-tiled roofs, the warehouses vary subtly in their details – windows are spanned by stone lintels or by brick arches for example – as well as in precise dimensions and internal planning. They all have robust timber floors supported by internal cast iron columns, and so can support heavy loads. Within the docks complex are other buildings of character: the lancet-windowed stone-built chapel, the main office building at the principal entrance (now the British Waterways Board), and the classically designed Custom House of the 1840s. Nearby, also in stone, are merchants' offices facing Commercial Road.

In recent years refurbishment has proceeded apace, though it was necessary for public authorities to show the way despite Gloucester's enviable geographical position with direct access to the M5 and a rail link to London. The North Warehouse, the one in the poorest structural state, was completed in 1986 and occupied by departments of the city council. In 1988 the Herbert, Kimberley, and Phillpott buildings were converted for the same purpose. At the same time the Llanthony Warehouse, the largest of all, was renovated to contain the National Waterways Museum which is expected to attract about 250,000 visitors a year. Regional offices for the British Waterways Board are also now in the Llanthony which is equipped with provision for parking 200 cars, as well as an outside exhibition area. Major commercial reuse is proposed for the rest of the Main and Victoria Dock basins. Outline planning permission has been granted to Pearce Developments (Bristol) for a comprehensive scheme involving building on sites fronting Southgate Street and north of the Barge Arm, together with the refurbishment of seven listed warehouses. Uses will include specialist shopping, housing, offices, workshops, leisure uses, and car parking. For the site west of the Main basin a planning brief has been prepared for development intended to include a 100-bed hotel, residential and community use, and further car parking to serve the docks as a whole.

Chatham Dockyard

Henry VIII's ships anchored at Chatham and some of Elizabeth's sailed from there to defeat the Armada; this was the seventeenth century's major naval base after James I had built the first dry dock. Workshops and stores were added to slipways, then more specialized facilities such as a mast house, sail loft, and a ropehouse. Fortifications were strengthened after the Dutch had sacked the Thames and Medway bases in 1667. Despite problems with shoaling most of the early eighteenth-century fleet was maintained at Chatham. Big ships such as the *Victory* were built in 1765. But by that time south-coast ports at Plymouth and Portsmouth had proved more strategically sited for the Atlantic and Mediterranean engagements of the French wars and Chatham was already being superseded. An expanding navy continued to find uses for the old buildings especially in wartime. Small ships were built and, between 1908 and 1966 submarines were launched.

Such are the habits of government departments that land was still being reclaimed from the marshes for expansion into the 1970s. That availability of space meant that new facilities were simply added as time went on and little was demolished. So it was that most of the eighteenth- and nineteenth-century structures survived in a largely unaltered setting and a reasonable state of repair. When the closure decision was taken in 1981, the preservation of the biggest collection of ancient monuments on one site, some fifty in all, many of them huge, seemed an impossibly daunting task – even to some conservationist groups like the Georgian Society. It says much for the imagination of Michael Heseltine and his successors at the DoE that, little more than a year after the navy departed on 1 April 1984, much of the historic site was open to visitors.

The Chatham Historic Dockyard Trust which commenced operations in March 1984 with responsibility in particular for the historic core of 80 acres in the 600-acre dockyard site, had the objective of 'the preservation and use of the historic dockyard for the benefit of the public in a manner that is appropriate to its great importance in terms of archaeology, history and architecture'. The trust also has to promote and spread knowledge about Chatham. New commercial, retail, residential, and industrial development has been carried out on the extensive outlying parts of the navy's former holding. The historic site itself, an irregular north–south rectangle along the Medway, consists of four parts differing somewhat in their character, history, and new roles.

In the centre is a little early-eighteenth-century redbrick 'town' of houses, offices, a slightly later church, and the 1720s sail loft. The buildings in terraces on sloping ground focus on a handsome 'manor house' built for the commissioner in 1703. On the river bank to the south is the

Anchor Wharf area, chiefly comprising two eighteenth-century storehouses, the largest ever built in Britain and the parallel ropery, completed in 1792, which at 1,140 feet is the longest. It replaced roperies dating to 1618. The more northerly half of the waterfront chiefly comprises the dry docks for shipbuilding and the covered docks, or ships, for fitting out and repairs, which dwarf most of the other structures. The earliest dating to 1838, of these covered slips, is a superb timber shell resembling an upturned boat, the others are scarcely less impressive metal structures. The last of them, built in 1855, will be the youngest fully conserved building on the site. Finally on the flat inland part of the site to the north is the industrial area. A group of nineteenth-century buildings is dominated by the sawmills of 1812–14 designed by Marc Brunel. Beyond is the mast pond with, on its further bank, the serene, white-boarded 'lower boat house' of 1844.

The site has a government endowment of £11 million, chiefly for the maintenance of the scheduled buildings and some of which was committed to the repair of the ropery when the trust took over. A lot of energy has gone into attracting others to 'bring their ideas, their skills and their money' to restore the dockyard to life. The trust's chairman, General Sir Steuart Pringle, the distinguished former marines commander, described his plans as having three and a half strands: residential, commercial/industrial, and, the most important, museum. The half strand consists of practical courses in some of the crafts appropriate to the reused dry docks, slips, and workshops. Ready for the opening was a vividly arranged museum in the former galvanizing shop, complete with information desk and tourist shop. Flag-making was proceeding in the sail and colour loft and rope-making in the ropery.

This latter activity had to be suspended only briefly during the period of repairs to the ropery carried out by the Property Services Agency, originally on behalf of the Ministry of Defence and latterly for the Chatham Historic Dockyard Trust in liaison with English Heritage. It was built in 1786–92 for the spinning of yarn and the manufacture of rope from natural fibres by means of machines which travel on rails the full enormous length of the building. The simple perspective of the apparently endless 'room' and of the loft above it, with machinery dating from 1818 operating in an entirely comprehensible manner by twisting endless lengths of yarn, is fascinating to visitors. The fact that the Falklands campaign underlined the superiority of the product to modern nylon rope in certain conditions adds to the sense of satisfaction. Built of red brick with grey headers, the three-storey building has a suitably functional exterior. Some casements still have original glazing bars.

Most of the expenditure on the ropery was concentrated on the double-pitched roof with its central valley gutter between the two cock-lofts (attics). Probably Kent-peg-tiled originally, the roof was recently clad in corrugated asbestos cement sheeting. The PSA replaced this covering with hand-made clay titles. Structural repairs to main floor beams and pillars and treatment of other timbers built into the brickwork were also carried out.

Another group of buildings of particular interest and which is now being restored with assistance from the European Commission are the mast houses and mould loft. Situated behind the covered slipways this is smaller in scale and more complex in outline than the ropery, and yet the primary space, the mould floor, has the quality of scale so typical of this site. Although 119 by 55 feet, it has no supports to interrupt the space which was required for laying down ships lines. These buildings, constructed in 1753 and extended in 1883, are the strongest in history and atmosphere in the whole dockyard. It was here that the *Victory* was laid out. They are ideally suited for museum use.

Battersea Power Station

A massive rectangular block with a fluted chimney at each corner, this building has often been likened – usually affectionately – to an upturned table. A closer view discloses the highly sculptural design of the brick cladding designed by Sir Giles Gilbert Scott, architect of Liverpool's Anglican Cathedral. Battersea was built in two phases, each with a vast turbine hall and two chimneys: the first of 1933 and the second, delayed by the war, not completed until well into the 1950s. This last, the B station, had three advanced generating machines each capable of 100 megawatt output. Surplus heat was fed through mains under the river to provide district heating for the Pimlico and Dolphin Square housing schemes on the north bank.

Battersea was the highest up-river coal-powered station in London, and one of its problems was the environmental pressure to remove sulphur from the exhaust gases. This had been at least partly achieved by attaching 'scrubbing' equipment to each flue. That process had the side effect of producing an acid precipitate which corroded both concrete and brickwork. It was expensive to operate, not to speak of the potential cost of replacing and repointing millions of bricks were the station to remain in use. In fact closure plans were announced in 1978. SAVE immediately sought admission to study the building and explore alternative uses. CEGB were not co-operative until, prompted by a letter from Marcus Binney to Tony Benn, the Minister of Energy intervened and a 'grand tour' was arranged in early 1979.

At that time turbine hall A, the more impressive of the two, was unfortunately in the process of being stripped out to sell the turbines for scrap. The architecture of the interior was expressionist in an almost 'Metropolis' way and was on a huge scale, the hall being 500 feet long, 100 feet

wide, and 120 feet high. Binney described the towering square pillars on either side of the main space: clad in tiles, the treatment 'was like two versions of the Hoover factory facing each other across a street'.[18] He also writes vividly of the control room, the work of the original architects, Halliday & Agate (Scott was brought in to aggrandize the exterior). The walls were marble panelled 'and the ceiling was worthy of a jazz age grand hotel or ocean liner. All the control equipment was still in place, and in one corner was a splendid scale model of the power station.'

In 1978 DoE officials had suppressed a Historic Buildings Council proposal for listing, not wishing to get in the way of the Electricity Board's plans for the redevelopment of the 15-acre site. On 14 October 1980 Michael Heseltine did list the station. SAVE commissioned a study of alternative uses from architect Martin Richardson. Offices would have been financially attractive, but architecturally difficult and unacceptable to Wandsworth Council in any case. An early conclusion was that there could be parking space for 1,300 cars beneath the main operational level, though it has to be admitted road access to the site, especially across the river, has always been a problem. An attractive proposal was for a giant European standard indoor sports centre with seating for 8,000 round a four-lane 160-metre track, for example, and this was approved by Wandsworth's planning department.

In October 1983 CEGB launched a competition. The financial requirements were daunting, but seven substantial entries were received and exhibited in April 1984. Public interest was considerable. A favoured proposal was for 'London's first leisure and entertainment complex of world standing'. And this, after several changes to the scheme and the make up of the consortium involved, is the core of the project under construction. A moving spirit in the enterprise has been John Broome whose entertainment

37. Battersea Power Station, London; Turbine Hall A had a splendid Metropolis-like interior with bold Art Deco detailing, some of which has been sacrificed in current £250 million leisure centre conversion

38. Dunton Staithes, biggest and only surviving Tyneside coal wharf, repaired with English Heritage grant to be a centrepiece of 1992 Gateshead Garden Festival

complex at Alton Towers is a major visitor attraction.

Many hurdles have been surmounted to reach the stage announced in *The Financial Times* of 22 September 1988. 'Sir Robert McAlpine ... has been awarded a £130 m management contract to convert Battersea Power Station into a £200 m leisure centre.... A series of halls and galleries will house a theatre and other entertainments. Part of the work will involve construction of a railway station with a direct link to Victoria, and parking for 2,200 cars. An existing jetty at the site is to be refurbished and there are to be new bridge links across the river.' The report concludes with the information that architects for Battersea Leisure, a company set up to run the building, is the Fitzroy Robinson Partnership. Completion is projected for 1990.

Dunston Staithes

This coal-handling wharf has recently been repaired with enthusiastic support from the Newcastle and Gateshead authorities. On the south bank of the Tyne, visible from both these towns, it was the largest coal depot ever built on the river, as well as the last one surviving.

A major fire had badly damaged the second staith, or jetty, which had been added in 1903 to the original wharf constructed in 1890 for the North Eastern Railway. When English Heritage offered a £250,000 grant in 1987 it was agreed that the remains of the later staith might be demolished in order to provide repair timbers for the proposed works to the earlier structure. The chief damage to this was found to be to the timber deck on which the trains originally ran. It had been alternately soaked with water and showered with coal dust for almost a century. The underlying framework of massive pitch-pine scantlings remained sound. Public access will be possible in future to both the upper deck and to an intermediate level, thus allowing Dunston Staithes to be a central feature of the 1990 Gateshead National Garden Festival.

This reminder of the coal- and heavy-industry-based infrastructure of Britain's wealth up to the mid-twentieth century will provide another example of 'conservation impact' encouraging efforts to breathe new life into the derelict industrial area of Dunston.

Ribblehead Viaduct

Built in 1875 for the Midland Railway, this is one of the most spectacular sights in the finest scenery on one of the outstanding railways in England. A scheduled monument, it is 156 feet tall at its highest point, spanning the Pennine Moorland valley. But J. S. Crossley's twenty-four-arched limestone structure has an uncertain future. British Rail applied to the Department of Transport in 1984 to close the line. The fame of the Settle–Carlisle route leading to intense public interest had been expected to keep it open if only as a tourist attraction. For that very reason, however, the line has been offered to private operators.

Meanwhile the railway continues to run and exploratory repairs have been carried out on one span of the viaduct.

39. *Ribblehead Viaduct, Cumbria; remote scenery enhanced by an industrial monument on the Carlisle to Settle railway which may be run privately as an alternative to BR's closure plans*

There has been some difficulty in agreeing the type and extent of necessary works on a structure virtually untouched for a century. Perhaps not unnaturally, British Rail, when seeking to close the line, did not belittle possible expenditure on works required to keep it open. Figures mentioned varied between £2.5 million and over £4 million. With just a touch of scepticism about even the first sum, English Heritage offered a grant of up to £1 million in May 1987 – representing its usual contribution to allowable costs of about 40 per cent. The expectation is that that will be taken up in 1989 or 1990 by whichever organization is then responsible for the line, the Ribblehead, and seven other viaducts, together with Victorian stations and associated historic structures.

As can be seen, the viaduct's every sixth support is a 'king pier' of extra thickness. Constructed in limestone, these have double 'chimneys', that is, vertical voids within. The ordinary piers are solid with hard limestone masonry cladding over rubble cores. In both cases there is surface cracking and some evidence of outer stonework separating from the core of the standard piers. Experts from English Heritage hope that only limited steel reinforcement will be required with possibly some resin repairs to stonework, with thorough repointing of mortar joints. The top deck, originally waterproofed with bitumen, will have to be made good to prevent water penetration to the basic structure and consequent damage through freezing. The exposed site is often cold, windy, and wet.

The recent specimen repair carried out by a private contractor for British Railways on behalf of the Department of Transport is expected to have yielded valuable information for later tenderers for work on the rest of the viaduct. It was assisted by the Railway Heritage Trust.

The heritage of railway architecture

Of all transformations of attitudes, both popular and corporate, the most remarkable one has been that concerning a future for railway stations and other associated structures, including bridges and viaducts. Among the largest of government historic building grants offered have been those for Ribblehead Viaduct and Dunston Staithes, described above. In 1977 SAVE Britain's Heritage mounted an exhibition, 'Off the Rails'. The introduction to the accompanying book started thus:

The purpose of this exhibition is to make you angry. Britain invented the railway, pioneered its application to passenger travel and built the most extensive network of lines and stations anywhere in the world ... an architectural and archaeological achievement without parallel ... an investment of effort, skill and even artistry comparable with the building of the great gothic churches in the Middle Ages. . . . Yet it is pitifully neglected.

Simon Jenkins, who wrote those words, is now a director of British Rail. He ascribed the neglect to the manifestation of a 'dying industry' and also to 'the continued reluctance of the British to respect the architectural achievements of their grandparents. The railways were the greatest of the works of the Victorian age.'[19] In the same publication Marcus Binney wrote:

British Rail's handling of redundant railway property shows a remarkable combination of financial ineptitude, managerial myopia and stodginess ... a sad failure to recognize that railway history and old railway buildings have the most marketable quality of all – sex appeal.

At the end of *Off the Rails* a series of proposals by SAVE included calls for 'a more energetic and flexible approach to the sale of surplus property', an end to 'corporate mania', where every region, indeed every sign, has to be standardized, adoption of 'multiple use' – 'Unwanted waiting rooms, ticket offices etc could be leased commercially or to local voluntary organisations' – the recognition of the potential of tourism, the appointment of conservation officers, and 'A trust could be formed to take responsibility, and where necessary raise money, for interesting railway buildings'. In various forms all this has come to pass; so has a suggestion for government (then HBC) grants for historic building repairs to continue to be offered, despite BR's then habit of refusing them. £65,000 for St Pancras was rejected on the grounds that it was insufficient, but really because British Rail did not wish to restore the famous linenfold-panelled booking hall but rather to replace it with a gleaming glass, aluminium, and plastic design. BR fought and lost a public inquiry over that booking hall, but in recent years it has supported the idea of the £50 million refurbishment of the hotel above it – long misused as offices.

Most symbolically striking of all was the establishment in 1985 of just the Railway Heritage Trust suggested by SAVE; both Binney and Jenkins are on the four-man board. Sums expended by the trust have been comparatively modest, but the fact that it was established by BR with a grant of £750,000, that it exists as a prestigious body aiming at 'the preservation of listed buildings within the BR portfolio', and that, contrary to former attitudes, BR now welcomes contributions to elements of major projects which relate to 'repairs and restoration of the heritage aspect of buildings and structures', point to a revolution in BR's thinking. This is just as well, for what used to be regarded as the onerous burden of responsibility for listed buildings unfairly loaded onto a transport undertaking has been increased by accelerated listing by the Department of the Environment. This has led to growth from 680 to 981 of BR-protected buildings and structures.

So far the Railway Heritage Trust has supported 106 schemes with grants totalling over £3 million and has attracted another £1.7 million from non BR sources. In the year 1987–8 grants were authorized for forty-five schemes amounting to £1 million which attracted £0.6 million from other parties. One of the major projects in progress, the restoration of Stockport Viaduct, was supported by a contribution of £2.2 million from the Manpower Services Commission. The very list of last year's grants is evocative: £300 was allowed for the Beverley Station clock while the clock at Malton, perhaps a more ambitious chronometer, was aided to the extent of £800; and Kettering, one of the most splendid of canopied stations, has been refurbished.

For all its valuable works the Railway Heritage Trust, with its annual budget of a million pounds or so, is of psychological significance as much as financial. For the multi-million pound projects the initiative has to come from elsewhere.

Manchester's railway stations

40. Manchester Central Station, the great train shed – now an exhibition centre rejoicing in the name of G-MEX

The two great cities of the north-west were the creation of the age of canal and rail. The Liverpool to Manchester

railway, one of the world's first, was opened in 1830 largely as a result of the efforts of George Stephenson. Its surviving bridges and goods warehouses and station buildings are among the earliest.

The station at Liverpool Road, Manchester, had a neo-classical passenger entrance building which was, however, soon overshadowed by larger warehouses. Passenger traffic ceased after 1844, but the station continued in goods operation until 1975. Five years later it was chiefly the warehouses which provided accommodation for the North Western Museum of Science and Industry as a co-operative venture between BR, the

Greater Manchester Council, and the Department of the Environment.

The story of the later and much bigger Central Station, Manchester is very different. Opened in 1880 as an integrated transport centre for passengers and goods via road and canal as well as rail, Central has a train hall rivalling St Pancras. Its 85-feet-high arches provide a clear space of over 100,000 sq. ft. The associated Midland Hotel was not opened until 1903, however. Closure of the station in 1969 was followed by eleven years of deterioration only halted after 1979 when GMC brought the site for £1.8 million. In 1981 £750,000 spent in stabilizing the iron train-shed structure was 50 per cent

41 (a) and (b) (overleaf). Green Park Station, Bath; the glamour of the Age of Steam cannot be reproduced in what is now a supermarket forecourt and car park – there is also a museum in the forebuilding

grant-aided by the DoE. That done, studies into new uses proceeded; the large space seemed ideal for exhibitions but the expenditure on the building and surrounding infrastructure was beyond the council's resources. Commercial Union Properties was brought into a public/private consortium. The station itself is but the core structure in an ambitious scheme to revitalize 26 desolate acres at the centre of the city, a task not rendered easier by the remains of multi-level communications on the site, including underground canals. Of the eventual sum of nearly £120 million expenditure some £18 million was devoted to the train shed and immediate surroundings. Only its

wrought-iron roof was protected by listing, and the 1950s corrugated iron and glass covering had to be replaced. Like that other Midland Railway giant, St Pancras, there were extensive cellars available for parking and other subsidiary uses.

Rather like the National Exhibition Centre at Birmingham, G-MEX, as Central is now known, is able to host concerts with seating for 8,500 and sporting events for about 5,000 spectators when not occupied with exhibitions. Great Victorian iron sheds are proving versatile assets – Islington's Agricultural Hall being another example. G-MEX had bookings two years ahead by the time of its opening show in March 1986. That was a promotion for the north-west with 180 local firms booking space for exhibits which attracted 25,000 British and overseas businessmen. Apart from Central Station Properties, the GMC and Commercial Union joint company, funds came from the government via urban development grants and from the EEC. Private companies have invested in other developments on the site.

The old Midland Hotel was renovated at a cost of £15 million and reopened in 1987 as a lavish Holiday Inn. Like St Pancras and the Langham, this 'apotheosis of Victorian hotel building', as Nikolaus Pevsner described it, is faced with red brick and brown stone. An interior rich in marble and ornate plasterwork evokes turn-of-the-century luxury while a health club and the usual conference and banqueting facilities are there to attract the modern businessman.

Bath, Green Park Station

Yet another Midland Railway venture, the Bath terminus, was opened in 1870 as the Queen Square Station. This being the city it is, the forebuilding is a little early-Georgian-style palazzo, a bit in the

manner of Burlington House in London with its columned and recessed centre. Behind it is a medium-sized train shed by J. S. Crossley, its single-arched iron main roof springing from elegant columns pacing down the departure platform on one side and the arrivals on the other. Around the corner were stables and horses provided by the railway company for local parcel and goods deliveries. After nationalization in 1947, the station was renamed Green Park and continued in use until 1966. Listed Grade II in 1971, the buildings were bought by the local authority in the following year. The unfortunately all too common period of disuetude allowed damage and decay

chiefly through vandalism and theft of lead. Bath Council carried out basic repairs to the stone buildings, envisaging reuse as a hotel, but as far as the train shed went the only action was to remove remaining roof glass as a safety measure. It was no surprise when an application for demolition consent was lodged, but learning that a public inquiry was in prospect the council withdrew its application in 1978. A search for alternatives led, however, to two public inquiries into various proposals the following year until, in October, the city council entered into an agreement with BR and the leading retailer Sainsbury's for the erection of a store and the renovation of the station buildings. Once again what must have seemed like intransigence by the DoE in support of conservationists paid off. The forebuilding and the adjacent part of the train shed was to be a museum and provide a picturesque pedestrian route towards the supermarket. The necessary parking would occupy the further, westerly, part of the former train shed.

Parts of both stone and ironwork were much decayed; a major refurbishment resulted in a return to original condition and materials as far as possible. The turned stone balustrade atop the stone facade was entirely replaced for example. Visitors now enter near one end of that façade through the former 'ladies second class waiting room' on to the restored wood-floored cross platform. The centre of the frontage to their right comprise the reinstated booking hall, stationmaster's office, parcels office, and beyond that, a narrow room which housed the 'foot-warmers' so appreciated by passengers before the heating of railway carriages in the early 1900s. Beyond that again are rooms for porters, lamps and stores, a third-class waiting room and toilets, and, finally, a 'fish store'. On the other side visitors may see the first-class ladies' and gentlemen's waiting rooms *en route* to Sainsbury's via the former third-class booking hall which houses an exhibition concerned with the restoration.

Brighton Station

The conversion at Bath is the product of particular alternative uses, but it is typical in scale and enterprise of a score and more renovations of still operative stations. Such was the recent £200,000 revamping of Brighton's Grade II buildings of the 1840s which was carried out with the help of donations of £30,000 from the Railway Heritage Trust and £2,000 from the local council.

Shrewsbury Station

In 1984 it was announced that BR, having failed to interest private developers, was 'going it alone' with a £1.2 million redevelopment of Shrewsbury Station dating from 1848 and also listed Grade II. In mock-Tudor and late-Perpendicular styles the stone buildings are extensive. By 1986 they were meticulously refurbished with much damaged stone and plasterwork detailing renewed to provide offices for rent in association with a still-busy station. The fact that the new booking hall and 'travel centre' in light coloured hardwoods and ceramic tiles partakes convincingly of neither modern nor period styles is a minor cavil.

42. Denmark Hill Station London; after a disastrous fire this handsome suburban station was reconstructed as a bar and restaurant

Cambridge and Chester Stations

At Cambridge Station the fifteen-arched, light-coloured brick and stone façade has been the subject of a restoration funded by BR, the Railway Heritage Trust, and Cambridge City Council in 1987. Part of the even larger, though less architecturally ambitious, buildings at Chester Station were fire-damaged in 1973 when classified as 'surplus office accommodation'. Sold in 1981, after the usual delay for further decay, they have now 'been magnificently restored as an architect's office with assistance of grant aid', and the BR Property Board's booklet of 1986 (encouragingly entitled *Heritage and the Environment*), continues: 'Further refurbishment of surplus accommodation in the original 1847 portion of the station is planned.' A notable feature of many of these projects is local authority participation, if on a modest scale. This can be seen as a response to a challenge issued almost a decade ago by BR, that if other organizations were so keen on the 'railway heritage' they should help to maintain it. They were and they have.

Thus the situation has been transformed. We can only lament some grievous losses in the 1960s and 1970s (of 3,500 stations closed less than half were sold for reuse and 20,000 acres of land were 'abandoned' according to the DoE) while rejoicing that now BR is back 'on the rails'.

Chapter 7

Looking after Modern Classics

*Voysey House,
Chiswick,
architect's
axonometric
from below*

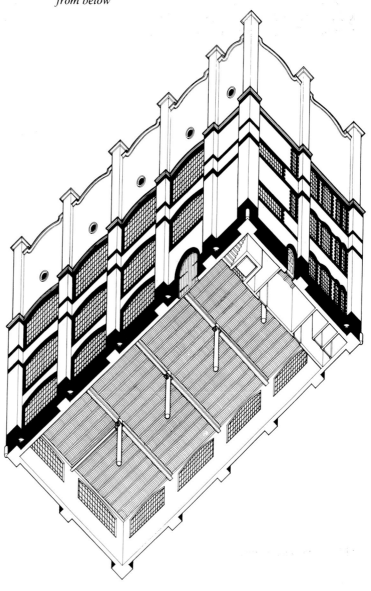

Introduction

The preservation, and, where appropriate, conversion to new uses of post-1919 buildings of merit is entirely consistent with conservation practice over the last century. If the best, most beautiful and interesting architecture and engineering of every period is to be looked after, there can be no reason – apart from judgement with limited perspective – to exclude the most recent. History is littered with appalling examples of losses of buildings simply because they were designed in that most unfashionable style, the one of the day before yesterday. Most Renaissance men regarded Gothic work as barbarous, Christian Gothic revivalists disdained neoclassicism except for the humblest of edifices, international-style modernists excoriated the unprincipled eclecticism of the Victorians, and, most recently, post-modernists have derided the naive certainties of the 1920s pioneers.

One problem, both theoretical and highly practical, complicates decisions in the matter of preserving modern architecture, namely that many examples were designed for a short life, sixty years at the most. Many indeed employ a technology into which a short life is built. Examples include tent-like structures such as those designed by Michael Hopkins at Cambridge for Schlumberger, and at Lords cricket ground for MCC. More fundamental is the dilemma posed by designs by Richard Rogers, for example the Lloyds building in London, and the Pompidou centre in Paris. In both cases exterior elevations are dominated by the 'guts' of the buildings, that is, air-conditioning, other service ducts, and, to a lesser extent, lifts and escalators. These are accessible partly in order that they may be changed, which, if they were listed, would be against the letter of listed-building controls.

In dealing with early twentieth-century concrete, or as was often the case rendered brick walls pretending to be concrete, with rusting iron windows

43. Boots' factory, Nottingham; this 1933 design by engineer Sir Owen Williams remains handsome and practical

embedded, there are difficulties again. Surely it would be foolish not to use metal which was coated or protected from rapid decay in some way? It is certainly necessary to insist as often as possible on repainting exteriors in the original colour, usually white. Ruskin's 'patina of age' here would be far from romantic.

It seems appropriate to face the fact that international-style buildings by such architects as Connell, Ward and Lucas, Lubetkin, even Maxwell Fry and Wells Coates are slightly poignant trailers for a future which never happened, rather than bright exemplars of a confident tomorrow, and simply another fashion, alongside the more commercial art-deco buildings of the 1930s. They shared many features – white walls, flat roofs, metal windows, balconies, glass bricks – but art deco, not taking itself so seriously, rejoiced in colour and decoration, polychromed glazed tiles, faience, bronze reliefs. This style is exemplified best by the prestige office fronts to factories on the western roads out of London.

Of course in some ways both these essentially European styles were widely influential in a popularized form in suburban and seaside villas. Very few were sternly internationalist, flat-roofed, and unornamented, though architects did design a number. Some are in the village of Silver End in Essex. More common was a hybrid of white walls and metal windows under a green-tiled roof and with a stained-glass sunrise in the front door. A telling juxtaposition in the suburbs was of these rather 'foreign-looking' houses besides rows of entirely English, sub-Lutyens, half-timbered semi-detached yeomen's villas. Recently a couple of such suburbs, such as Well Hall Estate, Eltham, have been declared conservation areas.

The vast majority of interwar architecture was backward-looking of course. While a few town halls echoed the stark brick elegance of Stockholm, Norwich and Hornsey, for example, most preferred a watered down neo-Georgian or a hyped-up Edwardian Baroque, like London's County Hall, listed but soon to be converted into a hotel. The best of these deserve protection too. Most forward-looking of all, as it turned out, were the concrete-framed, usually fully-glazed offices, factories, and newspaper works of Sir Owen·Williams, sometimes curved, often with black glass, always confident and competent. Boots, listed Grade I, is described below. Owen Williams's buildings were large in spirit even when not especially big in fact. Giantism was part of the excitement of a strain of design in the 1930s, inspired by Italian Futurist propaganda and films like Fritz Lang's *Metropolis* of the 1920s. Actual vastness

was occasionally achieved, for example in Battersea Power Station.

The Grade II* listing of Bracken House next to St Paul's cathedral, is recent. Its modest brick classicism by Sir Albert Richardson complements Wren more effectively than Lord Holford's clod-hopping efforts nearby. The irony is that contemporary fashionable opinion, at least as represented by the 'Anti-Uglies', was against Bracken House. Paternoster Square, to the north-east of the cathedral, is soon to be demolished. Let us hope that architectural opinion does not so change again that the loss of Holford's buildings will be regretted in future.

Voysey House, Chiswick

Sometimes referred to as the Sanderson Building, this is the only industrial structure designed by the leading Arts and Crafts architect and precursor of modernism, C. F. A. Voysey (1857–1951). It was constructed in 1902 as an extension for Arthur Sanderson & Sons, the wallpaper and fabric manufacturers, whose main factory is opposite in Barley Mow Passage. It is worth mentioning that the larger building has been occupied for a decade by the co-operative multi-occupation workshops and studios which are themselves an offshoot of '5 Dryden Street', the former Covent Garden warehouse converted in the early 1970s for use by small firms.

Voysey's connection with Sanderson's was, no doubt, his own work as a textile and wallpaper designer. He is best known for his influential country houses. They were often white, rough-rendered, with horizontal windows and prominent pitched roofs, it was their attempted 'absence of style' which provided the Modern Movement impulse. In retrospect, strains of Art Nouveau as well as Arts and Crafts date his buildings fairly precisely. Sanderson's left what was then aptly called the 'White Building' in 1928 after a fire had gutted the main factory. The remarkable exterior has survived largely unspoilt to this day. Rectangular in plan, 100 by 50 ft, it has four tall floors and is divided into bays by projecting piers which also serve as ventilation shafts – a motif picked up again in the 1960s by trend-setting American architects like Louis Khan. It is faced with white glazed bricks and contrasting bands of Staffordshire blues, now painted black. The piers extend above the tall, wavy parapet which hid the original roof. Both parapet and piers are capped in Portland stone, as is the string course over the uppermost of the large windows which occupy much of exterior of the three lower floors. These were steel framed, but were divided into small panes. As a complete contrast the lofty upper section of the walls was almost blank apart from a porthole dressed in Portland stone in the centre of each bay. The modernism of the masterly design is emphasized by the expression of four wide, structural bays and a narrower end bay containing what we would now call a service core – with staircase, lift shaft, and lavatories. Apart from that bay each floor was intended to be open-planned, with only a line of four central columns. But in this building Voysey was not only being 'modern', he was also being 'post-modern' in effect; the shallow arches over the large windows with their many panes are surely evocative of early textile mills, and the almost gothic oak doors must be the product of a lively wit. Even more quirky are the cast-iron quadrants fitting into the corners of the piers at low level 'to deter customers of the adjoining pub from using the corners as urinals'. Yet another humorous touch was the bridge to the main factory at third-floor level which resembled a train carriage. This has gone.

Distinctive features abound inside. Beams across the width of the building bear onto cast-iron columns which reduce in diameter on each floor. Resting on those beams are steel joists at 3 ft centres.

44 (a) and (b). Voysey House, Chiswick, is the old Sanderson wallpaper building renamed after its 1900 architect by the current owners, a firm of architects, one of whom has a flat behind the high curves of the roof parapet

These in turn support arched, corrugated permanent shuttering to the concrete floor above.

In 1928 the new owners, the Alliance Insurance Company, removed the bridge and used the building variously as a printing works, stationery store, and offices. Another insurance company, a subsidiary, taking over and using the building for offices, carried out a major refurbishment with all the sensitivity to be expected in 1968. Floors were raised, false ceilings installed together with the inevitable partitions and a new external fire escape. Most radical was the removal of the double north-light roof which was concealed behind the parapet; it was replaced by a flat roof with skylights.

In 1986 the Voysey Building, as it is now to be called, was taken over by an architect's practice and an engineering firm for their own use. They formed a trust which leases them each a floor and lets another to a third company. On the third floor, new offices have been laid out around a paved courtyard, and, above that, living quarters with a terrace have been created for occupation by one of the architect partners. The roof of this flat follows the undulating curve of this parapet and so is concealed.

Other alterations to the now listed Voysey House largely comprise removals of the accretions, including partitions and false ceilings and the external fire stair which has been replaced by a new internal one at the west end. All this work was supervised on a direct-labour basis by the architects, Lawrence & Wrightson, for a total cost of £150,000; they claim the price from contractors would have been double.

There is one drawback to this building (perhaps it would not be an early modern classic if it were not so) – it leaks. The water penetration through the white glazed brickwork, which has deteriorated badly in places, is proving troublesome in that it is difficult to find satisfactory

modern glazed-brick replacements to satisfy everyone, including English Heritage. There is even the possibility of a grant from EH – a rarity with a Grade II listed building – but then this is Voysey's only industrial design.

The Penguin Pool at London Zoo

Early Modern Movement monuments in Britain are rare. They are also vulnerable, very often being constructed in concrete, a material which is neither popular nor durable if exposed to the elements. Built in 1934 by the *émigré* architect Berthold Lubetkin in association with six Architectural Association graduates who called themselves Tecton, the Penguin Pool and its walkways are a classic.

As described by its recent refurbisher, John Allan of Avanti Architects, 'the strictly mathematical elliptical enclosure cut obliquely by two spectacularly cantilevered ramps provided an aquatic arena for the penguins to display alternatively their comic gait on land and consumate grace in water'.[20] It was a 'visual metaphor' for Antarctica, a complete break in the naturalistic tradition of zoological displays. Witty and rather beautiful, this design earned a fame disproportionate to its size. It was listed in 1970.

In 1985, after years of semi-neglect, superficial repairs, over-paving and other extraneous modifications, the structure had become 'a dismal shadow of its former self'. John Allan, a scholar of the architecture of the 1930s and a friend of the now elderly Lubetkin, secured the financial help of Peter Palumbo and grant aid from English Heritage as well as approval from Westminster City planners for restoration.

Here the poignant uniqueness of the scheme impinged on normal realities. Requirements such as increasing the nesting accommodation and the enlargement of the original diving tank surely constituted 'material alterations' to a listed structure. But since the original architect was engaged in the new work it could hardly be argued that these changes were not 'in the spirit of the original'.

Work started in April 1987. The additions were the most technically difficult part – 'rendering and lining with rubber sheeting the insides (of the new nesting boxes) required penguin-sized plasterers' says John Allan. Access to the site was very difficult and, although the work was small-scale, the delivery, forming, and finishing of concrete requires ponderous equipment. Thus the new reinforced-concrete tank needed eight separate concrete pours. In some respects standards are higher than they were half a century ago, thus thicker walls for the pool and much more complex water-filtration equipment are among the recent alterations.

Concrete is one of the more difficult materials to use; the theory is that being poured into wooden formwork it can effortlessly be made into fluid and daring shapes. Apart from the intricate construction of the formwork and of the steel reinforcement rods and meshes within, which all have to be covered with a sound and uncracked layer of concrete to prevent water penetration, there is also great difficulty in achieving crisp and strong edges. Thus all arrises had to be formed with stainless steel screwed to the concrete, and, even then, 'achieving smooth turns at the extreme ends of the ellipse was not easy'. The addition of drips on the underside of sections to improve weathering was abandoned as 'patently incongruous'. More important and more successful was the application of a thin veneer (of polymer-modified cement) to the surfaces of the free-standing structure. By limiting the thickness to 6 mm perceptible thickening of the elegant sections was avoided. When it was all painted it was, says Allan 'as though the sun had come out'. The grey, rather earthy object behind the hoarding began

45. Penguin Pool, London Zoo; half a century old and listed, this modern classic has recently been repaired and altered but the authorities could hardly object since the original architect, Lubetkin, was associated with the work

to look like something from another era. Although Lubetkin was associated with John Allan in this restoration, he could remember little of the original colouring. So the Penguin Pool was like any other listed building job – investigation was required. Like another 'modern' building recently refurbished, Michelin House in the Fulham Road, there was virtually no photographic documentation, and none in colour. So paint scrapes had to provide the answer, and under many layers the original deep blue was exposed. This was luckier than at the Michelin building where the stained glass had completely vanished since the 1960s.

Somehow typifying the attractive sim-

plicity of some Modern Movement think-ing was the alternating of grey slate and red rubber in the paving, so designed in order to encourage the sensitive-footed penguins to waddle about. Plain grano-lithic was retained as a surfacing material, rather than rubber, but the original rotat-ing pattern was re-created.

Although smaller elements were replaced – metalwork, plumbing, mosaic pool linings, and central fountain and perimeter sprays, it proved possible to preserve a crucial tree after some remedial surgery.

Silver End, Essex

The philanthropic provision of workers' model housing, already discussed in con-nection with Saltaire, was taken several stages further in social, stylistic and even planning terms by Lord Braintree, then Francis Crittall, in an assortment of 476 houses, 153 of which were pioneering Modern Movement examples, built on the site of a 200-acre farm between Brain-tree and Witham in Essex between 1926 and 1932. Founder of Crittall's Metal Window Factory in Braintree, he floated a rights issue in 1924, doubled production to meet surging demand, and found himself with a housing problem for his employees. At Braintree between 1918 and 1920 Crittall had already built sixty-five flat-roofed concrete cottages, arguably the first modern houses in Britain; their style was influenced by the enthusiasms of Crittall's son, W. F. 'Pink' Crittall and his architect C. H. B. Quennell. There was also the small matter that, apart from wishing to 'build something new, representative of the 20th century', Crittall had an interest in stimulating the sort of design which consorted with metal-window usage. He also had a genuine desire to provide a healthy rural environment.

There were houses of five types, ranging from one-off designs for larger detached dwellings of which Crittall's own 'The Manors' was a focus of the village, through detached four-bedroom dwellings, to three-bedroomed 'non-parlour' houses. Crittall brought in as planner Captain Richard Reiss, a garden-city protagonist with involvement in Letchworth, Welwyn, and Hampstead Garden Suburb. He laid down separate zones for housing, industry, and commerce, and the principle of eight dwellings per acre, to allow space for gardens and other facilities. It is more apt in such a setting to say that the village consisted of the Crittall factory, a village hall, a tea room, a department store, two churches, a school, hotel, canteen, sports ground and pavilion, a telephone exchange, and a farm. The essence was to be spaciousness and variety; wide, tree-lined boulevards lined with houses set well back, but with one projecting a little forward every now and again. Variety was also to be achieved by the employment of half a dozen architects. The most significant, in which Reiss's selection was probably crucial, included C. Murray Hennell, a man with garden city experience working under Parker and Unwin, Thomas S. Tait of Sir John Burnett & Partners, and C. H. B. Quennell. Hennell drew up the village plan, which consisted of a series of turnings, including several

46. Silver End Garden Village, Essex; 'Craig Angus', one of the larger houses built by architects Tait & MacManus for a manager at Crittall Windows for whom the model village was built in the 1920s

culs-de-sac off a main boulevard which turned at an angle when changing from Valentine Way to Broadway. Near the centre were the community buildings overlooked by Crittall's house, and which themselves overlooked the recreation ground. Beyond that were the detached managerial houses 'Wolverton' and 'Craig Angus' together with 'Le Chateau' built by Tait for Dan Crittall. The last was the grandest modern-style residence built at a cost of £3,000 – 'in terms of luxury a world away from the £500 workers cottages.'[21]

Hennell was responsible for the first houses, in Temple Lane and Valentine Way. They were rather dour workers' cottages in stock brick and with hipped roofs, a type which dominated the village numerically. Quennell built not only 'The Manors' in a sort of stripped down Voysey style, very different from his rather brutal concrete cottages in Braintree, but also about a score of fairly traditional semi-detached residences. It was Tait and his assistant, Frederick MacManus, who designed the futuristic houses which so exercised both the architectural and national press at the time. Sixty-three of the modern houses are by Tait and MacManus and ninety by the Scottish Architect James Miller who was brought in a little later. There was a far-

HOOVER LIMITED

cical element in these as in most prewar modern designs: intended to be flat-roofed concrete boxes in the best continental idiom, they were in fact made by the direct-labour team in painted brickwork, with a horizontal effect of window patterns, balconies, porch canopies and, on larger examples such as MacManus's 'Wolverton', some jazzy ironwork. Were Tait's corner windows on 'Le Chateau' the first in England? The three large houses by Tait (and MacManus) are listed, and the village is a conservation area with the additional protection of an Article 4 Direction. This last gives control over house colours, window alterations and wall finishes – just the sort of changes

47. The Hoover Building, west London; Art Deco prestige block in front of typical 'bypass' factory, may now be converted into a superstore

which, by accretion, can rob a place of the unifying identity which is its essential quality. But ownership is the only real means by which detailed control may be exercised and fragmentation of ownership has come as a result of legislation giving rights to buy. This well-meaning and no doubt freedom-enhancing law is not the friend of historic-building protection. In the rather different world of Mayfair, forced sales have threatened the unity imposed by the Grosvenor estate for good and ill for a century and a half; so it is in this Essex village.

Crittall set up the Silver End factory to make small component parts largely by employing war-disabled. Window parts are still made there, as are complete windows at nearby Braintree and Witham. In 1968 when ownership changed the complete village was put up for sale. Braintree Council had the foresight to buy it for £600,000, and now it is largely individually owned. The local authorities have taken all possible protective measures, including the securing of a town scheme through which repairs can be grant-aided by the council and English Heritage. Still, unsympathetic alterations persist and that subtle thing called character is slowly being lost.

The Hoover Factory, west London

During August bank holiday weekend 1980 the central block of the Firestone factory on Western Avenue was demolished. Like so many other spectacular conservation losses this led to the salvation of its peers. Knowing that the DoE intended to list Firestone on the following Tuesday, Trafalgar House, its recent purchasers, had committed 'the most brutal and despicable act of vandalism'[22] which had angered Michael Heseltine, the Minister for the Environment, among others. One of the buildings he listed a few weeks later was another of the streamlined interwar factories laid out formally behind lawns along almost a mile of the arterial road, the Hoover building. Both Firestone and Hoover were designed by Thomas Wallis of Wallis, Gilbert & Partners, architect of several such buildings in and around London which, often for US clients, reflected recent American developments.

The style was not universally admired. Hoover's factory was the best known of the type, and writing about it Nikolaus Pevsner was venomous: 'the most offensive of the modernistic atrocities along this road of typical bypass factories'.[23] Presumably what the Bauhaus enthusiast objected to was the decoration on the

powerful and simplified long white blocks in front of the production areas. Art Deco motifs occur everywhere, but at crucial points, such as the main entrance, coloured faience decoration bursts into Aztec splendour. Rightly Hoover is graded II*. In the mid-1980s Hoover disposed of its landmark premises to a developer whose proposals for the factory's future were architecturally benign but apparently financially impractical. The office block and its lower canteen wings were to be retained while the factory space behind was to be replaced. Ownership has again changed, and the buildings remain empty but in reasonable condition. Even the formal gardens in front are tended. There are hopes that a viable solution will emerge. The eloquence of the architecture of which the Hoover building is the outstanding example is now widely appreciated. In late 1988 architects submitted a proposal for conversion to a superstore for Tesco, the company which has similarly reused the spectacular Kaysor Bondor factory at Baldock.

Brynmawr, Blaenau Gwent

While it is no longer difficult to find admirers of the Art Deco architecture of the Hoover building and even for the more monumental 1930s style of Battersea Power Station, the concrete and glass buildings of the 1950s and 1960s remain a minority taste. The example in question, the Brynmawr Rubber Factory, has been empty, unused, and vandalized for years, is stained and leaks, but in 1986 the Welsh Office spot-listed Brynmawr. It is only when learning the views of historians that all becomes clear. The late Reyner Banham called the factory 'one of the first major pieces of post-war British Architecture. . . . The grand and still convincing conception of nine clustered domes covering the main work-spaces is one of the most impressive interiors in Britain.' While Banham spoke of 'The first post-war building in Britain to command world attention', Sir John Summerson wrote: 'I am inclined to place it with Owen Williams' Boots Factory at Beeston as one of the few British industrial buildings of this century which deserves to be called a classic'.[24]

The only significant postwar building in Wales was constructed during the period 1946–52 by Lord Forrester to bring employment to an area he had known during the worst of the Depression. It was intended to show how a new kind of architecture designed by socially aware young architects could revitalize impoverished parts of the country. In that it failed; if an equivalent quantity of built volume within a basically sound structure were available in almost any part of the country apart from inland South Wales, difficulties in securing new use would be less severe.

Sited beside an old reservoir from which it drew water for cooling at a rate of 1,000 gallons a minute, the main building is the factory floor consisting of a rectangle 450 feet by 325 feet providing uninterrupted production space. The roof consists of nine shell domes in 3-inch-thick concrete, naturally lit by arc-shaped clerestories on four sides and eight sky-

48. The former rubber factory at Bryn Mawr, Blaenau Gwent, is the only internationally distinguished early modern building in Wales. As such it was listed Grade II*, but remains under threat

lights in each dome. This pioneering design owed as much to engineer Ove Arup as to the group of recent Architectural Association School graduates who had constituted themselves as the Architects Co-Partnership. Beneath the factory floor is an equivalent area designed for storage of raw materials, supported on concrete mushroom columns. Other facilities on the site include a small office block, an elegant boilerhouse, and the social and welfare provisions for workers.

The eye always returns to the thin elegance of the concrete domes, the corner supports which are so attenuated that Frank Lloyd Wright on his 1951 visit declared that they should have been thicker! One reason for building the largest shell concrete domes in the world was the national shortage of steel at the time.

Taken over by Dunlop in the mid-1950s, Brynmawr ceased to be used as a factory nearly a decade ago. It was sold to a developer, Tenby Ltd, who announced plans to demolish the original buildings and replace them with a car park to serve adjacent shed factories. Claiming that the factory was too expensive to repair, Tenby was promised a grant of £200,000 towards demolition costs by none other than the Welsh Development Agency. The 1986 listing came just in time. A public inquiry found against the demolition proposals and urged that serious efforts be made to find viable alternatives – though even the inspector seemed a bit despondent about prospects. Planning studies of possible new uses ranging from warehousing and retail to sports and leisure activities were undertaken by a joint team from the original firms of architects and engineers.

In an effort to persuade local interests of the importance of the factory and seek fresh initiatives, SAVE convened a seminar in October 1987 chaired by Dame Margaret Weston, former director of the Science Museum. Hosted, after some hesitation, by the local authority, this stimulating event produced a lot of enthusiasm but, alas, no firm answers. A working party was set up consisting of representatives from Blaenau Gwent Council, Ove Arup, Architects Co-Partnership, SAVE, the Thirties Society, and the Welsh Development Agency.

As time runs out for this modern masterpiece ownership has passed to Michigan Investments, a company registered in the Isle of Man. The latest proposal is for conversion to a leisure complex, providing that the Welsh Development Agency confirms its offer to pay 80 per cent of the cost of removal of blue asbestos now spalling from the ceiling. Plans are complicated by the sale of the 30 ha. around the listed factory to house builders.

Chapter 8

H Country Houses

*Harlaxton Hall,
entrance front.
Salvin's Elizabethan-
style extravaganza
of the 1830s is now
a Texas university
outpost*

Introduction

The country house is arguably England's major contribution to European art. A combination of architecture, designed landscape, farmland, park buildings, collections of pictures, statues, books, and furniture, reflects a leisured way of life. This was supported by the infrastructure of a little community of service quarters, workshops, forges, sawmills, dairies, brewhouses, laundries, stables, coach houses. Political stability has bequeathed more complete survivals in this country than elsewhere. Large country estates dominated the social and political life of the nation from the sixteenth to the eighteenth centuries both locally and, through their control of parliamentary seats, centrally, until early-nineteenth-century reforms. Most aristocrats retained just sufficient roots, just sufficient reticence about their huge wealth, just sufficient sense to compromise in time with other rising forces to avoid revolutions. Britain was spared the despoilation and dispersals of works of art, of the kind which swept Europe between 1789 and 1848.

As is typical of most institutions, however, the greatest number and size of country houses was reached about a century later when the ranks of estate owners was swelled with the new rich from industry and commerce. Decline was comparatively rapid, starting with the agricultural depression of the 1870s, confirmed by the inception of income tax in the 1890s, completed by the permanent flight to the towns and suburbs of the former farm and domestic labour after the Great War. That last traumatic event also took the wind out of the whole enterprise; 'society' never quite took itself seriously again. Thus when James Lees Milne visited stately homes during and just after the Second World War to see how many could be preserved in the hands of the National Trust, he found many only part-occupied and then by decayed and often eccentric gentry who had 'given up the ghost'. That pessimism, which often led to the actual abandonment and demolition of great houses between the wars, was not wholly justified by objective circumstances. The resurgence of many a great house has come as a result of the energies of a later generation willing to work to retain their family home. To name but one example, it was a close-run decision for the present Duke and Duchess of Devonshire to move back into the rapidly deteriorating palace of Chatsworth in 1958, a time when they could have had no inkling of the huge inflation in world art prices which would render their vast art collection an almost limitless resource.

Although scholars and middle-class travellers had often viewed great houses out of season, when they would be shown around by the housekeeper for a few shillings, visiting as the weekend and holiday pastime of millions is a recent phenomenon. In 1939 the National Trust, already approaching its half century, was the owner of only two major houses. That the soap opera element is predominant over that of aesthetic study is well appreciated by most guides who let slip nuggets of gossip about 'the family'. Royal visits and use of the state dining room with its table sparkling with thirty-two settings in crystal, silver-gilt and Sèvres china are high spots – 'just think how many servants it took to clean all that silver!' Awe at the grandeur of vast, gilded salons can, however, be allied to growing appreciation of the old masters. In any case, sentiment about the Gainsborough portrait of the countess who was once a milkmaid does no harm.

Growing awareness of the interest and importance of the social history of 'ordinary people', reinforced by the ambivalently snobbish appeal of 'Upstairs Downstairs' and sheer nostalgia for the everyday past of our grandfather's generation, has all greatly increased the fascination of the servants' quarters and service courtyards. Great houses opened to the public in the postwar period simply allowed a roped-off route through the grand apartments. Now Burghley House at Stamford is entered via the great kitchen which is in part seventeenth-century and earlier. Here visitors are told the story of the house and its wonders. At Erddig Hall, Denbighshire, and the recently opened Calke Abbey in Derbyshire, as much effort has gone into the restoration and display of servants' hall, kitchens, lamp rooms, workshops, and laundries as to the state rooms. Calke is a veritable time capsule with drawing rooms, nurseries, and coach houses untouched, some hardly even entered by the reclusive family for a century. House as showplace is in effect a new use. But the point is unclear in those still in private ownership and still functioning chiefly as a home which happens to be opened to the public thirty days a year. That opening is necessary to justify the historic buildings grant for repairs.

Many visitors to country houses, perhaps the majority in recent years, do not actually enter the main house at all. They might take tea in the converted stable block, but they have come to see the gardens, the model village and railway, the zoo, the theme park. So country houses are part of an increasingly important leisure industry the clients of which hardly give them a thought as palaces of power or of art. Indeed the power association is barely present in the public mind, while that of art is only retained because of the frequent news of sales of pictures.

Once the house has lost its family and contents, perhaps been in another use for a generation – educational or scientific for example – it becomes a sort of semi-public institutional building bereft of the mystique of the associations described above. It is only of cultural interest for serious students of architecture, and they are lucky if they get a look in. Thus Tabley Court, a great eighteenth-century mansion owned, little used, and recently disposed of by Manchester University probably for conversion to old peoples' accommodation has very limited visitor attraction despite being largely intact, even to the extent of housing some important furniture and pictures. Hurstmonceux Castle was sold in October 1988 by the Science and Engineering Research Council; the story below the headline in *The Times*, 'Leisure developers buy "£10m" observatory site', explained that the Royal Greenwich Observatory had its 'home' in the castle since the 1940s, but nowhere mentioned that this had for centuries been a private residence. A study by the English Tourist Board called for a comprehensive leisure scheme, with a championship golf course, the use of the castle as a hotel, and a range of country activities'.[25]

Once the link with the past has been severed there is a vast range of acceptable alternative uses for country houses, but the public as a whole, and in recent years the government, have come to the view that the link is best maintained. Even the Treasury has been swayed by evidence that tourism is among the leading national-income producers, and that 'the heritage' is the core of that attraction. Add to this the sporting respect felt for owners willing to populate their broad acres with lions and tigers to enthral visitors and it is clear why there has been little substantial opposition to fiscal concessions in recent budgets. Not only are repairs to outstanding buildings grant-aided at the same time as incomes of owners have been augmented by income-tax reductions, but the rate of what used to be called 'death duty' has been reduced. There are also provisions for the establishment of trusts and maintenance funds enabling owners who are well advised – as the Harpur Crewes of Calke Abbey were not – to retain sufficient income-producing land to support houses of high quality.

Ameliorations in the predicament of the owners of country houses and estates only serve to slow down the sale of houses and dispersal of contents which so impoverished this country earlier this century. Then mansions were demolished and their collections travelled across the Atlantic. Largely through the agency of Lord Duveen the pride of American galleries, both public and private, was secured at British sales. Even in recent years notable treasures have been dispersed and often exported as a result of sales of contents of Belton House, Lincolnshire, and Mentmore Towers, Buckinghamshire, as well as selective disposals from Althorp, Chatsworth, Kedleston, and a score of lesser seats. But the difference now is that in no case is the house in danger of demolition: two remain in private ownership, two are vested in the National Trust, one is a conference centre (albeit of an eccentric variety – Mentmore is a centre for transcendental meditation). All can be visited by the public and only one, Mentmore, has not been improved in terms of the state of the fabric as a result of the sales. The new owners of Mentmore were obliged by the local authorities to install fireproof dividing walls and additional escape facilities despite the fact that their occupancy would be less than the numbers of a traditional country household – and the latter would have been without levitational powers!

Most outstanding country houses are in a better state of repair and decoration than they have been for at least a century or are in the process of being so improved. Those that have changed hands for the purposes of conversion to new uses and those that have recently been rescued from states of near or actual dereliction are subject to varying degrees of structural alteration. Dingley Hall, Northamptonshire, and Gunton Hall, Norfolk, were in the latter two categories and were both subdivided and converted by Kit Martin into numbers of individual houses.

In such cases domestic use is maintained – in fact re-established after a period of about half a century and a century respectively. They are no longer country houses with the rich associations of history, art, and snobbery attaching to the visited stately homes, but they are important events in the landscape, and their external architecture, and, in the case of Dingley at least, some interior features are beautifully preserved. Martin tends to convert houses without outstanding interiors and with plans of the rambling, additive, courtyard type not uncommon in the second rank of country mansions which have 'just growed' over the centuries. Christopher Buxton of Period and Country Homes, the ambitious pioneer in this field, has tackled seventeenth-century prodigy houses and eighteenth-century Palladian palaces with compact symmetrical layouts and first-rate interiors. He recognizes this major dilemma. At Charlton Park in Wiltshire the grand late-Georgian central hall formed by roofing the Jacobean courtyard is retained as a common space for use by owners of any of the dozen or so units. But the long gallery with its splendid plasterwork ceiling had to be divided into three flats after a scheme to house the picture collection of the house's original owners fell through.

The use of major houses for other functions besides domestic has precedent. Great country magnates were, in effect, the rulers of rural England for centuries; their seats were the essential institutional buildings attesting their power. When at the dawn of the eighteenth century, Sir John Harpur found himself the owner by means of inheritance and marriage of one of the most extensive estates in Derbyshire and adjacent counties, 'a prestigious country mansion was a basic requirement'.[26] Such a House of Parade had a suite of impressive state rooms usually occupying most of the first floor, the *piano nobile* in Italian terms. In fact Calke was more determinedly English, even provincial, than most eighteenth-century houses of that scale, the family sometimes used these formal apartments. Generally the institutional floor of great houses was empty apart from state occasions; other more modest, though often richly furnished, chambers were used for daily

life. If too big for normal use by vast eighteenth-century households these rooms are certainly unsuitable for domestic occupation today, a fact acknowledged by the increasing conversion of major houses to conference, educational, or hotel use.

Cliveden

As Hilary Rubinstein writes 'The opening of expensive luxury hotels, converted from private residences at many millions of pounds, is a common enough occurrence these days. But most of these enterprises belong to big chains and are aimed

49. Cliveden, Buckinghamshire; most famous as the interwar home of the political hostess, Nancy Astor, now a grand hotel – despite National Trust ownership

largely at the conference trade'.[27] Prices in such establishments are high – they offer all sorts of equestrian and other diversions for visitors. Perhaps the most expensive is that established recently in the Astors' former Thameside palace at Cliveden.

The only outstanding stately home converted into a hotel owes its origins to a four-storey brick mansion built for the second Duke of Buckingham in the 1660s. The arcaded terrace of that period survives, but the house was burned down in 1795. A short-lived successor was also destroyed by fire, though wings designed by Thomas Archer in 1706 to frame the entrance court escaped both conflagrations more or less intact. The main central block of the present house was built by Sir Charles Barry in 1850–1 for the Duke of Sutherland. To this massive Italianate villa was added in the 1860s a stable courtyard and clock tower in the less pure style of Henry Clutton.

William Waldorf, later Viscount Astor, made further additions after purchase in 1893, but these were largely in the direction of rendering appropriately classical some of the more stylistically bizarre features added by an intervening owner, the first Duke of Westminster. Astor graced the 375-acre gardens and parkland with

50. Dingley Hall, Northampton-shire; the early-eighteenth-century block was added to the Elizabethan courtyard house which by the early 1970s was in a ruinous state. Rescued and converted by Kit Martin

classical fountains and statues. He also converted an octagonal temple, built in the grounds in 1735 by yet another distinguished architect, Giacomo Leoni, into a chapel.

Cliveden was given to the National Trust by the second Viscount Astor in 1942, although his son continued to live there until 1966. The house is not open to the public. From 1969 to 1984 it was leased to Stanford University, California. After internal restoration and adaption the building was opened as a luxury hotel in 1986.

Compton Verney *Hotel conversion.*

One of Christopher Buxton's more recent purchases, the Grade I early-Georgian Compton Verney in Warwickshire, is also being converted into a hotel. The necessarily large investment is being financed by the preliminary adaption of the Gibbs-designed stables into cottages and flats and also by the sale of the walled garden for development – this last being a practical solution which is not regarded by anyone as ideal. The prize will be the thorough repair of a very fine house whose irascible owner refused to listen to any proposals for upkeep for a period of twenty years while 'water was cascading through the roof, destroying much of the exquisite painted plasterwork of the hall', according to Marcus Binney.[28] The hotel solution which allows great houses to remain entireties inside and out, is almost the ideal new use.

Dingley Hall, Northants

On the whole Kit Martin's conversions of houses have not involved tackling symmetrical Palladian compositions comprising sequences of great eighteenth-century apartments. He tends to choose large rambling houses with wings and courts which have grown over the centuries and are more easily divisible. Martin set up practice in Cambridge before completing his architectural training, and was very soon involved in historic building repairs.

In 1975 Martin began the first of his country house conversions at Dingley, which remains the most architecturally significant of about ten major buildings he has tackled. Originally built in the 1560s, though perhaps including fragments from a medieval preceptory of the Knights Hospitallers, the house was an inward-looking courtyard design attributed by Sir John Summerson to Thomas

Thorpe who probably built Kirby Hall not far away.[29] The owner, Sir Edward Griffin, was a courtier until Elizabeth's accession when his Papist sympathies led him to settle in the country. There was a similar end to the career of his great grandson, also Sir Edward, Treasurer to Charles II and James II, who, as a loyal Jacobite, followed the latter into exile in 1688. This was shortly after he had completed a fashionable remodelling of the house leaving only one complete range with its gatehouse and corner tower and a detached two-storey porch facing it. He inserted a larger L-shaped block in somewhat continental classical garb and with a high proportion of window to wall. The chief of the new elevations, that facing south, is dominated by a wide, three-bay feature, pedimented and with a central door which suggests Captain William Winde as designer rather than Hugh May who used to be credited. A fact now confirmed by the discovery of Winde's correspondence from Dingley.

In 1883, the then largely unaltered house was sold to Viscount Downe who later disposed of it to Earl Beatty, the hero of Jutland. He created the terraced gardens to the south. When put on the market again in 1958 Dingley was described as being in 'an exceptional state of repair ... consistently well maintained'. Fifteen years later this Grade I house was ruinous, its interior gutted, sections of roof missing, dry rot everywhere. Its last owner had used Dingley as a source of building materials. This disgraceful state of affairs remains a rebuke to local and national historic building protection bodies, and in particular to the local authority.

Following purchase in 1976 Kit Martin submitted plans for restoration and subdivision into fourteen separate houses (later reduced to eleven), leaving the exterior little altered apart from essential repairs. Despairing, after long negotiations, of receiving a Historic Buildings Council grant, and defying professional advice that conversion costs would exceed any likely return, he went ahead stage by stage. The idea was one that has become a feature of this kind of work, namely that funds could be recycled as parts were sold and also that trades would be continually employed following each other through the various parts of the house. Another key to success was that Martin saved by being his own architect and contractor; he lived with his family on site and so could answer all the problems that arise from day to day in historic-building work and which often justify contractors including large contingency sums in the quotations. Most of the work was carried out by his direct-labour team.

Repairs began on the sixteenth-century tower-like structure, another fragment of the original house which was embedded in the corner of the seventeenth-century 'L'. It was the earliest part of the house and to it a Victorian east wing had been attached until demolished in 1972 leaving the interface wall in an unsound condition. The creation of two new houses there was followed by the reconstruction of the 1560 wing behind the gatehouse. An extra mansard storey was added, almost invisible behind the parapet, which allowed space for two more units. When these first houses were sold so much interest was created that there were purchasers for the rest before completion. Dingley's plan, being roughly speaking 'H' shaped, was ideal for division: all of the houses have ground floor entrances, all are surrounded by well kept grounds and enjoy idyllic distant views, and, most remarkably, almost all have south- or west-facing living rooms. Variety in size is considerable, from 800 to 3,500 sq. ft and there is a consequent variation in prices. A buoyant property market at the time of the original sale helped the viability of a project which by no means made a fortune for Martin, but did enable him – emboldened – to move on to the next ruinous mansion.

51 (a) and (b). Gunton Park, Norfolk; the original 1740s mansion – only a fragment of the extended complex of state, family, and service wings – was gutted by fire a century ago. Reconstructed to provide three of the thirty dwellings carved out of Gunton

Gunton Park, Norfolk

Here once again was a sprawling extended plan which had grown over the centuries and was ideal for subdivision. Gunton was one of the largest houses in East Anglia, at the centre of a 1,800-acre park probably laid out by Bridgeman, Repton, and Gilpin, in succession. There had been a substantial Elizabethan mansion. Martin came across footings under the shell of the eighteenth-century house and beyond it. Matthew Brettingham designed the comparatively modest Palladian block in 1742 when he was supervising the construction of nearby Holkham, also, incidentally, in the oatmeal-coloured Norfolk brick. His client, Sir William Harbord, then turned to Robert Adam, in the arbitrary and fashion-conscious way of the time, to design a colonnade along the main south front overlooking parkland and lakes. The colonnade may not have been built until 1827, for after 1770 Harbord's son, the first Lord Suffield, concentrated upon vast family and service wing extensions in the opposite direction. Designed by James and Samuel Wyatt, these cost the then considerable sum of £40,000. Gunton is unusual in that its domestic offices and courtyard additions are Georgian. Little was developed in the nineteenth century except formal

gardens, extra parkland, and an observatory tower.

The remarkable extent of the house is demonstrated by the way the family could abandon one part and then another – often complete with their furnishings – and still be in residence in 1980. In 1882 the main mansion had been gutted by a fire, allegedly started by the family to curtail frequent and expensive visits by the Prince of Wales who enjoyed the shooting! So the interior of the house bought by Kit Martin in 1980 from the estate of the Hon. Doris Harbord had few complete interiors and no grand apartments, vast halls, or noble staircases to

inhibit his plans. The conversion of the house, lodges, and park cottages, occupied by two people less than a decade ago, has created thirty homes. Though even that will result in a population smaller than such a house would have had in its heyday.

As usual Martin dealt with it in phases; cottages and houses were sold on completion to finance the next part. But, even before that, the first need was to improve the infrastructure – the roads, drains, water, and electricity supplies. This was not a small task, including as it did a 1.5-mile water main and burial of wires for the new electric and telephone systems.

Construction was carried out by the usual direct labour team of about ten, with the addition of local subcontractors such as electricians, plumbers, and decorators. Martin was hugely pleased with the quality obtained from Norfolk specialists in plastering and ironwork.

Local planning and building regulation officers were helpful. There were few external additions and internal divisions were all by vertical party walls. Martin created three large houses in the family wing, the three storeys of which rather dominate Brettingham's original house alongside. The burnt-out shell of the

52. The Hazells, Bedfordshire; eighteenth-century home of the Pym family, a hospital after wartime requisitioning, abandoned, neglected, and due for demolition before a last-minute conversion by Martin into a dozen homes

latter he has made into a most attractive home for himself and his wife, planned around the open colonnade facing south. Rooms are large, determined by the windows of the original; there are historic fittings rescued from this and other houses, as well as a few pictures and items of furniture from Harbord days which Martin bought at the house sale and subsequently. The centre of the Brettingham block comprises an east–west courtyard open to the sky. Beyond are another house and part of a third which shares some of the Wyatt block.

At the opposite end of the scale was the

restoration of the old gardeners' cottages in the walled garden, five houses made in the stables, and others created in the brewery and laundry. An octagonal game larder isolated in the middle of a service yard, the wings of which provide more accommodation, has been made into a rather special little house with two bedrooms over a circular living room, 26 ft across. It is just such eccentricities that attract people to live in conversions. The bell yard was completed on one side by one of the rare new elements nearly always required, a line of garages. Prices varied from £35,000 for the smallest

cottage to £130,000 for a large wing. Several have since been sold for more than double.

The Hazells, Bedfordshire

The abandoned ancestral home of the Pym family since before 1790, this famous SAVE case was destined for demolition after almost thirty years of institutional misuse. Architecturally Hazells Hall has the sturdy grace representative of eighteenth-century gentlemen's residences that have escaped the attention of fashionable architects. There are two principle fronts: the south of eleven bays and the east of seven both have a three-bay central projection, though only the longer has a pediment, which presumably marked the main entrance before the plan was re-ordered. That occurred when Francis Pym altered an early Georgian house in about 1790, the date to which almost all the interiors belong. So also, presumably, does the neat single-storey tetra-style portico, marking what has been the entrance for two centuries. The impression of the exterior of Hazells is one of order – two apparently equal-height storeys with lofty and evenly spaced identical windows. Walls of dark red brick dressed at windows, and quoins with lighter ones, are convincingly finished at the top by a flat balustrade of stone, concealing any irregularities of roof and chimneys. The whole sits serenely in a flat but artfully landscaped park by Humphrey Repton.

So much for the show fronts; behind them is a fair degree of chaos, both in terms of an awkward plan for the main block and a series of disparate-looking eighteenth century structures around irregular courtyards. As at Gunton the rambling service wings far exceed the family apartments in area. All this only added to the ease of conversion into multi-residential units when the fate of the house was in the balance in 1979/80. It was a close run thing. Although the building was listed, the interior was undoubtedly in a distressing condition. This was the result of being stripped out and institutionally brutalized after none too gentle wartime requisitioning. Neglect of repairs had resulted in leaking roofs and widespread dry rot. All this was also fortuitous for the would-be converter, since it meant few grand spaces or features to preserve and a virtually negative value as a building.

But getting hold of the building was the problem. In some ways the ancestral family connection was remote, indeed they had only occupied Hazells for relatively short periods in the late eighteenth and early twentieth centuries. For much of the nineteenth century it was let privately, and in the latter part of this century publicly. For after de-requisitioning post-1945 the house was let for twenty-one years to a Hospital Board which, having cheaply converted Hazells and then neglected it, threw up its hands at the condition it had wrought and precipitately departed. Not unnaturally the Pyms now disliked the place, apparently a sad wreck beyond redemption as a home. It was also associated with a period of institutional use which, as near neighbours, they could not have found congenial. For they remained close by, still owning and farming the estate and living in a gracious post-war residence they had built a few hundred yards away. There was the added sadness of total wartime loss of the stored contents of Hazells. Undoubtedly the family would have preferred at that time to see an end to the house.

Nonetheless efforts were made to find new commercial or institutional tenants before an application for listed building consent to demolish was sought in 1979. This was the moment when SAVE appeared on the scene to campaign for the quality of the building in its setting and for an appreciation of its potential.

53. Cullen House, Banffshire, evolved over four centuries so that each wing and tower has stairs – ideal for conversion to multi-occupation. A spectacular wilderness garden is shared by all

Time and again the role of SAVE was to provide a new perspective for owners and indeed authorities concerned: to persuade them to lift their eyes above what might admittedly be the depressing current state and recent associations of a structure – it might be a 'Satanic Mill' (the title of a SAVE exhibition) as well as a decayed house – and recognize potential adaptive uses after refurbishment. People also had to be 'bullied', one might say, into looking beyond immediate cost-and-return equations, which have almost always proved short-sighted, to appreciate the real benefit of 27,500 sq. ft of solidly built

volume in the midst of the Bedfordshire countryside barely 50 miles north of London.

Demolition permission was refused after a public inquiry. The Pyms were eventually convinced that multiple residential conversion would be the least disruptive solution, and Kit Martin was able to buy the house and 14 acres of immediately surrounding land in December 1981 for a relatively nominal sum. This allowed for ample gardens for the twelve new dwellings that he created and also for access along the old main drive, quite separately from the Pyms' current home.

As before, no external alterations were necessary, apart from the addition of a small garage range of similar materials and roof pitch to the adjacent service and stable ranges. Not surprisingly Martin spent something over his estimated £700,000, but property price rises again allowed a reasonable return on sales of units for from under £50,000 to over £100,000, depending on size. Once again a listed building was secured without a penny of grant money.

Cullen House and Tyninghame

Following pioneer rescues of doomed mansions in the English midlands and eastern parts, Kit Martin's attentions moved northwards. His very success and that of others before and immediately after, together with the property boom of the 1980s and the general recognition of both the attraction and value of country houses for conversion to a variety of uses, obviously reduced the number of opportunities in southern parts of the country.

After Gunton he had purchased Cullen House on the Banffshire coast. This splendid baronial house of 1600 evolved over four centuries, being hugely enlarged by the successful Scottish architect William Bryce. The contents at Cullen had been auctioned in 1975, so when Martin bought it in 1982 it had stood empty for a number of years. At Cullen the spectacular wilderness garden is being jointly maintained by the residents for their shared enjoyment.

Another of the properties he bought was Tyninghame, a fifteenth-century tower house enlarged in the seventeenth and eighteenth centuries. Its wings and towers, each with their own turret stair and entrance, adapted ideally to several

54. Keith Hall, near Aberdeen; former seat of the Earls of Kintore whose heraldic achievement can be seen over front door on left. Now converted into apartments

55. Callaly Castle, Northumberland; not very castle-like since the eighteenth century. Typical of remoter houses whose price still makes multiple conversion viable. A family wing was retained

houses. Tyninghame had been much aggrandized in 1829 by an even more fashionable Scottish architect and teacher of Bryce, William Burn. It had rather more in the way of interior features than Dingley, though mostly of a later date, so several quite large houses were created. But Martin takes a particular delight in making small homes available in such settings, and the kitchen wing at Tyninghame has provided opportunities to do that. He is also pleased with the way he is able to integrate the only necessary additions, garages. At Tyninghame garage pavilions will be designed in the language of the place with crow step gables, stone walls, and slate roofs.

Much the same is being done at Keith Hall, another Scottish mansion which has recently undergone extensive restoration and conversion to several houses.

Callaly Castle

Just one other house to receive Kit Martin's attentions should be mentioned. It has significant differences as a case and shares some features with Christopher Buxton's creation of a comfortable family wing for Lord Londonderry at Wynyard in Durham, previously described by Marcus Binney as 'the draughtiest house in England'. Martin saw Callaly Castle in its ancient park in remote Northumberland countryside as he drove every fortnight from Gunton in Norfolk to Keith in Aberdeenshire. Much less like a castle in appearance than many Scottish mansions, Callaly has at its core a fourteenth-century Pele tower but that is concealed behind major seventeenth-century and Georgian additions which provide the courts and entrance doors so desirable for sub-division. The interesting factor is ownership: after being largely created for a couple of centuries by the Clavering family, Callaly was sold to a Major Browne, a major landowner, in 1877. He employed a local architect to add a museum wing to house a collection of

56. Callaly Castle, music room, hung with game trophies and spears, and demonstrating the uncouth fascination of the Scottish baronial hall

antiquities acquired by an uncle. Little has changed since that work was completed in about 1900. From 1925 the house has been occupied by Browne's grandson, also a major. He has maintained the house, opening to the public in the summer, and gradually retreating into the kitchen wing himself. A sale of contents became necessary in 1985, in preference to the sale of the house or land.

At that stage Kit Martin was brought in. He produced a scheme enabling Major Browne, aged 91, to keep a main wing of the house together with family portraits and furniture. The rest is being restored and divided into twenty houses, cottages, and flats. As usual the garden with its series of lakes is to be shared, and there is also a small but dramatic museum for new residents and their visitors to enjoy.

At Callaly Kit Martin broke with his normal practice of using direct labour, chiefly in order to make the wing ready for Major Browne as soon as possible. He went to tender and appointed Laing and Stanley Miller. The architect working with the design team was local, as usual, in this case Tony Barnes of Ainsworth Spark. At Dingley the architect was Robert Weighton, at Keith, Douglas Forrest, and at Tyninghame, Mandy Ketchin of Simpson & Brown.

Castle Ashby, Northants

Not every house in need of an adaptive use can be regarded as suitable for subdivision; for the greatest mansions it should be unthinkable. So it was for the seventh Marquis of Northampton when exploring various possibilities a decade ago. One idea was to convey Castle Ashby to the National Trust, but private enquiries suggested that although the house was certainly of appropriate quality, an endowment of £4 million for its upkeep would be required to accompany the gift. Perhaps the sale of the 10,000-acre estate, leaving Castle Ashby in its mere 200-acre park, would have sufficed, but it was asking a bit much of his lordship to voluntarily part with so much of his birthright in one swoop. He accepted the challenge of finding a new use and converted the house into a hotel and conference centre. The geographical situation in the heart of England, within easy reach of the M1, was clearly helpful in the success of the venture. Meanwhile the marquis and marchioness have repaired to their other ancestral home just a little further west, Compton Wynyates in Warwickshire, itself described as one 'of the most romantic buildings England has ever seen'.[30]

Personal references are fitting in the histories of houses. This is the story of one family, the Comptons, and its two chief homes. William Compton, Squire of the Body to Henry VIII, rebuilt the Warwickshire manor which had been the property of his ancestors since the twelfth century. Irregular brick-built ranges cluster around a quadrangle. Within a moat and the shelter of a wooded valley, it was for its date surely deliberately backward-looking, more than a little medieval. Through his friendship with the king, Sir William was very rich, and bought the Northamptonshire estate on which the remains of an eleventh-century castle stood, but did not build there.

57. Castle Ashby, Northampton- shire; the Earl and Countess of Northampton – having withdrawn to their more picturesque Warwickshire home of Compton Wyngates – have converted Castle Ashby into a hotel and conference centre in the best possible taste

Work was started by the first Lord Compton in 1574. He created a house round three sides of a long courtyard, across the open end of which a lower, but imposingly classical screen was erected in about 1630 by William Compton, friend of James I and by him raised to the first Earl of Northampton in 1618. Nikolaus Pevsner and the current Lord Northampton choose to regard Inigo Jones as the architect of the subtly designed addition, Summerson and Cornforth do not. In any case here is first-rate architecture of court quality. The principal seat of a great aristocratic family for almost four centuries is now, as the brochure proclaims, 'the perfect setting' for conferences, exhibitions, promotions, launches, board meetings, film locations, rallies, wedding receptions, medieval banquets, 'or indeed any special event'. All amidst 'priceless paintings and antiques', with first-class cuisine available, alongside a 'versatile cellar' offered by 'our chef and his fully trained staff'. As if that were not enough, 'guest groups may live in pampered luxury for the duration of their visit'. The house which has been host to visits by royalty including Elizabeth I, James I, and William III has now been 'lovingly restored to its original grandeur and refurbished under the personal supervision of the Marchioness of Northampton'. Those fortunate enough to enjoy 'these celebrated rooms offered to our Clientele as exclusive accommodation' may also have the benefit of expert tuition in clay-pigeon shooting, archery, horse riding, croquet, coarse fishing, and tennis. 'Golf is available nearby'. It would appear that the marquis and marchioness are as adept in their entertaining of those who matter as were their predecessors. They have the advantage nowadays of not needing to be actually present to do it. For, after all the centuries, they have returned to live in the home of their squirarchic forebears, Compton Wynyates.

Brocket Hall, Hertfordshire

Not so great a house but a far more exclusive conference centre, Brocket was thoroughly decrepit when the present Lord Brocket's grandmother left him the mansion thirteen years ago. The 23-year-old former guardsman had to lay chipboard over the holes in the floor of his little flat over the front door when he took possession.

Brocket Hall was designed by James Paine in 1755, but not completed internally until about 1780. Though surrounded by an extensive park it has what Pevsner calls a 'utilitarian' exterior – somewhat in the vein of Hazells, though loftier and more compact. Of red brick with minimal stone dressings it consists of nine bays on the principal front, the centre three bays extending up to a fourth floor. Paine also built a bridge spanning one end of an irregular lake created out of the river Lea which flows through the undulating landscaped grounds.

Brocket is distinguished above all for its grand apartments. From the entrance hall a central stair leads to a gallery which is Palladian in character. But the chief room, a large saloon converted by Lord Brocket into a conference and dining room, has many of the characteristics of a major Adam interior. Its sumptuous coved ceiling or rich plasterwork is inset with striking paintings by John Hamilton Mortimer, though completed after his death in 1779 by Wheatley. The picture collection includes portraits by Van Dyck and Lely. The house's colourful history includes more than a few salacious incidents in the life of Lady Caroline Lamb, a relative of Lord Melbourne, one of two prime ministers who lived at Brocket. The other was Lord Palmerston.

To return to the more straitened circumstances of the current occupant, Lord Brocket had an uphill struggle financing necessary works to the hall. The major banks were unforthcoming; American Express loaned him the essential first million. Once converted the place was an almost instant success thanks chiefly to Lord Carrington who set the tone by holding the 1981 EEC summit meeting at Brocket. Other governments have convened meetings here, attracted by proximity to London combined with the comparative isolation which facilitates security. Nevertheless the largest number of visitors are American executives who enjoy the 'incentive' side of the conference centre as well as the lavish lifestyle. Among those incentive activities are archery, shooting, and hovercraft races on the lake.

In common with other business fields, the running of a conference centre requires regular improvement and updating of facilities. Fortunately this can usually be achieved without serious effect on historic fabric. At Brocket much of a recent £3 million programme of expenditure has gone to ensure the 'bug-proof' qualities of a conference chamber to accommodate secret inter-governmental talks and sales conferences. On a lighter note there are all sorts of other profit-earning activities such as filming for cinema and television from time to time. Indeed filming takes place at many country houses, not excluding the grandest such as Belvoir Castle, home of the Duke of Rutland.

As can be seen from the foregoing examples, the conferences/hotel/leisure centre mix can vary from house to house. Some conference centres are run virtually on an institutional or trust basis; examples are Leeds Castle in Kent or Ditchley, near Woodstock in Oxfordshire, or even Selsdon – a hotel which lent its name in the 1970s to a brand of Conservatism. Some are luxury hotels where informal conferences can be held: Castle Ashby, Stapleford Park, Cliveden. Others with varying emphases on work, entertainment, and sport are Middlethorpe Hall, Yorkshire, Bodysgallen Hall, Gwynedd, and Normanton Park, Leicestershire.

Calke Abbey, Derbyshire

The story of the salvation of this magical house, its 'time-capsule' contents, its unworldly family, and the complex financial 'package' which was assembled at the all-too-familiar last minute, is all fairly well known now and has been touched upon earlier in this book. In 1982 only a handful of architectural historians seemed to have heard of the house and fewer had seen it. There is something particularly appealing about the discovery of hidden treasure, an unexpected seam of gold. When the future of an architectural shrine like Kedleston is in question, as it recently was, it is difficult to get excited – there is an underlying assurance that in this day and age, unlike most others, an answer will be found. But Calke Abbey, so obscure and eccentrically English, no milestone in architecture and without a single item of international quality inside, has immense appeal. This was demonstrated a year or so ago when it was opened for a day to National Trust members and was besieged. It is not quite true that there is nothing first-rate: there is an early-eighteenth-century state bed of superb quality and immaculate condition which was probably a royal gift to a newly-wed, but then no one knew about that because it had never been unpacked from its cases in nearly 250 years! What was unique about Calke was the totality of the house, its park, its stables with carriages and tack ready for a drive, its penny-farthing bicycles only a bit rusty, its kitchens, and brush rooms, and lamp rooms, its hundreds of indifferent pictures and infinitely more treasured stuffed birds and bits of animals, its state drawing room with almost every item of furniture and painting in the same position as shown in an early photograph a century ago, its nurseries with Victorian toys spilling out of cupboards, its little private sitting room with a novel which someone had put down open and unfinished on a table in 1923.

58. Calke Abbey, Derbyshire, no more an abbey than plate 57 is a castle – nor even a great stately home; a unique 'time capsule' of fully furnished rooms untouched for a century or more. Roof repairs in progress

Of course Calke had never been an abbey – that was a name adopted in 1808 because it sounded romantic. But there was a short-lived priory of Austin Canons in the twelfth century which had declined into a 'cell' of Repton Priory by the Dissolution. After that it passed through various grubby hands before being bought by Henry Harpur in 1622. By further acquisition, marriage, and the purchase of a baronetcy from Charles I, the family raised itself in status and wealth to minor aristocracy. It dominated the southern half of Derbyshire as the Cavendishes did the northern. To match all this a grand three-storey stone house was built in 1701–3. The design was both

sophisticated and gauche, it had corner pavilions marked by giant pilasters and a splendid frieze in a version of the Composite Order derived from published designs by Philibert de l'Orme, yet the general massing of the four-square block might best be described as Midlands Baroque. There are similarities with the slightly earlier Chatsworth which was also built to incorporate substantial remains of an Elizabethan courtyard house and has the awkward and irregular plan resulting from such origins. There was no known designer for this mansion, and even the grand flight of steps to the *piano nobile* entrance built to drawings apparently dispatched by James Gibbs

were swept away when the elder William Wilkins added a portico to the entrance front in 1806. Then for a couple of generations main access was via a rather flimsy pair of metal flights up to the first-floor portico level and into the nearly central grand entrance hall. A century ago the hall was converted into a saloon, the stairs were removed, and visitors, of whom few were encouraged, entered under the portico into a gloomy basement hall hung with mounted heads of prize oxen.

A number of the principal rooms were remodelled in the early nineteenth century but then nothing changed; the family became increasingly eccentric and reclusive although still the wealthy owners of estates in several counties. Rooms were abandoned, staff reduced, such inventions as electricity, motor cars, and telephones resisted for many decades. The death of Charles Harpur Crewe in 1981, with no trust settlements to preserve house contents and park, meant that there were massive tax liabilities. These increased over several years to £10 million with added interest as negotiations proceeded with unsympathetic government departments. The Treasury was disinclined to accept Calke under the 'in lieu' provisions because it had not been declared to be of outstanding status. Eventually the Treasury gave way to the extent of accepting that all, except the essential land to provide the endowment, would be accepted in place of capital taxes. This was little help as the intended recipient, the National Trust, calculated that a total of £7.5 million would be required for repairs and endowment. Even the unworldly and almost elderly Henry Harpur Crewe who had succeeded his brother baulked at the idea of completely beggaring himself for the privilege of being allowed to give his home and all its contents away. He was patiently reassured by the scholarly Howard Colvin while public and eventually parliamentary opinion was mobilized, first by SAVE with the National Trust, then by Lord Montagu of English Heritage, and finally by the full establishment battery of letters to *The Times* culminating in a magnificent leader in that paper. Still there appeared to be no solution until, to everyone's amazement, Nigel Lawson, in his first budget in March 1984, announced that the government was providing the National Heritage Memorial Fund with additional finance to save Calke Abbey. An unknown country house became unique in being mentioned by name in a budget speech. Conservation had come a long way.

The sums required were £4 million for capital works and £3.5 million for endow-

59. Calke Abbey required £7.5 million for repair and endowment. Quarries on the estate were reopened but provided insufficient stone of a high enough quality for recarved cornice sections

ment. The total of £7.5 million was obtained by the £4.5 million NHMF donation, £1 million from English Heritage, £1 million from Mr Harpur Crewe, and £1 million from the National Trust itself. Of that last sum, 75 per cent was provided by legacies and anonymous donors and 25 per cent from a public appeal. On top of his contribution the owner still had to meet an £8 million tax bill by selling large parts of the remaining 14,000 acres of the family estates in Derbyshire and Staffordshire – some of the latter going to the Peak Park.

Architect Rodney Melville and his associate John Bucknall, who had already been involved for years in helping to put the Calke case, set about a major repair programme in 1985. Several stages started with first-aid measures such as patching fractures in the lead roof, clearing and unblocking gutters and downpipes, and attacking outbreaks of dry rot. Next they embarked on a pilot programme of specimen major repairs to the massive stone cornice and releading part of the roof in order to discover where the main difficulties were likely to arise. Then came the key phase which included refurbishment of most of the rooms to be on show, the formation of flats for the donor and some staff, the repair of stables and conversion of outbuildings to form a tearoom, shop, information room, and lavatories. The architects regarded themselves as fortunate in being able to appoint an established traditional contractor with his own craftsmen, Messrs Linford-Bridgeman.

This proved particularly important when it was realized that the whole of the stone cornice under the balustrade, a chief feature of the building, would have to be dismantled and much of the decayed carved stonework replaced. Radio scanning had revealed that every stone was held by four rusting iron clamps which were causing damage and had to be removed. The upper part of the building has been restrained from outward movement by the insertion of stainless steel

rods and a reinforced concrete ring beam. Being former SPAB scholars, both Melville and Bucknall were happy to employ modern technology to assist in retaining as much of the carved stonework as possible. Thus only structurally fragmented blocks were replaced, and weathered but sound stones were put back. Each stone in the three courses of the cornice is man-sized, and the foliate detail of the upper course and egg and dart of the middle course meant that there was a major undertaking for Linford's masons. White Hollington sandstone was used as efforts to reopen a quarry on the estate was unsuccessful.

Structural roof and wall repairs, the eradication of rot, the releading of the vast low-pitch roof with heavy cast lead carefully ventilated to prevent chemical reactions leading to corrosion, together with the provision of fireproofing and smoke-sealing, resistant and retardant installations after the usual exhaustive discussions with regulatory authorities – these are a few of the tasks involved in this conversion of a private home into what amounts to a national museum. The reordering of routes in the grounds to provide extensive but unobtrusive car-parking, which is approached and left from different directions, was another task which is common to all major properties open to the public. Calke welcomed its first visitors in spring 1989.

This chapter has discussed but a few of the agencies successfully caring for country houses. Different organizations include the Country Houses Association, a charity founded in 1955, which has bought a number of outstanding houses, and restored and converted them into flats for letting, often to retired people. Its properties include very important houses such as Aynhoe Park in Oxfordshire, largely by Sir John Soane; Danny, a fine Elizabethan house near Hassocks in Sussex: Flete near Plymouth, an ancient house to which Norman Shaw added substantially; Gosfield Hall in Essex with its

Tudor courtyard and eighteenth-century wings; the Palladian Pythouse near Salisbury, Wiltshire, and Great Maytham Hall designed by Edwin Lutyens in 1910, which is near Cranbook in Kent.

It is questionable whether such fine buildings in rural southern England will be affordable in future by charitable foundations. The market in country houses, especially if at the centre of large estates, has become one for multi-millionaires in recent years. It is to be hoped that these purchasers will not soon become as bored and neglectful as those who bought Heveningham or Mereworth Castle. Both of these beautiful buildings have been in sorry states until a splendid refurbishment of Mereworth in the last few years. Heritage organizations will no doubt keep an eye on Daylesford, bought by Anthony Bamford for £10 million from Baron Thyssen-Bornemisza, together with its 1,000 acres of Gloucestershire countryside; on Glympton Park with an estate of nearly 2,000 acres near Woodstock in Oxfordshire which went to Alan Bond for £11 million recently; and on the most expensive purchase of all at £15 million, Ascot, sold by the widow of Sir Jack Heinz to Mick Flick, with a mere 500 acres of gardens and woodland.

Chapter 9

Rural
Buildings

Introduction

Computer staff salary increases in Wales, the South West and the Midlands have overtaken those in the South East as employers search ever harder for scarce skills. (*The Times*, 25 November 1988)

The depopulation of the countryside which has been continuous since the late eighteenth century is in the process of being dramatically reversed. In much of England booming property prices already evidence a revolution which will eventually reach even the remoter parts of the UK. The reasons are clear. First is the perceived higher quality of rural life, especially if it can be enjoyed in weekday daylight hours by the breadwinner as well as his or her family. Universal car ownership has largely removed the problems inherent in all but extreme physical isolation. Second is that increase in house prices which has forced many would-be homeowners away from the immediate south-east and as far afield as Doncaster. Third is the reaction to that dispersal, a resentment at the sacrifice of time and temper involved in long-distance, or even relatively proximate commuting – road conditions worsen daily and BR's 'Network South-East' is not greatly loved. So those who have moved from London and other major cities start looking around for alternatives to travelling back daily. The fourth and most significant long-term factor is that which supplies the answer to the problems of the other three. The rapid growth in affordable information technology will allow an increasing number of people to work some or all of the time from home. Eventually this will even moderate urban house prices.

Equipped with a computer and/or word processor, a Fax (facsimile transmission) machine and perhaps a photocopier, as well as a couple of telephone lines, workers in many creative and administrative fields can be more efficient during a longer and less stressful day in infinitely nicer surroundings. Those who miss social interaction or, alternatively, find there is too much from an ever-present family, can set up with others in communal workplaces. Design studios, computer bureaux, craft workshops, and office co-operatives already exist in or near many villages.

An increased demand for housing is being followed by a scarcity of premises suitable for conversion to workplaces. At what might be called the top of the market country houses are already greatly in demand in much of the country as was seen in the preceding chapter. Other redundant rural buildings, barns, schools, churches for example, are at a premium in attractive areas. So information technology is transforming work and travel patterns, it will reduce pressure on commuting facilities and inner suburban houses, and will continue to intensify and geographically broaden demand for refurbished space and, indeed, new building in the countryside. Already local authorities, having yielded to DoE pressure barely a decade ago to look at new-use applications for old farm buildings in particular, are reversing such policies to preserve just a few barns in an unconverted state. Financial incentives can distort use patterns, and if a farm building is even marginally economic in agricultural use, and a farmer is willing to keep it in basic repair, that is preferable to any conversion.

A historic reversal of the flow of population to the cities started a quarter of a century ago with the growth of outer suburbs. London's population loss – exacerbated by misguided postwar redevelopment policies – led to a huge growth in the south-east as a whole. That region was the most, some would say the only, prosperous part of the country; but that trend is also showing signs of reduction. On a much smaller scale a similar pattern was seen in, for example, the north-west, where people who were able (and who didn't make the trek to the south) moved from inner Liverpool and

Manchester to the Wirral, Cheshire, and north Wales. All such moves were determined by available facilities for people to travel to work. Now that in many occupations it is not people who need to travel, but information, and that this can be conveyed in seconds even if it has to be bounced off an earth satellite, the spread of people over the countryside is likely to return to a pre-industrial pattern. The only trouble is that there are far more people, so the pressure on rural land and buildings will render them extremely valuable. This chapter looks not so much at bright ideas for reuse – there will be no shortage of them – but at sensitive conversions which retain the maximum original character.

In order to understand the essence of that character it is a good idea to re-examine its origins which are, broadly speaking, vernacular as opposed to the architecture of towns, much of which is 'polite'. That is, it has been preconceived and planned. In the Middle Ages most of England's population of under a million lived in hovels – earth-floored huts of wood, wattle, mud, and thatch – or in low and virtually windowless stone bothies which survive in parts of Ireland and the isles of Scotland. Wooden shacks were often thrown up overnight on the edges of common land or in forest clearings by 'squatters'. They have not survived. What we now choose to call cottages were the homes of substantial peasants; if of two storeys with several bedrooms they were probably the residences of franklins or yeomen, that is, freed men who owned a little land.

Such buildings, together with most farmhouses and many manors, were also vernacular in that they were made of materials which came to hand, by customary methods to standard plans and without stylistic flourishes. Some eighteenth-century landowners did build model cottages, even villages, for workers, and they were designed and laid out by architects or surveyors. But these were few. When we speak of rural buildings we generally speak of structures erected by people who had no alternative patterns in their heads of how it might be done. That does not mean that decorations were entirely absent, but they too would have been of a customary kind. Well into the nineteenth century cob cottages were built in Devon of plastered mud and thatch in a manner oblivious of the Renaissance, or even of Georgian architecture. Vernacular building was essentially instinctive and it is impossible in the twentieth century to think ourselves into a state of mind which recaptures that instinct. To add to and adapt a rural building which appears to have no 'style' is a great deal more difficult than to amend a Victorian building in a self-conscious style. The talents of a Lutyens or a Voysey are appropriate.

Vernacular buildings have a 'rightness' which attracts the sophisticated and often something called the 'picturesque', neither of which qualities are reproducible. Polite Georgian architecture, on the other hand, being classically inspired and reliant on rules of proportion and decoration, is fully susceptible of reproduction in 1988 as demonstrated by Quinlan Terry; indeed, as he has shown, it is even possible to play games with its rules. Furthermore, it is nearly impossible to build alongside rural buildings without disfiguring them because regulations disallow appropriate ceiling and therefore roof heights and window sizes. These factors are discussed elsewhere in this volume.

Larger buildings dating after 1714, such as some west country textile mills in the Stroud area, have a regularity of span and materials, calculable floor loadings, larger windows, and acceptable ceiling heights – all of which render them ideal for conversion and adaptation to new uses. Once into the nineteenth century and dealing with buildings constructed with machine-made bricks and sawn slates the conservationist's task is comparatively straightforward. The really difficult area is that of timber framing. That form of construction, as well as being among the most picturesque to modern eyes, was also among the most advanced. For the primitive cruck frames of little thirteenth-century cottages, as well as the great roofs of later medieval barns, were prefabricated, their joints pinned to allow a degree of movement. Their infill of boarding, or wattle and daub, were also capable of allowing for temperature movement, moisture transfer, and some settlement. It is the lack of these facilities which have led to so many failures in rigidly constructed modern buildings. Thus it is necessary to approach vernacular architecture with humility on a technical level as well as in terms of aesthetics.

Oak frames should not be repaired with modern glues or epoxy resins which render their joints rigid. Lime plaster or whitewash should not be removed just because we find half-timbering attractive to look at. Interior lime-plastered walls and ceilings should not be replaced with modern plasterboard and skim coat which do not 'breath' and which crack. Old cottage or church walls which have been lime-washed for centuries should not be repainted with emulsions which are impermeable to vapour and encourage mould growth. Such technical mistakes are not the worst, they are reparable with time and money, but some alterations involving the scraping of oak beams and the replacing of old plaster have led to the loss of medieval painted decoration, fragmentary evidence of which not uncommonly comes to light.

Another factor in rural building demands great restraint on the part of the modern 'improver'. Just as a barn will retain no 'barn-ness' if its conversion involves the addition of large windows, dormers, chimneys, let alone external extensions, so it will also lose its 'local-ness' if materials unknown to its original builders are ostentatiously employed. There are limits to purism here; few people would complain about a correctly rethatched roof even if the material used

is Norfolk reed in a part of the country where combed straw would have been traditional. As always the importance of a building, as determined by DoE listing, will be the relevant determinant, especially if grant aid is sought.

Speke Hall, near Liverpool

Having spoken about vernacular architecture our first case study is a large country house, but, as has been suggested above, timber-framed buildings have a great deal in common whatever their scale. A magnificent example like Speke allows us to read the lessons writ large, for it is one of the most extensive surviving timber houses. Before the nineteenth century Merseyside was a rather isolated country area dotted with many fine manor houses; even Victorian visitors praised the beauty of the remote marshy shore beside which Speke was sited.[31]

The Norris family had built themselves a hall in about 1390. The manor was enlarged in about 1500 and took its present courtyard form in Elizabeth's reign. The great hall is splendidly 'wainscotted' or panelled and has an exuberant stone overmantel often thought to be of the Victorian Gothic Revival but was in fact a fascinatingly uncouth creation of about 1550 for Sir William Norris. Around the courtyard are predictable ranges of large and small chambers, some with fine wainscot and plasterwork as well as galleries, kitchens, and servants' quarters: the plan is quite muddled.

The Civil War saw the house partly emptied of furniture. The Norrises and their successors neglected it but there was a double attraction according to sale particulars of 1795: romantic views over the estuary to north Wales and the possibility of coal mining on the estate. The purchasers, the Watt family, were wealthy, and lived intermittently at Speke until 1921. At times, in the 1850s for example,

the house was quite lavishly redecorated and refurnished. It may have been at that time that pitch was applied to the exterior timbers, many of which were irregular and of poor quality. In any case the remarkable black and white patterning of the infill panels to the main frame is the most vivid impression retained by visitors, whether the diagonal or chevron patterns of the four-gabled north range overlooking the dry moat or the quatrafoils which predominate on courtyard elevations and elsewhere.

Miss Adelaide Watt, the last private owner, had taken good care of Speke Hall, but her wish that it go to the National Trust was not realized until

60. Speke Hall, near Liverpool; one of the few surviving half-timbered mansions near a once-isolated coast, now an oasis amidst highways, chemical plants, and an airport

1942. Meanwhile the Liverpool Corporation had purchased 2,000 acres at the break up of the estate in the 1930s. This has resulted in the house being bordered on three sides today by Speke Airport; though concealed by earthworks, jets can taxi to within 125 yards of it, added to which the further panorama is of petro-chemical works and power lines. This lack of surrounding tranquility is reflected in the evolution of ownership and occupation. The National Trust leased the hall to the Merseyside County Council for a dozen or so years until the abolition of the latter in 1986. Nevertheless that council, together with the NT and the Historic Buildings Council, set in train the most thorough repairs possible of a building the very survival of which was said to be in danger as a result of roof deterioration and death-watch beetle.

Architect Peter Lock of Donald Insall & Associates tackled the building in several large phases coinciding approximately with courtyard ranges. In all over £1 million was spent. The fact that the approach was very much that of the SPAB's conservative repair method, which means carrying out the minimum work to keep the building weatherproof and safe from decay, indicates the extent of decrepitude. In any timber building there are likely to be two distinct types of problem: the first involves large-scale structural weaknesses in major framing members or junctions, the second concerns local breakdowns in subsidiary members in walls or roof, or in the infill panels between framing members. Obviously the first could cause building collapse whereas the second is only likely to result in water penetration through wall or roof which will lead to a cycle of decay which would be fatal to the building in the longer run. Major structural failure can be caused by distortion or even fracture of members or junctions as a result of uneven settlement or undermining. It can also result from injudicious alterations; it is remarkable how apparently sensible people will remove roof ties so that they can move around a loft space more easily. All members in a timber frame have a job to do. Because such building was not an exact science there is usually more material in the structure than strictly necessary, so taking away one or two timbers may not result in immediate signs of distress. Such weakening is progressive, however, and if other members become overstressed the building is more vulnerable to serious damage when decay occurs at another point.

Both types of framing problem are most likely to be caused by water penetration which encourages immediate decay by wet rot and, more importantly, provides the conditions for the spread of

61. Speke Hall; timbers were generally small-dimensioned and treated with tar to compensate for poor-quality oaks in the area. The effect is decorative

the all-pervasive dry rot. At Speke beetle attack was as serious a problem as rot, affecting timbers in a variety of situations. Eggs laid in the timber spend years boring their way out to the surface before emerging through the tell-tale holes as beetles to fly, mate, and lay fresh eggs in crevices or runs in other timbers. Apart from the hole, the wood surface often looks superficially sound, but inside it is brittle and if stressed it can disintegrate in a cloud of dust. Oak is especially vulnerable to beetle, less to rot. The web-like fronds of dry rot travelling almost invisibly behind skirtings or panelling remove all the moisture and cellular strength of softwood especially. The 'fruiting body' of

the fungus is not the real danger, except to its immediate host timber, so destroying that achieves little. In fact killing all apparent manifestations of growth will be ineffective unless the conditions which encourage outbreaks are removed. Dry-rot spores are in the air almost everywhere. Wherever there is damp timber, not too cold, with a hint of a passsing air current and a little gloom the spores will settle happily. Peter Lock is renowned for his all-out campaigns against *merulius lacrymans* (dry rot) in the most distinguished buildings such as Trinity College, Cambridge. A timber-framed building is tackled by surveying every member on annotated drawings, and

62. Speke Hall; reconstruction of a bay in the west wall. Members were replaced where necessary and pieced into the existing structure

tracing all areas of decay back to rot outbreaks and places of water ingress so that causes can be cured and damaged or brittle members repaired in a manner which retains the maximum amount of original fabric. Some years ago the present writer inspected roof repairs in Lincoln Cathedral, where the splendid craftsmen were replacing whole long baulks of oak with well-seasoned new timbers and were proud that 'it would be good for another five hundred years'. With the best of intentions they were destroying a rare and majestically scaled medieval carpentry structure. It is the actual timbers, the surface marks of tooling, the particular way the joints were made, even the numbering of members and the setting-out marks, all of which are to be seen, that make an old roof a historic artifact.

In a house like Speke the idea is to retain as much as possible not only of the surviving frame, but also of the wattle and daub infill and even plaster surfaces where practical. In a country cottage this would matter at least as much, for the original material which gives it character will exist in much smaller quantities. Where accessible oak members are cut back to sound wood without removal from their position in the building, new sections of seasoned timber are spliced or scarfed to them (with the addition of metal straps if the stresses seem to call for them), and new or partly new pinned joints are created with all the strength and flexibility of the old. Joints are often in vulnerable positions such as at junctions of wall and roof, so water damage or insect attack are common. New wood should not be artificially aged, or even stained; the repair becomes part of the building's history. Where decay occurs at vital points, notably the bearing of roof trusses onto the tops of walls – that is, in the vicinity of parapets or gutters which are often the seat of problems – not only new timber beam ends but iron or steel straps, even complete 'cradles', might well be called for. Again there is no need to hide these additions. What is important is that they be designed to allow a modicum of movement. All buildings move with changes in moisture, temperature, or settlement of foundations – except monolithic concrete structures which simply crack.

The 'conservative repairer' does not reject all scientific interventions, especially where they can be called in aid of preserving old fabric. If an important wooden member such as a fireplace beam, perhaps even with carved decoration, is in danger of fracturing because of increased loading above it, or beetle attack within, the injection of epoxy resin, perhaps with nylon rod reinforcement, may be used

to restore its strength without moving it from the spot. Such materials should never be used to glue a junction together, as one member is bound to be over-stressed and will be liable to fracture.

The other use of science – apart from in investigative processes – is in the chemical warfare waged against dry rot in particular. Contrary to all that has been said above, it is sometimes necessary to remove large areas of plaster, panelling, or boarding, even demolish parts of brick walls for example, to get at sources and routes of outbreak, and then impregnate the timbers and surrounding walls with chemicals (dry rot strands will travel distances over stone or metal to reach fresh wood). After a period the removed coverings are replaced.

The methods described in outline have been employed on many significant repair projects in recent years: at Thaxted Guildhall in Essex and Little Moreton Hall, Cheshire, another notable timber-framed house in the care of the National Trust in the north-west. That and Speke, together with Rufford Old Hall, which is not quite on the same scale, are among the few survivors among hundreds of manor houses in the region which was affected more than any other by the Industrial Revolution.

Barns

The introduction to this chapter spoke of the virtual mania to convert farm buildings, and especially the grain-storage and threshing barn which has always been the most impressive type, into homes or other new uses. Certainly in fashionable parts of the country such as areas of Gloucestershire or the Cotswolds there seems to be barely an unconverted barn. That is not true in remoter regions, or those too near industry or those on the land of farmers disinclined to allow access.

As recently as 1987 there were more applications to demolish listed barns than any other single building type, and in fact farm buildings as a whole comprised one in five of all applications for total demolition. This is not to speak of the hundreds of unlisted farm buildings that have been swept away. Barns in that year also suffered from the blight already touched upon – loss of character and interest through unsympathetic conversion – more than other sorts of buildings. A record number were delisted because domestic use had destroyed their architectural interest.

At a time of trend reversal it is possible to suffer from opposite effects, in this case loss of buildings because of redundancy and neglect in some areas and loss of quality through too much attention of the wrong sort in others. The previously underlying movement was of agricultural labour from the land – indeed this continues alongside the influx into the countryside of townees. Thus Britain's famously mechanized and productive farms employ less than 3 per cent of the working population, the lowest in Europe. Not only have machines replaced men and the concentration into larger units made whole farmsteads surplus to requirements, but grain dryers and concrete-framed storage sheds have proved more economical in use than old barns. The latter have occasionally come into their own recently to provide shelter for stock where farmers are diversifying into animal rearing instead of concentrating on arable production. But on the whole farmers have preferred to see old buildings destroyed rather than converted into new uses which would bring strangers onto their land. Until the 1980s even the Ministry of Agriculture advisers (ADAS) at least tacitly supported such views. Now all is changed. EEC quotas and reduced farm incomes have obliged landowners to look at all kinds of new activities. Even the Country Landowners' Association holds competitions for sympathetic conversions.

63. Fisher's Pond Barn, Eastleigh, Hampshire; conversion of a basically sixteenth-century structure into a private house, with quite radical external alterations by skilled architects; but the 'barn-like' quality is retained

64. Fisher's Pond Barn; the decision to place bedrooms and bathrooms at ground level allows roof structure to be admired in the living room

Fisher's Pond Barn, Eastleigh, Hampshire

This barn, converted into a private house, elegantly demonstrates several rules of the game. First, the exterior is still barn-like despite a by no means over-modest design approach. The ridge of the roof is continuous but below it on one side is a dramatic horizontal gash of terrace and glazing. The point is that lines continue, they are not broken up by inserted chimneys, dormers, or spotty rooflights. The barn's only original large opening, the cart-entrance, is also glazed and there, as elsewhere, the wooden detailing around the opening is robust. Apart from an area of glass, the original brick infill to the exposed frame at the gable is retained. Clay roof tiles and fragments of stonework of the sixteenth-century building are also kept. Such details as the shadows under the eaves are only noticed if they are lost in the process of a conversion which doesn't 'look right'.

The architects, Stevenson & Thomas from Winchester, have a firm precept about internal arrangements in such conversions: owners are obliged to live 'upside-down', with bedrooms and bathrooms downstairs and the main living area above so that the chief feature of such buildings, the splendid timber roofs, are fully displayed. The Queen post trusses, and such features as the curved wind braces which indicate the fairly late date, can all be admired in an interior which is, nevertheless, unashamedly 'modern'. Of course it would not have been beautifully plastered in the sixteenth century, but some compromises are allowed! This conversion was one which received a commendation from the Country Landowners' Association.

65. Great Priory Barn, Panfield, Essex; listed Grade I, this, the older and larger of two barns, has been repaired as a display area by the furniture maker who bought the farmhouse and yard

Great Priory Barn, Panfield, Essex

66. Great Priory Barn, this, the smaller barn, is now the furniture workshop

This barn dates at least in part from the thirteenth century, and is part of a historic farmhouse group in the rural heartland of Essex, although the buildings are no longer the centre of a working farm. The priory's foundation was shortly after the Norman Conquest, and traces of its buildings survive in a nearby field. In 1982 a furniture designer and restorer moved into the Tudor farmhouse. He had an antique restoration workshop in Wapping which, after some essential repairs to the smaller of two barns at Great Priory Farm, was resited there. This building, listed Grade II, retained

some early structure but was mostly rebuilt about 1680.

The larger of the two barns, listed Grade I, was a far more serious proposition. The 700-year-old timber frame was in need of extensive and expert repair and the roof had to be rethatched. The next few years unfolded a tale of patient co-operation with various local and central government grant-giving and supervisory agencies, together with private contractors and craftsmen, to produce a fully restored historic structure. The use is as a display and storage area for the furniture being made in increasing quantity in the smaller barn. The owner was encouraged by his move

to spacious rural surroundings to fulfil an ambition to make his own furniture, a decision which reflected his interest in William Morris and the Arts and Crafts Movement.

Generous financial support from HBMC (that is, English Heritage) was the key. Technical guidance came from county council conservation officers who helped to supervise repairs – and whose account of the project has assisted the present writer.[32] The contractor chosen was one of the few in the country with recent experience on a comparable building – Bakers of Danbury had just completed work on Grange Barn at Coggeshall. Panfield Barn was tackled before it had approached the disastrous state of Coggeshall. Repairs involved the minimum of new timbers, but missing members such as curved braces between posts and main beams had to be replaced. Traditional methods were used, repairs were carried out without recourse to epoxy or other plastics. Metal straps were fabricated to appropriate profiles to secure some joints. In connection with the rethatching the advice of COSIRA (Council for Small Industries in Rural Areas) was helpful. A local Essex thatcher was knowledgable enough to be ready to reproduce a rare traditional feature, tiled valleys between the thatch of the main roof and the gabled entrance porch. Work was completed by the end of 1986 and, as conservation officer Peter Richards says, 'the most satisfying part of the whole exercise is that the farmyard still looks much as it did [when] a working farm'. There is no sign of the squalor often accompanying small workshops. And this despite the Grade I barn being the busy showroom for the products of half a dozen or so employees working in the smaller barn. Such a scheme as this demonstrates the various profits available in the conversion of ancient structures to new industrial uses. Not only is a group of fine buildings preserved but employment opportunities are expanded; two recruits from the youth training scheme are now permanently employed.

67. Harmondsworth Barn, Middlesex, near London Airport; this great aisled grain store, built in 1426–7 for Winchester College, is now a builder/developer's showcase

68. Harmondsworth Barn was recently surveyed over a period of eighteen months prior to repair by Peter McCurdy who has assembled unrivalled data on such construction

which, as a creation in 1426 of Winchester College, it was not unconnected.

The college received the manor of Harmondsworth as an endowment from its founder William of Wykeham, who had purchased it from the French Abbey, St Catherine's of Rouen, in 1391. Wykeham, bishop of the immensely rich see of Winchester, had, in 1394, specified the cladding of the Norman nave in the latest Perpendicular style. As McCurdy writes: 'This congregational part of the cathedral impressed, not by mystery and darkness or by the surprise of soaring elevation, but by the sheer hypnotic majesty of so many clearly defined units repeated one after another.' Both barn and cathedral have a nave and aisles, both have twelve bays; Winchester at 230 feet was a bit longer – but was the longest nave in Europe.

McCurdy describes the medieval Harmondsworth barn as being not only full to the 'brim with produce and labour like a combined factory floor and storehouse', but as also having a second function 'to subdue by its bulk and manifest order one of the most notoriously rebellious and litigious manorial holdings in England at a time of class warfare and social change'. Its very survival long after its threshing floors ceased to function is proof of the awe such a building continues to instil. That may be part of the reason why the John Wiltshier Group, builder/

Harmondsworth Manor Barn

Interiors of great barns have frequently been compared to those of cathedrals, and William Morris, founder of the SPAB, did exactly this in relation to Great Coxwell Tythe Barn. Here in Middlesex, on a semi-rural, semi-real island between motorways, is an example which its scholar/craftsman-repairer, Peter McCurdy, has found to be virtually a simulacrum of the nave of Winchester Cathedral with

developers, bought the barn together with the rest of the Manor Farm property three miles from Heathrow in 1986.

The company is repairing the building as a prestige showplace for its work. McCurdy has spent eighteen months carrying out a detailed timber-by-timber survey, photographing, drawing, and noting the condition of every part of the fabric. His interest in the subject has led him to invest far more time than can be financially justified. He has been joined by the Museum of London which is carrying out archaeological work on the site of this scheduled Ancient Monument and by a historian who is researching the estate records.

69 (a) and (b). Grange Barn, Coggeshall, Essex, one of the oldest timber-framed structures in Europe, this twelfth-century building largely collapsed in the 1970s while the owner sought to destroy it. It was reconstructed by Essex County Council architects using

McCurdy has made himself an expert in the study of how such frames were set out and marked for erection, how the joints were scribed. He has recorded innumerable markings on these 700-year-old timbers. Each component of the building has been drawn separately to scale showing all scribe marks, waney edges, and rot so that a repair schedule is made for each piece showing required patching or replacement. The result is a complete archaeological record and an understanding of how the building was made as well as a detailed proposal for repair. For example, the 14-inch-square arcade posts of good-quality hewn oak sit on squared blocks of green sandstone

resting on subsoil with no footings. Movement in one wall has caused distortion of the frame. About half of the original oak weatherboarding survives. It is fitted to a rebate in the underside of the wall plate and fastened with wrought nails. Boards have pit saw marks.

Thus far most of us can follow Peter McCurdy. It is when he ventures into international comparisons of scribing and of construction methods that his almost unique expertise impresses: 'Unlike most English timber frames which are set out from the face sides [these] have been set out from centre lines ... this type ... is characterised by certain constructional relationships more typical of the French

traditional methods and reinstating fallen timbers and tiles wherever possible

system'. It is something of an anti-climax to learn that one end of the barn was damaged by fire in the 1970s. What we can be relatively sure of is that it is being immaculately repaired in the late 1980s.

Grange Barn, Coggeshall, Essex

A magnificent, aisled, six-bay, double-porched threshing barn, one of the oldest wooden-framed structures in the world, was almost destroyed in the 1970s because the farmer who owned it wanted space to turn his lorries round. By the time various local and national voluntary groups and local and national government authorities had convinced themselves and others of the building's transcendent importance and then secured the powers and funds for repair, the structure was virtually a ruin. The reconstruction, skilfully carried out by Essex County Council architects, was perforce so extensive that a substantial part of the building was new. The lesson to be learned in this case is that attitudes were revolutionized in the 1970s, but the processes of procrastination during that change resulted in vast expense at the end of the period to preserve and reuse fragments of the building which had been nearly intact and economically repairable at the beginning of it.

Another conservation issue raised during the long struggle to save a rapidly collapsing building was that of removal to another site – never the best solution. But is it always wise to stick out for the best rather than compromise? During a decade in which the tide has flowed in favour of conservation it has generally been wise to avoid compromise. But when in 1974 the would-be preservers of Coggeshall Barn were first offered the structure as a gift so long as they removed it to another site, their dilemma was painful. By then it was rapidly deteriorating, with vast areas of tiling missing. Despite this the main components of the frame were still capable of being salvaged. A not unsuitable site was available in the vicinity, near a chapel which was once the *capella ante portas* of the abbey. There is also the argument that medieval carpentry structures, unique among major historic buildings, were largely prefabricated and then secured by oak pegs, so that dismantling is practicable. A large number of barns – too many – have been re-erected, usually for domestic use, as far afield as the USA. If Coggeshall barn had been moved in the mid-1970s a greater proportion of the fabric may well have survived than proved to be the case. The idea did find reluctant support among conservationists at the time, including the present writer.

The truth, however, is that a building separated from its original site ceases to be a historic building and becomes largely a facsimile. Quaint it may be, even instructive, which is presumably the justification for open-air museums, but much of its meaning is gone.

The barn dominating the view to the south from the nearby valley owes its existence to the Cistercian abbey of Coggeshall, founded in 1140. The crucial importance of arable farming to such a community is shown by the building of the barn as an essential store for grain – the source of the monks' wealth – ten years later. Only in the 1970s was the mid-twelfth-century date proved by a combination of historical and scientific (radiocarbon-dating) evidence most satisfactorily reinforced by the research of medieval-carpentry expert Cecil Hewitt. He dated the main timbers to the twelfth century by analysing carpentry joints. It was also recognized then that much of the roof had been reconstructed in the second half of the fourteenth century, the form of construction as well as the survival of some of the large clay tiles of that period proved this.

In 1539 the monastery was dissolved; the barn and the land were sold off. Although altered in both the eighteenth and the nineteenth centuries it was essentially the same building that came into the ownership of Mr Cullen in 1958 when he bought Grange Farm. From then on it fell into disuse and disrepair for a period of over twenty years. While farmer, conservationists, and authorities argued about its fate the building collapsed at either end and that which remained was badly fractured and distorted. An abbreviated account of the to-ings and fro-ings can perhaps ensure their non-repetition. In 1966 the barn had been listed Grade II*. The Coggeshall Society first expressed concern about its condition the following year. In 1969 there was the first request for the service on the owner of a repairs notice and also an offer of purchase by the parish council, but both were rejected. Essex County Council, precociously interested in historic buildings as early as 1968, surveyed the building and also sought government financial help. While awaiting a reply the county served a section 101 repairs notice itself in 1972 and thereafter carried out works to stabilize the three most easterly bays.

By this time the farmer, realizing that he was not going to be allowed to let the barn fall down, made his offer to the county to take it away. Repair, then estimated to cost £25,000, was preferred. It was prevented by the discovery that access to the site required the permission of an adjoining owner, and this was refused. A newly formed Grange Barn Trust was unsuccessful in a search for new uses; the idea of vesting in the National Trust was explored, but the provision of an endowment for the repaired building was a stumbling block. Removal was still resisted and, in 1975, Mr Cullen was thought to have agreed to lease the barn to the trust. He changed his mind and applied for demolition consent which was obviously refused. At a subsequent public inquiry the inspector judged the structure to be of 'extreme importance' and urged local people and public authorities to strive towards a solution to the problem. Meanwhile there was a major collapse of two bays at the west end and repairs were costed at £45,000 according to an emergency schedule prepared by the county council. Nothing could be spent, partly because the local planning authority, Braintree District Council, continued to be unwilling to take the necessary legal steps. It was nervous of financial commitments, despite guarantees from the Grange Barn Trust that any expense would be reimbursed.

At last in 1978, with only about half of the barn standing, the HBC chairman, Jennifer Jenkins, called a round-table meeting of interested parties and experts. Subsequently the DoE agreed to a sub-stantial grant – but for removal. After much local heartsearching, particularly by the redoubtable 'ladies of Coggeshall' who had provided the backbone of village support – the oft-derided middle-class do-gooders – this was agreed. Ironically it was at least in part the continued dilatoriness of Braintree Council which allowed time for another rethink. A change of mind by that council after a last-minute campaign by the county, the SPAB, and the Grange Barn Trust finally tipped the balance. A compulsory purchase order resulted in a change of owernship, the provision of access, and the stabilization of the near-ruin in 1981. With the support of the SPAB the Grange Barn Trust asked the assistant county architect, James Boutwood, to supervise the reconstruction of the building.

Repairs were carried out using traditional techniques, although often in an innovatory manner. With the exception of one post, all the remaining Norman carpentry was rescued, together with the greater part of the crown post roof. As has been indicated this upper roof was of fourteenth-century date and there were other, though comparatively minor, modifications over the centuries. But there was no attempt at conjectural restoration; the structure was reconstructed almost entirely as it had been before the collapse started. The work was carried out as a Manpower Services project under the careful supervision of a local builder. This last was important to all concerned and the job turned out successfully in more than one way. Of the eight men employed under the scheme, five were taken on to the contractor's permanent labour force.

Even with effective subsidy of labour costs by the MSC, and of some professional costs by the county council, the total sum expended on repairs amounted to £192,000. Grants were received from the Historic Buildings Council, Essex County Council, Braintree District Council, and the National Heritage Memorial Fund, who contributed

£30,000 towards the acquisition of the site. The Grange Barn Trust raised some £30,000 by voluntary effort and is approaching a number of private charitable trusts. Thanks to an enormous legacy to the National Trust from a local businessman it has been possible to provide sufficient endowment for the NT to assume ownership of the barn. Management will remain in the hands of a local committee.

Chapter 10

Building in
Context

Puma Court,
Spitalfields,
London, new
infill follows
original
proportions
rather than style

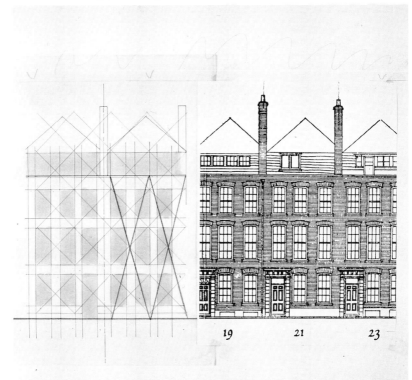

Introduction

Aesthetic problems associated with the insertion of new buildings, including large additions, into historic settings have exercised architects and, indeed, planners since the last war. At least until 1975 modernist dogma implied, via its 'form follows function' tenet, that there could only be one right way of designing – straightforwardly modern. In exceptional circumstances pastiche was allowed but was only really acceptable for gap-filling, as in the case of the bombed Nash terraces around Regents Park, London. Even then, says John Summerson, there were fierce arguments before rebuilding in facsimile was adopted as policy. In practice a timorous 'keeping in keeping' attitude often resulted in a sort of committee-designed solution, watered-down neo-Georgian or, worse still, watered-down modern. The famous British compromise is misplaced in matters aesthetic; for one thing it precludes originality and wit, whereby an intruder into an established environment can make a contribution. The days of timidity are now past; in architecture, especially among younger exponents, there is an aesthetic free-for-all. The result is an increasing number of lively and successful new-with-old designs not only by young architects like Piers Gough but older ones such as William Whitfield.

Size and the scale of a building's grain, or detail, are as important as its particular architectural language. A new house is almost impossible to intrude into a village street tactfully, even if dressed in all the old materials, simply because the storey heights and ratio of window to wall required by modern regulations and taste results in wrong proportions. Style, in terms of presence or absence of period trimmings, is of almost no consequence set-alongside the appropriateness or not of the bulk and grain of a building. There are exceptions however. A reflective glass building can assume the modelling of its surroundings, and the dark glass-walled Willis Faber office building in Ipswich, designed by Norman Foster in the late 1960s, is generally regarded as a success. Its curved form occupies most of an irregularly shaped block on the edge of the old town centre, it is only three storeys high, its walls dissolve in reflections of the idiosyncratic architecture of surrounding streets, and I. M. Pei has inserted a sizeable glass pyramid in the Louvre courtyard – a formal object in a formal space. All that is required for the rewarding addition of a new building in an old setting is for the genius of the place to be complemented by the genius of the architect!

Like so many of our recent, if not current, preoccupations the idea of stylistic 'keeping in keeping' is comparatively recent. The daring Parisian pyramid could symbolize, if in rather an extreme form, the historic attitude that the builder of today adds his contribution to that of his forefathers without undue nervousness about those forefathers' sensibilities. It may be salutary that the progressivist concept that anything we do will be an improvement has fallen into disuse, but the general lack of confidence in any architectural design is certainly not healthy. Apart from the style argument which we have suggested is drawing to a close, there is one objective difference between building in the later twentieth century and building at any other time – that is, the triumph of technology. Modern materials' strength to weight, together with engineering advances, mean that there are almost no limits to the height and span of buildings. The process started in the mid-nineteenth century; great train sheds of iron could arch 200 feet – and with reasonable economy. For 2,000 years the world's greatest civilizations could devote huge resources and their best brains to build arches and domes with one stone upon another in combined forms to enclose awe-inspiring spaces – such as Santa Sophia, St Peter's. But most buildings, certainly domestic ones, were composed of rooms the smaller dimension of which was determined by the span of a wooden beam, 4–5 metres. Panes of glass, sizes of lintels, pitches of roofs, number of stairs, width of floor boards, were all limited 'naturally' in buildings made of timber, baked mud, stone, and plaster, and occupied without mechanisms such as lifts. These factors, again more than style, meant that throughout the centuries there was a natural homogeneity in all architecture except the very grandest. Now we have to strive for that homogeneity by, among other things, forgoing some of the facilities science has provided. But since such restraint is going to be essential to mankind's future in every sphere from aerosols to atomic power, there would appear to be no reason why architects working in conservation areas should be excepted.

Until the eighteenth century there were only isolated examples of deliberately anachronistic architecture, that is, of building to match something older. Most masons were not self-conscious enough, they had neither the historic perspective nor the knowledge to allow the creation of 'period pastiche'. As usual there is an exception to be made in the case of the nation's major monuments and those who designed them – William of Sens and, several centuries later, Henry Yevele for example. They were capable of continuing a cathedral nave in the style of earlier times. Even then the details of carving and the extent of undercutting of mouldings, for example, would provide evidence of actual date for the scholar. Normally in the medieval period new work added to even a great church or castle would be undisguised.

In the latter part of Elizabeth's reign some of her courtiers built mansions in a deliberately antique style, reversions to romantic medievalism, as at Cowdray in Sussex where the turreted gatehouse was, almost unbelievably, built a generation after the Italianate classicism of Somerset House, London, which dates to the 1540s. This was a literary-based 'post-modernism'. The English landowner's addiction to ideas of chivalry, especially if he be parvenu, had already been foreshadowed in old-fashioned castles, built with quite thin brick walls, of the fifteenth century at Tattershall and Hurstmonceux. It was to persist into the seventeenth century (as at Bolsover) and see revivals in the late eighteenth century and at various times in the nineteenth. Until that last period these exercises were games-playing, no more intent on being confused with the real thing than Wren's 'Gothic' church towers. Evocative, not accurate. Much the same can be said of Robert Adam's castles, or even more elaborate fantasies such as Strawberry Hill, though there was in the eighteenth century a less well known continuation of a much more archaeologically based church restoration. Architecture was not yet a profession, and the descendants of medieval masons, who had patched up many churches with considerable skill after Cromwell's depredations, were still building small manor houses in remote parts of the country in a style almost innocent of the Renaissance.

So it is also possible from an historic perspective to dethrone Style from the crucial position in architectural thinking it assumed in the late eighteenth and nineteenth centuries and which was reinforced in the period when the Modern Movement saw itself fighting historically-based eclecticism. Now that architects are dismantling the profession as created in the nineteenth century, there seems to be a consonant freedom of practice as well as language. Before surveying the much more fluid current situation it may be worthwhile to sketch in the route by which architects arrived at the neurotic condition from which they are only now showing signs of recovering. Nineteenth-century eclecticism ran riot, and every version of classical and Gothic in foreign (especially North Italian) forms were exploited together with Byzantine and Romanesque. Motifs were added from Chinese and Egyptian decoration. Designers were concerned with stylistic forms, yet what we see are nineteenth-century products which happen to be dressed up in this or that costume. The only exception being SPAB-inspired church repairs, even Pevsner remarked that in many west country churches he had difficulty in separating that late Victorian work from ancient fabric. It was not just the good quality of later-nineteenth-century workmanship, materials, and scholarship which identify their origin, it was the way the buildings were imagined in an imposed pictorial way. The 'conservative repairers' on the other hand saw the buildings from the stones in the rubble walls outward, more as their original builders did. This approach, together with closely allied Arts and Crafts practitioners, was one origin of modernism in this country, the homespun route. The other derived from the work, and then in the 1930s the actual influx, of central European intellectuals and the designs and writings of the French/Swiss architect Le Corbusier.

Both modernist strains were enormously influential, partly because of the coincidence with huge population increases, worldwide urbanization, and, in Europe, postwar reconstruction. Interwar suburbia of the 'Metroland' variety evolved from Arts and Crafts filtered through the genius of architects like Mackintosh, Lutyens, and Bailie Scott, and then turned into a cheap, mass-produced product. Public-sector building after 1945 was based on a species of the German socialist functionalism of the Bauhaus. Traditionalism, usually a watered-down version of Edwardian Baroque and neo-Georgianism, staggered on through the 1930s and 1950s especially for commercial and institutional buildings. Mainstream modernism has become the language of a rapidly urbanizing world except in the predominantly nineteenth-century cities of Europe, where modern architecture began.

It is hardly surprising, given this complex and rich architectural background, that in Britain where, despite all the redevelopment and new building in the last forty years, the majority of structures predate that period, there are many approaches to designing new buildings in old settings. At the risk of over-simplification, a number of these are described. The most straightforward is embraced by the dogmatic view that there is no way to build in any context except in the language of 'our own age' which may have a mainstream modernist accent, or may have a High-Tech one. Their argument is irrefutable, as it has been since stated by William Morris. The only problem with this theory, now held by mostly middle-aged architects, is that the products it produced while it held sway in terms of both individual buildings and larger environments are almost all cordially loathed by almost all the population. They have also failed in the two areas where they promised to succeed best – technical and social performance. If, nonetheless, this becomes one architectural language among many, as seems likely, there remains a case for the juxtaposition of the slickest of reflective, thin-skinned walls against the most solid and sculptural of historic façades. Foster and Manser are among architects who have shown how.

All the other approaches, if illiterate and timid neo-Georgian is admitted to have died out combine historic references with contemporary inventiveness in varying proportions. One school limits its borrowings largely to traditional materials; this might loosely be called 'contextual modernism'. Practitioners include Edward Cullinan, Robert Maguire and Richard MacCormac following in the tracks of Powell and Moya. Most of these architects have been chosen to design new buildings for Oxbridge colleges. Stone, brick, timber, lead, even concrete to a limited extent, are detailed in a bold, almost expressionist manner by these contextual modernists. It is an abstract language; there are no historicist references although there are hints of recent moves in that direction in the work of MacCormac. A more poetic version is the somewhat mysterious and unfortunately still rather small-scale work of John Outram. Via an abstract and symbolist classicism he transmutes orders and hints of mythology into a cerebral version of post-modernism. Because the actual detail of, say, the Ionic order, has been drained of significance, Outram re-invents the grammar. He introduces unexpected imagery as, for example, of the power of the sun, or of flight.

Some architects, Anthony Richardson for one, straddle this modernist/symbolist divide. Firmly on the other side are all the burgeoning variants of post-modernism. More concerned with visual effect than intellectual content practitioners working in historic contexts would normally limit their cheerfully eclectic picking up of classical or other quotations to those inspired by the context.

Some architects, like Terry Farrell and Piers Gough are such instinctively gifted designers that the combination of forms they arrive at when working (almost it would seem 'on automatic') are more than just witty. Starting from the same point as the 'keepers-in-keeping' architects, that is referring to both language and materials of the adjacent important building, the current 'English Extremists', choose to play with and even grotesquely exaggerate the mannerisms of the earlier architects and thereby actually add to the architectonic intensity of the scene instead of diluting it. They and not their timid predecessors are in the historic tradition, as witnessed by any old high street or complex of college courtyards.

Even those transforming interiors, behind valued façades, are only mimicking Robert Adam who thought nothing of inserting his lavish up-to-date rooms behind sixteenth- and seventeenth-century walls. Old Northumberland House and Osterley Park were thus transformed for the Percys. Nowadays it is only indifferent or already ravished interiors that listing protection allows to be so used. Eighteenth-century architects had no such inhibitions. Thus in the reconversion of St Pancras Station Hotel, Scott's several magnificent rooms and great staircase must be painstakingly preserved while the inferior Langham Hotel, its public rooms bureaucratized out of existence by the BBC and others, will be new behind the cleaned Victorian brickwork.

What is very difficult to find historic precedent for is Quinlan Terry's exercise at Richmond Riverside. In clothing adjacent new buildings in imitation first-hand Palladian and imitation second-hand Palladian, he intends them to look as if they had 'just growed' over a century or two. They have identical characterless interiors only a generation out of date.

Professions are normally dominated by those in their mid-50s, and Terry is roughly a contemporary of Richard Rogers and John Outram; he almost alone refused to be seduced by the modern movement as a student. Now there is a younger generation of born-again classicists, more fundamentalist – as is the nature of things – than Terry or his mentor Erith. Today's neo-classicists generally allow themselves to be less witty in design than Terry and less morally serious in their credos; he genuinely believes that his architectural language is the only civilized one. The younger set partially by-pass the Renaissance and return to Rome for inspiration. Leon Krier did this in his Spitalfields Market area redevelopment scheme and Simpson in his proposal for the replacement of Holford's Paternoster Square. Another of this generation, Robert Adam, even echoes Roman vernacular architecture, rather than the usual temple ethos, in his offices and shops project in Winchester High Street.

Unlike High Art classicists like Krier and Simpson, who dream of towers and temples, loggia, atrai and fora, Robert Adam is a jobbing revivalist who can turn his hand to a reasonable Victorian Gothic. Similarly Roderick Gradidge, of the rather older generation again, is also competent in various styles including a seductive Lutyens/Blow turn-of-the-century country house manner. He has been in great demand recently. Almost all Gradidge's work is in far from timid additions to, and adaptions of, listed buildings in a language close to the original. His work, unlike that of Quinlan Terry, does very subtly admit that twentieth-century architecture has happened.

A nod to this century is often achieved via echoes of the designs of the early nineteenth-century genius Soane – the only classical architect, with the possible exception of the even more mannerist Hawksmoor, universally admired by modernists. Taking revivalism another couple of rungs down there are just two further trends to mention. First is commercial facsimile work where office development behind listed façades is found to be most expeditiously executed by demolishing and rebuilding façades. No. 49 Whitehall by former 1960s trend-setters HKPA (Howell, Killick, Partridge and Amis) is but a fairly recent case of the practice which might be said to have started in the early 1950s with the rebuilding after nearly half a century's absence of much of the early-eighteenth-century front of Schomberg House, Pall Mall.

Finally there is neo-vernacular revivalism currently fitting itself into most vacant sites in the towns of southern England. Born out of Essex County Council's *Design Guide*, now almost twenty years old, this style is still exemplified well in that county's fake old New Town of Woodham Ferrers. In the popular shopping centre a large supermarket masquerades as a tithe barn, there is a town square with a clock tower and cupola, lots of bay and oriel windows and any amount of allegedly traditional building materials such as clay tiles, wood boarding – some of which turns out to be plastic – decorative brickwork, lead dressings to chimneys (mostly false) and window sills and lintels (mostly real). Cobbles and sets underfoot are all part of

70 (opposite). 'Christmas Steps', Bristol, rise up behind the rather Austrian-looking building fronting the arterial road in plate 71. Its gentrified 'boutique-y' quality is preferable to demolition

71. St Bartholomew's in Bristol, which was once the kingdom's third city but one which did its best to destroy its historic character in postwar decades. The medieval stone arch between the houses in the angled row led into the hospice

a cheerful ambience which fools almost no one and makes most people feel comfortable because of the generally accepted myth that the past was cosy

Important saying

carriageway towards Christmas Steps embraces examples of much of British postwar architecture. On the left a decentish late-1960s horizontally sliced tower of a type seen much in London at the time. Below that is a slab built a few years earlier which is of a shoddy banality now inviting replacement by the sort of 1980s commercial vernacular block beside it. With its superior detailing and materials, but coyly arch and eaves-less pitched

roof, this is the present scheme's money-spinner. Anything but lacking in eaves is the much smaller block at its foot designed by the same architect as a transition into the refurbished precinct. He explains the overhang by the need to be able to stand upright in a reasonable proportion of the roof-space office floor. Robustly scaled in every way for its size, this rather continental-looking building typifies once again the new confidence of architects adding to old settings. It works well at ground level, contributing a gravitas to the cramped space prefacing the medieval arched entrance to St Bartholemew's facing it at one angle and the boutiqueized and cobbled pedestrian street descending the hill towards it on the other.

The important achievement is the rescue of the walls of the hospice built beside the former River Frome in the thirteenth century. This had been engulfed and concealed in centuries of development culminating in the roofing over of the courtyard for a printing works. Moxley Jenner's client was the Bristol Municipal Charities, a body which in 1856 had converted one range to 'model dwellings for the industrial classes'. Funding for the £¼m project was assisted by the city and by the government via the Historic Buildings Council. Flanking the hospice entrance were a couple of houses

72. Christmas Steps; the seventeenth-century building at the foot of the pedestrian street was in a sorry state a decade or so ago

73. St Bartholomew's; inside the reconstructed courtyard of the old monastic hospice (now health offices), the architects have contrived an attractive medley of new and old

with shops below, one of which still sells fish and chips, but behind the decayed rendering and metal windows has now been exposed one of the best survivals of timber framing in a city once largely composed of such buildings.

Archaeological investigations indicated where it would be most practical and least harmful to pile foundations to reinforce the four ranges which have been transformd into 'collegiate style' offices for the National Health Service Training Authority. Each range round the courtyard has the character of a different period: one an eighteenth-century school, another the workers' flats (which has also been a shoe factory since the flats failed), the third is dominated by the arched entrance porch of St Bartholemew, and the fourth by an attractive new range of the contextual modern form. In fact the block is based on medieval foundations and has a rear wall with elaborate Tudor mullioned windows. With a sort of jetted first floor and bold iroko timber detailing evocative of Bristol's half-timbered past, this elevation also has fretted wooden screens with a vaguely eastern air. Only long stretches of unrelieved white-painted rendered blockwork, especially at parapet level, fail to reward the eye. Random stonework and a couple of cushion capital columns once in the hospice chapel, combine to make the new range at least as interesting as the old fabric. Indeed any qualms are limited to the presentation of the latter. Random rubble was hardly ever exposed originally.

Puma Court, Spitalfields, London

There was no question of facsimile in eighteenth-century Wilkes Street for architect Anthony Richardson. For one thing the building had gone, and it was a matter of gap-filling. For another he wished to build in means appropriate to the 1980s. In the shadow of Hawksmoor's

Christchurch, Spitalfields is a remarkable area of Huguenot merchants' and weavers' houses occupied over the centuries by waves of increasingly poor immigrants also in the 'rag trade'. In the last decade Bangladeshis have been surprised to find themselves neighbours of middle-class aesthetes carefully re-converting garment-makers' sweatshops into exquisite panelled drawing rooms over provençal kitchens. But this site, towards the edge of the conservation area with much war-damaged and derelict property, has been set aside for a development of six new houses for large families erected by the Newlon Housing Trust and funded by the Housing Corporation. A limited amount

74. *Puma Court, Spitalfields, London; gap-filling for housing. The architect's drawing indicates a sensitive but hard-edged approach to the translation of the early-eighteenth-century language of neighbouring housing into a contemporary equivalent*

of repairs to what remains of the old buildings has been assisted by English Heritage.

For his street elevation Richardson decided to analyse the proportions of the houses opposite and adapt them for the new buildings. Although simple dwellings of the middling merchant kind constructed in a manner natural to craftsmen of 1725, they had fine brickwork with features in the soft red 'rubbers' only surviving in isolated London examples. He decided against reproduction and noted that one nearby Wilkes Street house had been rebuilt in an Arts and Crafts vein a century ago. While 'doing what came naturally' in the 1880s, it too had echoed the form and proportions of the early eighteenth century. Richardson reasoned that his own twentieth-century interpretation would also soon blend in.

Thus he has used plain, unquoined bricks of a pink-red colour which he says will weather to dirty brown. Window lintels are of concrete with terracotta facings, not so much replicating rubbed brick segmental arches as providing a modern paraphrase. Doorcases are in hardened-aluminium welded sheet with a 'synthapulvin' plastic finish. The roof and cleresory, echoing the long horizontal weavers' lofts of the area, are made of aluminium folded sheet. Given these twentieth-century translations it is a bit surprising to find that copings and sills are in limestone.

Neither the Spitalfields Trust nor the Georgian Group were impressed with this reinterpretation of the early Georgian aesthetic, but the Royal Fine Art Commission, among others, regards it as at least a worthwhile contribution to the problem.

Richmond Riverside

Quinlan Terry would prefer his buildings to be made in as traditional a manner as possible, or at least to look as if they were. His successful redevelopment and infilling of a stretch of sloping riverbank between the town centre and the Thames is the most extensive essay in classical revivalism completed in the 1980s. Its 'sparkling facades' were admired in the *Sunday Times* and it is likely to be influential; already a vast regional shopping centre near Heathrow has been designed in what claims to be the shape of a great Palladian palace – though one with 6,500 car parking spaces.

Commissioned by Haslemere Estates, a company well known for its refurbishment schemes, Terry has created about 106,000 square feet of offices, some shops, two restaurants totalling over 9,000 square feet and twenty-eight flats,

75. Richmond Riverside; here an unashamedly traditionalist approach uses solid structural brickwork and various eighteenth-century styles, as well as echoes of Palladio untranslated, as costumes for standard air-conditioned office blocks. Original listed buildings are over-restored

together with parking for 135 cars, for £20 million. The partly derelict site was in a conservation area. Old buildings already there included a late-nineteenth-century Renaissance style town hall, roofless since the war, a decayed coaching inn, a handsome house of 1716, and a prominent Italianate stucco terrace with a tower dominating the bridge end of the site. Starting from that mid-nineteenth-century pile which he has refurbished, Terry's creations commence with a Venetian-style gateway building giving access to the new Town Square. Next is the rather thoroughly restored early Georgian Heron House and beyond that, in a red-brick, late-Wren manner, the new and large Hotham House. This has four main floors below deeply overshadowing eaves, a slate-hipped roof culminating in a balustraded flat on which sits an elegant cupola disguising air-conditioning outlets. Cupolas, it might be noted, are a common revivalist feature, combining impact with economy.

Beyond Hotham House the site's major cross axis is formed by a wide stepped and landscaped way through to the town via the reroofed town hall. Beside this route and traversing the hill is a palace-style terrace of late-eighteenth-century stuccoed type with end pavilions. Highly mannered and grotesquely proportioned pillars support a central entrance. That

terrace, at right angles to the river, manages to be one of Terry's less elegant designs; the square, arcaded, two-storey restaurant block with cupola, downhill of it is the prettiest. Appropriately at the riverside and so with views in several directions, this is a Venetian-style building scarcely attempted in England before.

The ensemble of different buildings, of different apparent dates and designers, is attractive especially from the river. It is difficult to believe that this is skin-deep architecture – albeit in places a skin 2-feet thick. There is a handsomeness, wit, and thoroughness about the external detailing. It could be argued that few people will see the banal office interiors. The distant views, the newly-arcaded part of Bridge Street and Hill Street are enhancements of Richmond. So is the Town Square with its fascinating variety within the theme – there is even a crenellated mock Gothic gate tower and, of course, a fountain. There is amusement in the Regency-type iron balconies added, as so often happened in real history, to earlier façades – both built at once in fact. Experts can detect an occasional short cut to craftsmanship, but such quibbles do not seriously devalue the creation of one Richmond Riverside. A rash of them, especially by inferior designers, would be unfortunate.

76. Richmond Riverside; the Town Square shows the élan with which period styles may be revived by a skilled practitioner untrammelled with modernist dogma – while creating premium-priced development

77. Bryanston School, Dorset, a new block for computer studies; post modernists of wit like Piers Gough design an equivalence rather than a reproduction of – in this case – Norman Shaw's exuberant brick and stone mansion epitomized by the gate posts in the picture

interpretation of just the red-brick and stone-dressed English classical style in which Quinlan Terry seeks to build. Since 'Wrenaissance' was adapted from Italian Palladian and Baroque strains which in turn owed allegiance to ancient classical models more than a touch of decadence might be expected in an architectural language removed from its origins by nearly 2,000 years and several civilizations – even when purged in CZWG's case by the astringency of modernism *en route*. It is instructive to compare this 1985 essay by Piers Gough with William Whitfield's more literal quoting of Shaw alongside another of his buildings in Whitehall. Designed three years after the Hayward Gallery's homage to Sir Edwin Lutyens which Gough designed in free mimicry of that great architect's style, at Bryanston one sees a fully liberated interpretation. True, as in Whitfield's design, there is a suggestion of stone and brick banding to echo the Bryanston gate piers, but it is limited to a dressing of the semi-circular gable. Elsewhere the 'English Extremists' embellish the Craft, Design and Technology Building with 'screw columns [which] support upper floor windows hooded in a paraphrase of computer screens'.[33] Between the columns are 1930s/1950s type metal windows. Remarkably the result, while wilfully idiosyncratic on one level, on another

Bryanston School, Dorset

Wit is evident in the approach of Campbell, Zogolovitch, Wilkinson, and Gough in their new block, intended eventually to constitute one side of a courtyard at this public school. In case any non-British readers are in doubt 'public' in this context means 'private'. That is the least of the eccentricities here. For Bryanston was one of the more individual country-house designs of Norman Shaw, a turn-of-the-century architect with a very personal, and mannerist

comprises a brick and stone composition in contextual tune. 'It is Norman Shaw with a twist' and it does 'stop the rot' at a Bryanston 'being swamped by a dissipated campus of weak buildings', according to the authors of a 1988 catalogue to a CZWG exhibition at the RIBA. Gough obtained this commission by persuading the school governors that recent buildings at Bryanston had failed to show due deference to Shaw's masterpiece of a country house. The result shows that he was serious.

China Wharf

Similarly, CZWG's new China Wharf, sandwiched between the refurbished New Concordia and Reed's wharfs in London's docklands, respects both neighbours and riverside architecture as a whole by making a bold 1988 contribution. This firm's designs pick up essences rather than superficialities.

Winchester High Street

A notable feature of recent classical revivalist buildings and, indeed, of unbuilt projects such as those of Leon Krier, is their espousal of tradition by novel routes. Robert Adam, a young architect practising in England's most prosperous town, says 'I think of myself as a revivalist and I started being most interested in late Roman architecture and the Romanesque'. Among other modes he can work in a late Victorian Gothic style, as a small speculative housing scheme demonstrates.

In Winchester High Street a few years ago he chose to import late-Roman, brick-arched massiveness. With deeply shadowed eaves, arcading based on a simple circular geometry, this four-storey building is neither self-effacing nor, in any obvious way, contextual. The local

78. China Wharf, London Docks; the same architect has inserted a new – bright red – block of flats among recently converted warehouses near London Bridge

79. Winchester High Street; an early Roman-style infill in a typically variegated high street is no more reticent than many a Victorian architect's contribution would have been

chapter of architects, however, sees this building as 'a positive sympathetic contribution to the street'. It is overscaled in just the sort of way confident Victorian architecture might have been.

In the case of additions to other historic settings Adam is capable of being more assertive than the original. The heavily modelled and rusticated treatment of a major country house extension for commercial use, Dogmersfield Park, Hampshire, where Adam was elevational consultant, is remarkably interesting in terms of 1980s architecture. Imperial Diocletian cum heavyweight Soane are recurring features these days, but not often clothing a large building tacked on to an inoffensive mid-eighteenth century-style manor.

Thorncroft Manor and Henley Park, Surrey

Of architect Michael Manser's designs for conversion and major extension of country houses for commercial clients, one was completed in the early 1970s, the other is about to be built. The approach is equally confident though much less obtrusive than the foregoing revivalist examples; the language is of late-twen-

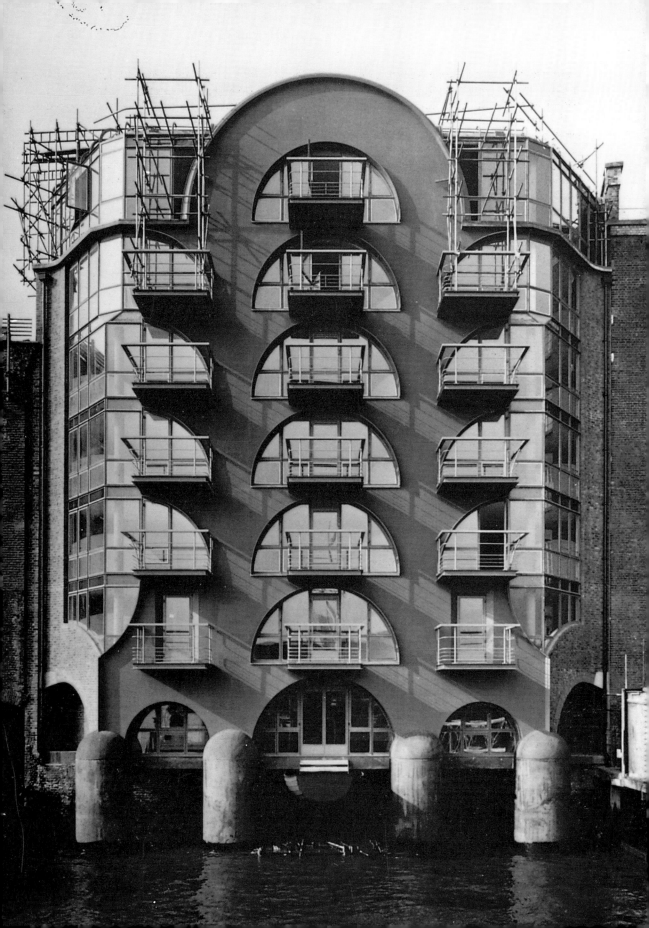

tieth-century glass-box type. It is a type epitomized by a handful of structures as near-perfectly beautiful as has been given to man to create; the problem is that once done – by Mies van der Rohe or the early Philip Johnson – the thing can only be done again, perhaps by architects seeking ever more elegant proportions and junctions. Manser's two projects will be separated by two decades; few architects except those who have stayed in the mainstream of modernism could make two designs differing so subtly.

The addition of a totally contrasting yet entirely unassertive building which is larger than the historic original can only be achieved with a minimally detailed,

80. Thorncroft Manor, Surrey; reflective glass walling to an extension at least the size of the original can be both tactful and confidently modern

81. Henley Park, Surrey; a more recent design by the same architect

flat-surfaced, reflective-glass-walled construction. It is a pity that planners lacked the courage to allow it, perhaps architects to propose it, in the middle of an historic town like Oxford. Until Norman Foster showed the way in the late 1960s in London's docks and in Ipswich, British practitioners seemed to lack both the skills and the components to produce such architecture. As a standard approach the time of the glass box has passed, as serried ranks of them repeated on the outskirts of Los Angeles demonstrate. But in the context of historic architecture this approach will surely establish itself as a classic answer.

Unlike almost any other modern skin

the transparent glass wall has the potential for infinite variety, depending on differences in light conditions, reflectivity, weather, and the relationship in space of neighbouring structures and ambient viewers. A person approaching a building which is almost 'not there' sees trees, sky, other buildings, himself and/or the interior. At night, if the interior is lit that is dominant, although floodlighting the exterior could change the balance again. The problem is that clear glass, while aesthetically the most rewarding, is technically the least. Requirements for heat insulation, glare reduction and, indeed, for privacy, can be answered by glass which is coloured or laminated to render it opaque.

Michael Manser had a three-and-a-half-year struggle to secure planning permission for the Thorncroft manor project from Mole Valley Council, which claimed that 'additional buildings here . . . would damage the pleasant rural character' and then allowed a much bigger and more obtrusive leisure centre nearby. That authority in more recent years has, while taking visitors to admire Thorncroft Manor, opposed a second expansion alongside the first. At a successful appeal the inspector had expressed the view that the 1973 building could be more than doubled with no impact on the surroundings.

Originally built by Sir Robert Taylor in about 1730, the manor was dilapidated when Manser's clients, an international firm of consulting engineers, bought it and the nine-acre park in 1969. It was felt that the house, having dominated the site for 250 years, should continue to do so. Links between the new buildings and the refurbished mansion and its stable blocks were made in clear class, to be as self-effacing as possible. The rest is in silver coated reflecting glass which greatly reduces the air-conditioning load. The penthouse floor has sloping walls 'in order to reflect the sky and thus give form to what might otherwise have been a confusingly formless structure', says the

shows the main approach to the house unaffected by the major office extension behind

82. Henley Park; looked at from the side, it is clear that separation, both physical and stylistic, can allow mutual respect

architect. He notes, that Taylor designed according to rules of formal geometry here as elsewhere and adopted the 'golden section' rectangle for his new elevations and for all the main pieces of glass. Presumably this has a subliminal impact on the viewer. Anyway the new building has won awards.

At Thorncroft Manser spent about £750,000 in 1973, and the cost of a similarly scaled job at Henley Park is expected to be of the order of £2.5 million – comparable when inflation is allowed for. This house is also thought to be by a distinguished early-eighteenth-century architect, Colin Campbell. At the rear is what the architect describes as 'a

substantial and overbearing Victorian extension comprising ballroom, kitchens and many bedrooms'. On the site of the latter Manser has designed and obtained planning permission for an extension of almost 26,000 sq. ft, which with the house's 11,000 will comprise office accommodation of 37,000 sq. ft. He was appointed at Henley on the strength of the work at the other house, but in this case the client is a developer, so detailed implementation may depend to some extent on the whims of a tenant.

It was important to the architect that, as at Thorncroft, the extension be invisible during the approach to the mansion. In this case that is down a mile-long drive through a thirty-acre park. Entrance to both buildings will be via the original main entrance, then through the door in the restored rear elevation and along a link bridge which is to be made 'as delicate and insubstantial as possible'. Most striking is the fact that the large new block runs at a diagonal 'to simplify circulation'. Visually the interrelation will 'reveal something of a trompe d'oeil as the rear of the mansion is seen reflected in the glass of the new offices. This will be complicated by the reflective pool between (the old and new buildings) and the splayed glass at the bottom and top of the elevations reflecting in turn the sky and the water.' In this enthusiastic

RG del 83

description Michael Manser makes it plain that he is not content to settle for the geometrically proportioned, smoothly detailed glass box, as a glance at the design suggested. Like the other architects discussed in this chapter he has the confidence to wish to play more daring games.

Tancred's Ford, near Farnham, Surrey

Equally confident, though again quite different, are the extensions to historic buildings by an architect not in the least

83. Tancred's Ford, Surrey; the opposite approach to a country-house extension is to design as if the original architect has just returned to his drawing board after lunch – the arch and buildings to its left are new, the swimming pool building beyond has not yet been built

concerned at making buildings 'true to their period', to employ Manser's phrase, in the sense of being modern. Roderick Gradidge's work is true to the period of whatever building he is extending. He goes further and seeks to enter into the language and spirit of the original so that it looks as if the same architect, or a near and sympathetic contemporary, was commissioned to come back a decade or so after the completion of the main building. Thus there is no slavish imitation, still less a timid repetition of motifs, rather a new development along the lines of the maturing character of a person.

Roderick Gradidge's practice is strong on country houses. In 1983 he enlarged

84 (a) and (b). Michelin Building, Fulham, London; the best of commercial architects now restore and extend old buildings as part of their practice. One way of leaving the old wall undisturbed is to duplicate it alongside

85. Eastcheap and Philpot Lane, City of London; YRM, the same architects as at Fulham, have refurbished these colourful Victorian warehouses and offices incorporating a new block behind which respects both street line and heights – unlike the 1960s tower further along Philpot Lane

Tancred's Ford in the style of its 1913 architect Harold Falkner which is described in *Country Life* as 'romantic, Surrey vernacular'.[34] As the writer went on to remark he had also been, or was presently engaged in extending, two other large houses – Charleshill Court and Fulbrook also on the southerly ridge near Farnham – 'while only 10 miles to the south Mr Gradidge is at work on New Place'. The last was by Voysey, Charleshill was Detmar Blow's, and Fulbrook was Lutyens's third major house.

In the country of the mind this is predominantly Lutyens land, but in fact Falkner had a notable impact on the appearance of Farnham and environs. In terms of a contemporary architect's life Gradidge is a remarkable example of a man whose time has come. His lifetime passion for turn-of-the-century architecture in both its Arts and Crafts and Wrenaissance moods saw expression in a book, *Dream Houses*, a decade ago. Then the interest was still a minority one and Thatcher's revolution had not provided the wherewithal for much country-house work.

Having recognized the persistence, skill, and luck – the owner of Tancred's Ford bought the book before the house – there is still more than a touch of perversity in the way this fairly modest pile was doubled in size, and that is taking no note of the flashily mirrored and partly Soane-inspired interior works. Falkner's original building, despite numerous eccentricities in proportions and irregular placing of windows, especially dormers, for example, was nonetheless a basically regular, nearly symmetrical, Lutyens-influenced, Queen-Anne-style gentleman's house. Gradidge's new wing, with great sweeping roofs, fewer and smaller windows on outward facing elevations, uneven gables and tiled dovecotty turret, has more of the Surrey yeoman's farmhouse spirit of Munstead Wood. And the more formal new elements on the extended entrance front, the octagonal staircase tower with walls dominated by projecting quoins and the garage arch with hugely mannered voussoirs and a keystone invading an attic window over – all these and more features in various witty connotatory styles surely tip over from the one extreme of reticence towards the other of indulgence. Here at last it really can be said to be a matter of taste. For Aslet in *Country Life* it all makes a bland house more interesting.

What is unarguable is the matching in new work of quality of materials and craftsmanship of that Edwardian standard long thought to be unapproachable. That the bricks might be specially made is less remarkable than the aptness of their laying and pointing and of all the other Surrey builders' work supervised from day to day by a local architect's practice, Stedman & Blower, which has been in Farnham since Edwardian times. It is all as if the Bauhaus had never been.

Chapter 11

High
Conservation

Wells Cathedral, figure on west front. Victorian photograph shows timber and rope scaffolding

Introduction

Ancient monuments, churches in use, a minority of outstanding buildings, and, indeed, engineering structures, are so intrinsically fine and owe their interest, character, and beauty so much to what they are, rather than any possible reinterpretation or new use, that they must be preserved intact, unaltered, and, if necessary, unused. It is a mark of a civilized society that this be so. A small proportion of barns, parish churches, viaducts, and – to widen our scope a little – eighteenth-century landscaped parks are, to misuse an expression of DoE secretary of state Nicholas Ridley, 'perfectly useless'.

Even if Christianity were to become as anachronistic in the land as stage coaches it is to be assumed that the Angel Quire at Lincoln Cathedral, even the mausoleum at Castle Howard, will be safe from internal alteration or conversion to new uses. Even the foregoing pious hope cannot be held with complete confidence, for aggressively iconoclastic regimes – Oliver Cromwell in England, Stalin in Russia, or Ceaucescu in Romania – take a pleasure in using such buildings as stables, or even destroying them. On the other hand we are, on the whole, ready to see less important ecclesiastical buildings, such as the former Welsh Presbyterian Chapel in Charing Cross Road, transformed into a night club, or a church in Bradford converted into 'Sheikh's Restaurant'. Such goings-on would have outraged our grandfathers. A century ago many churchgoers would have been more than a little doubtful about secular music being played at a cathedral concert; neither we, nor our medieval forebears would regard such a thing as anything but appropriate.

Very few values are absolute or unchanging either in those buildings which we might now regard as architecturally significant enough to 'save' in some form, or in acceptability of new uses. In the world wars even the greatest country houses were used to billet troops or converted into boarding schools or nursing homes. The consequent, perhaps even anticipated, damage to many and loss of a few were regarded as irrelevant in the context of wartime priorities. Though there was a considerable effort to preserve the greatest picture collections.

All that can be done at any time is to preserve those works of art and architecture that seem pre-eminent, while at the same time trying to foresee likely changes in taste and values in the near future. The term 'useless' is, in any case, misleading, for all such unalterable buildings are of educational, re-creative, and aesthetic use. In a period of increasing leisure and rampant tourism 'perfectly useless' works of architecture may produce more income than imperfectly useful ones.

At least in the field of pure preservation there are a few absolute laws and they are essentially those encapsulated in the term 'conservative repair' coined by William Morris's Society for the Protection of Ancient Buildings. They can be summarized as 'Thou shalt not fake'. Conjectural restoration of what has long been destroyed or perhaps never completed – both frequently the case in gothic structures – must be avoided. Likewise new work must not be 'faked', that is deliberately 'aged' to be indistinguishable from old. The second law is that all major alterations or new work functionally or structurally required, must be reversible. Much of what has been said above can be seen to refer to the cases discussed in this chapter.

West front, Wells Cathedral

English Gothic sculpture cannot in general compare with that of the Ile de France. Nonetheless the assembly of figures adorning the west front of Wells Cathedral is exceptional by any standard.

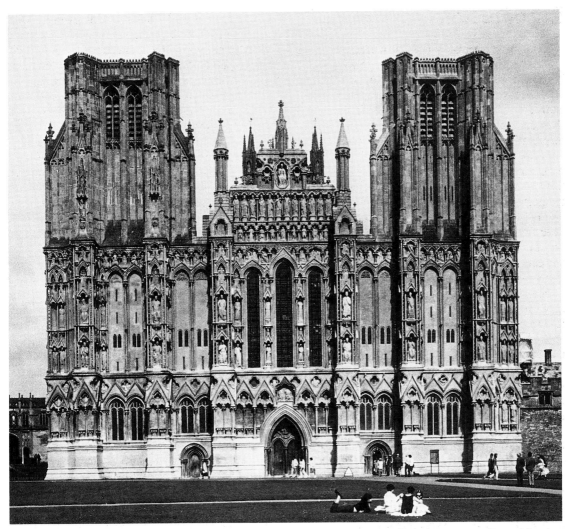

While not constituting so dynamically architectural a totality as the west front of Rheims or the south transept of Chartres, nor rivalling the French work in proto-rennaissance grace, this great screen of sturdy English thirteenth-century carving has unique impact. When gorgeously painted and gilded the giant tabernacled display must have been awe-inspiring, which was its purpose.

The hierarchy of hundreds of figures of kings and nobles, saints and biblical characters, constitutes the finest sight of its kind in England. Above the central gable is a figure of Christ in Glory, below are tiers of angels (in better condition than the original figure of Christ, perhaps

86. Wells Cathedral, Somerset; the west front, once glowing with gold and polychrome, is still an incomparable ensemble of medieval sculpture although the detail of limestone carving has deteriorated rapidly in recent years

because a little less exposed), and further down again are rows of angels and a panelled sculpture of Doom. Niches articulated by slender shafts and shadowed by little roofed canopies continue round six projecting buttresses, the four outer ones of which support towers completed at a later date. Nearly all the higher niches contain a figure, most of which escaped Puritan vandalism but not the effects of seven and a half centuries of weather and one and a half centuries of restoration work.

Unfortunately such an outline description has to be offered somewhat tentatively for changes have taken place in the last decade. The much damaged, but crucially important Christ has been removed to museum care and a conjectural modern figure of doubtful quality has replaced it 'experimentally' on the façade. Other figures of varying eloquence have been inserted into long-empty spaces, though far fewer than was proposed when the recent restoration programme commenced. A great deal of most careful cleaning and protective work has also been carried out, as well as some experimental treatment of priceless sculpture. For, little known to the general public, who have contributed millions to the cathedral's appeal, Wells' west front has been a battleground for the restorers versus the SPAB's 'anti-scrape' methods as fiercely fought over as any of the nineteenth-century controversies which inspired Carlyle to exclaim that 'all restoration is a lie'. As usual everyone had the best of intentions and, perhaps not always the case in the past, the figures definitely required attention. It is possible to go further and say that there have been mistakes, but considering that virtually everyone working on the façade was 'trained on the job' – a strange procedure for the outstanding example of its kind, but apparently inescapable – very few major and irreversible ones. The painful compromises arrived at have meant that overall a good job has been done.

The cathedral, not the first on the site, was started in about 1180. The west front dates from 1220 to 1240. A random rubble core was faced with Doulting, 'a course Jurassic limestone'. The west front, its undercut surfaces at the mercy of the prevailing Atlantic winds, is in much worse condition than the rest of the building, and the architect, Martin Caroe, said in his report: 'The major cause of decay is crystallisation of salts within the stonework caused by constant wetting and drying action of the weather.'

Of some 380 figures, 297 survive at least in part. But their condition was so decayed by the 1960s that action was vital. Not that the great assemblage had been totally neglected through the cen-

87 (a) and (b) (overleaf). Wells; figure of a king before and after treatment with poulticing and lime-washing. Pressure from 'museumizers' to remove the figures and replace with fakes was resisted, as was that from those who favoured irreversible chemical impregnation

turies. After the Commonwealth refurbishment was carried out in 1664, another series of repairs was undertaken, on small areas at a time, between 1827 and 1868. In 1870 the whole west front was scaffolded for a typically thorough restoration with Gilbert Scott as consultant, though under the immediate supervision of Benjamin Ferrey. Further work was carried out before the Great War and again in the 1930s. Then strong Portland cement was poured between the figures and the walls behind them in many cases, effectively bonding them to the building. Repairs to the statuary, Martin Caroe believes, were conservative at most of these times in contrast to treatment of masonry and decorative stonework. A number of statues were coated in Roman cement but very few conjectural additions were made. Work was generally confined to the replacement of rusting iron shoulder cramps with copper, to pinning and bonding loose parts in the same metal, and to stopping holes, cracks, and scabs with mortar, unfortunately usually based on dense Portland cement. The architect's difficulty in determining such matters is, however, conveyed in his remarks that 'whenever stones – whether structural or decorative – had decayed beyond reason they were replaced in new stone ... to match the original as closely as possible'. He does go on to state that 'One figure received a new head and shoulders in the 1840s, another was comprehensively (and brilliantly) repaired after falling some 40 feet in the early 1850s, the Bishop below received a new face after the original was destroyed in the crash and a number of figures were coated in Roman cement on the south tower.'

In the last half century decay had accelerated with increased pollution, even by Somerset air. Exposed and projecting features such as arms, noses, and toes had eroded away; original thirteenth-century leaded dowels had expanded and caused figures to shatter, and concentration of rain water had dissolved some features.

There had also been a deposit of disfiguring dirt.

Shortage of funds delayed work on either masonry or figures for several more years, apart from the experimental treatment of two figures. The development of technical and philosophical arguments over proposals for the major figure compositions had sufficient time to issue in the setting up of an advisory committee of experts before the erection of scaffolding in 1975. Meanwhile there had also been a successful appeal for funds.

To return to the 'philosophy': before major works are started on a building of such significance it is important to understand its nature. What was the west front of Wells for? Until a few years ago a great deal of nonsense was talked about 'the poor man's bible in stone', now regarded as even less apt than speaking of the 'bible in stained glass' for the illiterate. For one thing much of the details of medieval windows are invisible to the naked eye from ground level. As medievalist and iconographer Dr Raymond Winch of Oxford avers[35] the images were put up to the glory of God, to aid veneration rather than learning. To the medieval visitor the front was an awesomely huge technicolour tribute to the Almighty and his works. Not only figures, niches and canopies, but much of the background masonry was brightly polychromed and gilded. There could be no intention of returning this 'wonder of Europe' to that medieval condition.

So is it best to accept the front as an imperfect but beautiful record of not only the original intention but also of the intervening centuries? In this case the repairer would alter little, and add nothing but essential protective filling of dangerous crevices and holes in a material softer than that surrounding it. Essentially he would gently clean and attempt to slow down the effects of weather and time. But he would accept that decay is inevitable. He would regard himself not as the owner, or even the arbiter of the future of such a monument, merely as 'the trustee for those that come after'. Alternatively the restorer will say that our scholarship is more profound than that of former times, our technology superior, we are capable of treating stonework in such a way that erosion will cease. It is not only our duty to do that so that future generations may have the opportunity to see what we can see, it is also our duty to take down those figures so decayed already, so fragile that only carefully controlled museum conditions will prevent total loss. In order that visitors will be able to get an impression of the front, of the whole design and the original intention, replicas of removed or lost figures can be carved by artists with guidance from scholars and theologians. After all, such insertions are reversible, since there would be no intention of 'glueing' them to the original stone with hard mortar as was done in the 1930s.

Most people would agree that there is much to be said for the second view. The trouble is in putting it into practice, so the 'conservative repairers' would say. How do you know that your radical chemical treatments of priceless stone carvings will work? None of the innumerable methods tried in the past – with oil, wax, or silicone – have done any good and some, like Roman cement, have done a lot of harm. Indeed siliconesters, one of the most recent materials, formed a shallow surface skin, trapped salts underneath, and allowed freezing in winter to expand under the skin and 'blow' whole sections of the face. By making such decisions not only are great risks taken, but also the rights of future generations to make decisions are pre-empted. Secondly, the judgement, more a guess in fact, about missing figures or parts of figures, or even of some ornamental motifs, can only be imperfect, subjective indeed. Again what right do we have to 'interpret' a great medieval work of art for today's visitor, to impose our own view on him? Thirdly, such is our distance from the vision and methods of gothic carvers of mouldings, let alone mystical figures, that the results time and again are either timid and lifeless, or else caricatures. It is not necessary to be a scholar to recognize a Victorian restoration of part of a church; it is widely recognized that, in imposing their own vision and technical proficiency on ancient buildings, nineteenth-century craftsmen often mutilated them. And those carvers were not trying to revive a dead art, they were comparatively close to their forebears.

These, briefly, are some of the arguments. European restorers are enthusiastic 'museumizers'; they are also great producers of silanes and even, in Germany, of cocktails of chemicals with which to impregnate medieval stone. So bright, clean, and perfect are Denmark's old parish churches that the visitor experiences nothing of history in stone, only history in facsimile. They might as well have been built yesterday. In fact to a considerable extent most of them were.

At Wells four alternative strategies emerged: 1: replacement by copies on a large scale; this proved impractical on grounds of cost when the expense of building a large museum was included, and, more important, was impossible because most of the figures were firmly fixed to the façade and would have been destroyed during removal; 2: impregnation with the newly developed alkoxysilanes, a technique favoured by representatives of the Victoria & Albert Museum which was intended to stabilize the figures as Kenneth Hempel of the V&A had done for the Venice in Peril Fund; 3: minimalist preservation repairs in the hope that future generations would find a lasting solution; this was based on fears of employing any irreversible methods because of almost total lack of experience in the UK of any techniques for consolidating limestone; 4: use of lime-based cleaning, repair, consolidation, and shelter-coating techniques developed by Professor Robert Baker and used by Mrs Eve Baker on two south-tower figures some eleven years before with apparent success.

While debate proceeded two further figures were treated *in situ* by the Bakers and two by the V&A, one on the building and one at the museum.

Apparently the first alternative had been favoured by art historical opinion. The second strategy was favoured, naturally, by the V&A, less categorically by the Building Research Establishment (BRE) which had developed its own version of silanes, and more open-mindedly still by the DoE's own Ancient Monuments and Historic Buildings division. The SPAB, with more than a backward glance at the third approach, favoured the lime-based technique. The cathedral architect, Mr A. D. R. Caroe, who was to be succeeded by his son, Martin Caroe, in 1981, seemed initially to be impressed by V&A claims that stone would be 'frozen' for sixty years. Deep silane penetration would preclude surface decay or dusting, as well as mould, moss, or lichen growth, but still the stone would be vapour permiable. As Martin Caroe said after his 1987 inspection, 'that has proved to be untrue', and what is more, discolouration took place in some cases.

In the event a compromise policy was agreed, namely that a small number of figures would be 'silaned', then observed 'for a number of decades' to see how external stone so treated would behave. The remaining figures would be treated with the lime processes, on the understanding that the use of this homogeneous material, weaker than the base limestone, acted 'sacrificially', was reversible, and, if ineffective, would allow silane treatment later. A small number of figures (a maximum of thirty) would be taken down, protected, and replaced by copies. Furthermore, and here the architects' report is quoted; 'The vandalised "Coronation of the Virgin", the chestless "Christ" in the high gable and possibly the "Virgin and Child" over the west door gable would also be taken down and replaced by *completed* copies in the spirit of the original'.

After a dozen years' experience of that

policy being carried out – though the number of figures removed and replaced was reduced further – it is clear that no method of conservation of external sculpture in the British climate provides 'the answer'. An inspection in 1987 showed that results depended very much on the skill and experience of the operative, and even on such factors as the weather. For example, the surface of King no. 177 (V&A 1975) showed dusting, breakdown of the resin, 'unfilled sulphation cracks and hollow-sounding surfaces', all because penetration of the silane was 5 mm instead of the desired 50–60 mm, and this was thought to be because of inadequate drying out in a period of wet weather. A figure treated by the BRE with their silane, called Brethane, but not filled or repaired, had further deteriorated. The architect determined that if figures were to be left *in situ*, which is the general policy, they must be made weathertight.

Experience, more extensive than anywhere else in Britain, had been very instructive and, on the whole, reassuring. Baker proved that virtually invisible 'dental' repairs and fillings are possible, contrary to long-held belief. Of course this success in itself raises questions of a philosophical kind: whereas it is generally agreed that a repairer should not try officiously to conceal a stone inset or mortar repair, it is a bit obtuse to ask him to mix a colour deliberately as a mismatch in order to prove his integrity. In fact the professor did not achieve a match in this case, since the additive he mixed with the white-lime putty to darken the filler, crushed Hornton Blue stone, oxidizes (rusts in effect) and becomes an orange-coloured limestone. So the original perfect match developed rather unfortunately. Doubts were also raised about some other details of the lime treatment. It might be as well to establish here what Mr Baker's method originally comprised: inspection of figures was followed by the application of a hot poultice of recently slaked lime which was then covered and kept damp for some three weeks; next

came manual cleaning with timed water sprays, then removal of external metal cramps and bands (replaced with new 'secret' fixings) and of all cement repairs. There followed the time-consuming application of 30–50 coats of calcium hydroxide in perhaps five drenches a day, after which the figure would be wiped down to remove lime 'bloom'. Seriously weakened stone showing no signs of original detail was removed and replaced with pozzolanic mortar (basically lime putty with aggregate matching existing stonework in colour and texture) textured to resemble decayed stone. Exposed or loose original details were strengthened at edges with this material too.

Exceptions to much of the above would be delicate areas and many of the heads which, being protected under canopies, often showed signs of polychromy. All but these areas would now be protected with a very fine 'sacrificial' shelter coat of putty and aggregate. Modifications introduced as the work proceeded included the abandonment of the poulticing which seemed to achieve neither of its stated aims – drawing salts from the stone or consolidating it. Dry cleaning with small scale air-abrasive pencils gave more sensitive control and was used alongside water cleaning. It was also found that limewater applied to consolidate the painted surfaces, which were clearly of great art-historical value, had not succeeded. Nevertheless the chief point was that the shelter coats, while worn away in some exposed positions, had achieved exactly the protective function intended. It was decided to retain certain figures intended for removal to a museum in their original positions.

A further problem highlighted in the architect's 1987 report was the 'positively disgusting' pigeon droppings, which light netting had failed to deflect; he suggested the insertion of steel spikes.

So in general the lime treatment was successful; four figures out of 152 treated 'have failed quite badly', but these were among early efforts by operatives who later improved their skills. Results of silaning were worse. The figure treated at the V&A was greyer in colour than the surrounding stone and the particular dry-cleaning method had left its surface 'gritty'. More important was the 'local breakdown of the surface' in several places. Also the epoxy-based repairs were 'not well modelled and are starting to discolour'. It has already been noted that resin penetration on one figure was insufficient. Since to an extent the treatment of these three figures was agreed to be experimental, an emphasis on failings might appear unnecessary. The 'Brethaned' figure fared better, with very slight surface dusting, though the experiment of leaving it unrepaired, so leaving water traps and vulnerable edges, is regarded as mistaken.

The dean and chapter were not to be dissuaded from the replacement of three minor thirteenth-century figures and one transcendently important group. Two were in niches, a kneeling bishop in poor condition and an 1840 addition of a top half to a medieval lower part. The third of the minor figures was that which had fallen to the ground and been stitched together with innumerable metal dowels and then coated in Roman cement. The approaches to recarving varied. The workaday carver perched on the scaffolding was cheaper and more successful in catching a suitable spirit – it is generally agreed – than were the artist/sculptors in their studios.

The replacement of 'Christ in Majesty' at the summit of the front was an expensive exercise. Of five sculptors invited to submit ideas, four were too modest or conscientious to do so with serious intent. David Wynne has produced four angels, two each side of his new Christ. There was no evidence for those minor figures in the flanking niches and quatrefoils and much mystery about the attitude of the missing upper half of Christ. Was He a judgement figure? Was He crowned? holding a sceptre, or perhaps a book? Was He displaying his wounds? Mr

88. House of Lords Chamber, London, where part of the gilded ceiling fell, just missing the members; both glue and timber itself had been 'denatured' by a century of heating. A meticulous repair operation has secured the ceiling for at least another century

Wynne's resolution of these and the many other dilemmas in replacing a gothic masterpiece, the lower part of which is now in a museum, has not been universally admired.

But the addition of a sculpture is something that can be undone; experiments with acrilic resins on small-scale figures, carried out on the advice of John Larson of the V&A, cannot. He has expressed the view 'that it would be a mistake, after such delicate work, to leave sculpture of this importance to the mercy of the weather'. Another expert, Dr Clifford Price, late of the BRE, agreed 'in effect' because stonework so treated 'should not, in the present state of knowledge, remain out of

doors'. That is one way for museumizers to prevail!

Despite all arguments and doubts it is necessary to leave this discussion of an important, influential, and classic historic building repair with the positive conclusion of the architect responsible. Martin Caroe writes: 'What was achieved by Robert Baker and his conservators (Professor Baker retired in 1982) was a highly successful holding operation which is likely to preserve the Wells figures for at least several more decades . . . until such time as tried and certain methods of conserving external stone are proven in use.'[36]

House of Lords ceiling

Buildings very rarely fall down. The Houses of Parliament, or Palace of Westminster as the renowned Thames-side group of buildings is more correctly known, are among the least likely to do so; many millions have been spent on fabric repairs in recent decades. This can be asserted notwithstanding the recent discovery of the vulnerability of the floor structure, supported on an arched undercroft, which apparently requires reinforcement to cope with the intensive use now prevailing. Signs of strain are to be expected after nearly 150 years; nevertheless it was a considerable surprise when on 21 July 1980 a heavy pendant boss section of the gorgeously carved, gilded, and painted timber roof fell on their lordships – or rather just missed several of them.

Westminster had been the seat of royal government since before the Norman conquest, the buildings only extending eastwards up Whitehall during the time of the Tudors. The minster was both a royal abbey and a chapel where most royal marriages, funerals, and coronations were solemnized. The Exchequer was run from offices in the cloisters. Naturally, when the monarch summoned noblemen and, later on, prosperous commoners to advise him and vote funds, they met in chambers attached to the palace. Sometimes this was in the great Westminster Hall itself. That was the only substantial structure to escape the fire of 1834.

Charles Barry and Augustus Pugin, designers of the replacement, were expressing the even then theoretical dominance of aristocratic power by ensuring that the lords' chamber was among the most sumptuous. Its ceiling of course looked very substantial, with apparently massive beams dividing it into eighteen great compartments of coffered and painted panels, but what appears from below as the structure is nothing of the kind. It was constructed as a softwood canopy suspended from a network of iron joists and trusses, which also supported an ingenious cast-iron roof. Barry had been constrained by many factors, including stringent finance; he even set up machines to mass-produce carved features, though all the detailed elements – trophies, bosses, rosettes, and fretted inscriptions – were superbly hand-finished.

Immediate observation after the 1980 incident revealed degradation of the timber. A scaffold platform was erected to permit detailed inspection and to protect their lordships. The government's Property Services Agency appointed architects Donald W. Insall & Associates to prepare a full report. Completed in early January 1981, this disclosed extensive, though unevenly distributed, damage to the timbers of a kind characterized by the Building Research Establishment as 'brashness'. A significant reduction in the cellulose content of the wood had induced it to crack across the grain and rendered it so dry and brittle that sections would disintegrate when touched. Glued fixings to certain carved elements, such as the coronet boss which had fallen, were badly affected. Causes were not to do with the original construction but rather with the conditions to which the ceiling had been subjected since its completion in 1847. Various heating and ventilation systems employed and, especially, the effect of powerful gasoliers hung only 5 feet below the ceiling, had resulted in prolonged exposure to high temperatures and changes in moisture content. The timber itself was found to be very acidic.

The architects found that the ceiling would have to be dismantled and repaired by expert craftsmen off-site – a procedure entirely consonant with its initial prefabrication. As much as possible of the fabric was to be reused. It was found that the carvings, the gilding of which had been a protective factor, the heraldic panels, and complicated arched braces and spandrels, were capable of being consolidated and restored. The fact that the decorative painting to the bed of the ceiling had been applied on canvas rather than timber meant that most of this was intact and salvageable. The irony is that if Barry and the inspired designer of the decorations, Pugin, had been allowed sufficient time to produce the ceiling out of traditional plasterwork these troubles would not have arisen. As it was all the structural carpentry and straight-moulded joinery, some of which was barely strong enough to support itself, would have to be renewed.

The decoration of the new work was to follow the original scheme and tone in with surviving gilding on the carvings and the paintwork of the restored heraldic panels.

The access platform was strengthened and made dustproof so that business could proceed below. It remained in position until the restoration was complete in August 1984. In order that the ceiling could be dismantled without causing disturbance, independent access was arranged from an adjacent courtyard. Before being taken down the ceiling was photogrammetrically recorded. Some of the most important carvings such as the trophies were photographed stereoscopically, in case their condition dictated replacement. Each item was referenced and the carvings carefully boxed. Painted segments of canvas were protected with a layer of 'mulberry tissue' before being individually cut out.

Degraded timber of carvings was consolidated with epoxy resin impregnation under vacuum. In fact all 543 carvings in their constituent fragments so treated were able, when cured, to accept fixings and receive new carved work. The process had the added advantage of cleaning the surfaces without damage to original gilding. Epoxy adhesives were reinforced by wooden dowels and stainless-steel pins and cramps to ensure a mechanical fixing. New timber was matched to original yellow pine. Basic regilding was executed on the bench, using $23\frac{1}{4}$ carat English gold leaf to match the existing. Toning of the new gold was left until final redecoration of the ceiling. Helped by the DoE's former chief carver the PSA agreed costs for repair of every item with the consultants before work started.

Most of the painted heraldic canvas panels were painstakingly remounted, then laminated to a three-ply birch backing with epoxy adhesive. Tissue was then removed and the paint surface cleaned and restored. In the few cases where new sections of canvas had to be cut in, missing parts of the design were drawn upon them and painted. In the case of the great arched braces and spandrels new yellow pine was pieced into damaged

areas in G. E. Wallis & Sons' joinery workshops at Maidstone. There new members were moulded from the plank with mitres and joints preformed for reassembly on site. Moving upwards in scale, the old carpentry support frames were taken down from their seatings on the iron trusses and immediately replaced with new ones made, as before, with Scots pine. Fixed to their undersides were new panels of highly durable 'marine' plywood to which much of the decorative ceiling was to be refixed. All new timber was treated against rot and beetle attack. The joinery was then fixed and primed ready to receive final decoration. The idea was that the ceiling should look as if it had been cleaned and restored rather than rebuilt. So new gold leaf was 'toned' to the duller colour of the old by the application of a tinted layer of parchment size. This technique is, of course, somewhat out of line with the SPAB's code of 'honest repairs', but on the other hand the size is water soluble, so can be removed if required. Paint finishes were prepared in much the same way as when the chamber was built. After painting, a black glaze was applied to 'complete the graining effect of the original'. Areas of red paint were built up in a number of semi-transparent coats to give depth and richness. Finally the carvings were refixed, not with anything like the original animal glues which could theoretically be 'denatured' again in the distant future, but with stainless steel bolts and fixings of the kind used throughout this most intricate of repair and restoration projects in recent times.

A year or so after the House of Lords chamber ceiling was reconstructed a fire destroyed the transept at York Minster, the restoration of which provided yet more proof of the availability of dedicated and skilled craftsmen to make good the ravages of time or accident.

Brighton Pavilion

89. Brighton Pavilion, Sussex; the Indo-Chinese-style Regency extravaganza has been the subject of a thorough restoration at the direction of the local council

Already the home of the licentious Duke of Cumberland, Brighton was an ideal setting for his nephew, a young man of flamboyant tastes determined to enjoy himself at a distance from the restrictions of Court. It is piquant that a local district council should find itself responsible for this, the most extravagant royal palace in Britain. The authority is unselfconscious about Brighton Pavilion, 'one of the most remarkable buildings in Europe. With its instantly recognisable outline, it is Brighton's proudest symbol, known throughout the world and visited by many thousands each year. It is unthinkable that this unique ... palace with its superb interior and furnishings should be allowed to decay.' So commences a leaflet describing current major structural restoration.

George Prince of Wales, later Prince Regent, had a mania for display which found its most costly expression in his numerous building projects. Architect Henry Holland's comparatively modest neo-classical marine villa of the 1780s was enlarged and transformed for the prince by John Nash into a mixture of 'Indian and Chinese motifs in an orgy of refinement and bad taste' between 1815 and 1823. Banister Fletcher's apparently contradictory description is apt. For here at the end of the Georgian period was the last moment in history when even bad taste was good. The Hugh Heffner of his day was not a philistine; the prince was expressing, through means of the highest art and craft, Britain's widened imperial horizons following the triumphant end of the Napoleonic wars. There was an intense fascination for the Near and Far East.

In the maturity of Queen Victoria's reign it was impossible to be frivolous about the 'imperial mission'. She did not find the pavilion to her taste, and it was nearly demolished. In fact her Office of Woods and Forests practically sacked the interior in removing decorations and fixtures and fittings before the building, which had cost over £500,000, was sold in 1850 to the Brighton Town Commissioners for £53,000. The latter repaired the pavilion for civic use. In 1864 the queen relented and returned much of the furniture which, in any case, had never been unpacked.

So the ensemble was largely preserved. But Nash's construction techniques were notoriously gimcrack, and problems recurred. Under an exterior of Bath stone and stucco-faced brickwork was a frame of timber and cast iron, which was one reason why the building has been subject to fire damage. The main causes of decay were, however, 'time, the sea and more recently pollution [which] have eroded the original stone exterior while water from leaking roofs has rusted and rotted the iron and timber within'. The restoration leaflet continues: 'Moreover, additions and alterations in many parts of the building over the last hundred years have obscured important features of the original design; in many cases these alterations themselves have accelerated the structural decay'.

Thoroughness is a frequent and welcome feature of historic-building repairs in recent years when it has been possible to raise sums for such causes which would have been unthinkable a decade ago. Thus while spasmodic work was carried out during the 1960s and 1970s – including a programme for replacement of minarets and pinnacles, the most exposed and therefore eroded parts of the structure – short-term economies were made. Glass-fibre reinforced pinnacles replaced stone ones at a cost of about £12,000 each. The SPAB protested at this procedure and predicted, quite rightly, that the plastic would soon be damaged by sand- and salt-laden sea winds. The society was also concerned that, in the long run, no original Bath stone examples would remain as models for future replacements. With the support of the Historic Buildings Council it was agreed that at least a few of these features

would be replaced in stone, even though the cost was at least five times as great. In the event erosion and delamination of the fibreglass was so rapid that it was abandoned as a material.

Upgrading of specifications has been symptomatic. Since 1980 Brighton Council, with continuing EH support, has been engaged in a thorough restoration costing no less than £9 million. The council's architects are fully conscious of the obligation to retain as much early-nineteenth-century fabric as possible. They are employing 'materials and methods compatible with those originally used'. The pavilion will be in a better condition than ever.

The Alhambra Theatre, Bradford

Horse-shoe shaped, many-tiered, elaborately proscenium-arched, with rich plasterwork and murals, the whole being refulgent in crimson and gilt – this is everyone's mental image of 'a theatre', despite the more utilitarian versions of our own age. The most influential designer of this late-Victorian and Edwardian type was Frank Matcham. Many local authorities, wanting to preserve at least one example, have managed to raise the several million pounds required to restore such auditoria. At the same time they have attached greatly enlarged backstage facilities as well as additional foyer, bar, restaurant, and administrative accommodation at 'front of house' to provide an 'entertainment and conference complex' up to today's standards. An early and comparatively modest example of such a project was the Lyric at Hammersmith, London, and a more recent and ambitious case is Bradford's Alhambra.

Theatre restoration may seem an unlikely part of urban regeneration, yet many places have found that as tourist attractions, as centres of evening sparkle, and of daytime business conferences or product launches, as well as as examples of conservation impact, they have helped to transform run-down central areas. So the Belfast Opera House has attracted new cafes, bars, and shops since its reopening in 1986. The Theatre Royal in Nottingham, enlarged and refurbished a few years earlier, has stimulated not only the construction of a new concert hall nearby, but also the building of a hotel and the upgrading of adjacent shops and restaurants. Newcastle's Theatre Royal and Cardiff's New Theatre will probably do likewise, and so, it is hoped, will a current restoration of the Hackney Empire and a proposed one at Wimbledon where a very ambitious multi-use project by architects Renton Howard Wood Levin will include three auditoria, a cinema, night club, health centre, and restaurant, all centred on a spectacular steel and glass foyer and exhibition area designed by engineer Anthony Hunt. Since the theatre at the core of all these schemes is often a listed building, English Heritage grants have sometimes been available and so have EEC contributions – the latter met half of the total costs at Newcastle and a third of building expenditure at Bradford.

The Alhambra, built on the eve of the First World War, was a late and lavish example. Occupying much of a prominent city block it was a civic building in its own right. A landmark with three domes, the rather lumpen massing made up in confidence what it lacked in elegance. The outstanding feature in architectural terms of this Grade-II-listed building was the sumptuous 1,500-seat auditorium with its elaborate plasterwork, murals, gilt, and plush.

The interplay of innumerable curves forming the dress and upper circles and boxes beneath a domed ceiling adds up to a textbook example of the Edwardian theatre, a fact which its owner, the Bradford Metropolitan Council, had the good sense to appreciate. Even so, it was fortunate that the building's fate was not settled until the early 1980s; bearing in mind the obviously considerable expense of refurbishment an earlier decision might well have led to demolition, followed perhaps by the construction of a new municipal theatre.

Bradford decided on an ambitious plan for an entertainment complex based on the old Alhambra. The best does not come cheap. The £6.5 million conversion and extension project involved the purchase of an adjacent cinema building as well as the reduction in width of streets bounding the site in order to extend in both directions. There were skyward ambitions too – the fly tower was rebuilt on a larger scale.

The Alhambra had virtually no backstage facilities and precious little administrative or sanitary accommodation. At front of house the foyer space was extremely limited. It was designed in the Edwardian tradition where patrons entered their respective tiers via a series of staircases leading from street entrances where separate box offices were also sited. In 1982 architects Renton Howard Wood Levin produced a feasibility study proposing alterations and extensions, the most important implication of which was the purchase of the Majestic Cinema which was on the further side of the stage tower. This was approved, thus permitting a near-doubling of the stage size as well as the provision of rehearsal rooms and a 400-seat hall for studio theatre productions and conference or community use. More visually prominent was the addition of a new entrance building attached beside the original columned and domed rotunda into which has been inserted a new grand staircase. A fully glazed, double-height, colourfully decorated entrance hall allows for promenading and conversing, drinking, buying of books and programmes – all the more social activities now expected of an evening at the theatre.

Nineteenth-century audiences paraded and talked quite animatedly in the auditorium itself; now there is more respect for what goes on on the stage. A mezza-

90. Alhambra Theatre, Bradford; another successful municipal enterprise, this late Edwardian building has extensions to provide all modern facilities for conferences and social events as well as a beautifully refurbished and re-equipped auditorium

nine gallery overlooks the entrance and links the pit bar and its eating area with the grand stairs and stalls lobby, a small and ornate compartment which previously contained the dress-circle stairs. These foyer spaces are designed to be open during the day as meeting places and for occasional lunchtime entertainments.

As at Nottingham and Hammersmith, the forebuilding is frankly modern in style. The only exception among recent proposals of this kind, where a large theatre is to be expanded both backstage and front of house, is the largest example of all, the Royal Opera House, Covent Garden. Part of the extensions there will be clad in a stripped-down neo-classical manner, but that abuts remnants of Inigo Jones's seventeenth-century piazza and will in effect re-establish a segment of it.

In all such thoroughgoing projects, almost as much is spent on unseen technical installations as on built extensions. At Bradford there are new ventilation, sound, and light systems, for example. Indeed some £500,000 was spent on electrical works, almost £750,000 on mechanical apparatus and a further £500,000 on specialist theatre equipment such as scenery and passenger lifts, sound systems, production lighting, and stage engineering gear.

The new fly tower has been constructed with fifty-five counterweight sets. The

greatly enlarged orchestra pit in front of a flat, lightly sprung stage floor, together with ample wing space, allows the Alhambra to present ambitious dance and musical shows. Either of the auditoria can be used for conferences. Film projection facilities are provided. Exhibitions, wedding receptions, trade launches, and a wide variety of other events are all catered for in the smaller space. All in all the facilities provided, as well as the offices from which to administer them, are on a scale undreamed of in 1914.

At that time almost all the expenditure was concentrated on the richly decorated auditorium itself. This has been comprehensively restored in a range of gilts and subtle shades of warm reds, with whites and blues highlighting the tier fronts and proscenium boxes. Carpets have been specially designed and the high-level paintings have been cleaned and restored.

Chapter 12

Churches
a delicate balance

*Trinity Church,
Irvine,
Strathclyde,
converted to
community use in
New Town centre*

Introduction

Anglican churches constitute the most significant architectural legacy from the Middle Ages. There exist a score of majestic cathedrals, almost as many minsters only a little less remarkable, and about 8,500 pre-Reformation parish or other local churches, most of which can be expected to continue in ecclesiastical use for the foreseeable future. But there will be exceptions even among medieval buildings: Norwich with a cathedral and thirty-two ancient churches and York with an even grander minster and nearly as many medieval places of worship, both still probably have too many despite a number of imaginative redundancy and reuse schemes in the last decade or so. Pre-Reformation churches exist in numbers disproportionate to the density of population in the eastern counties. Nonetheless the majority of redundant church buildings occur in major cities in the midlands, north, north-west, Scotland, and Wales and are, naturally, of eighteenth- and particularly of nineteenth-century date. This does not alter the fact that as places of worship they enjoy particular status under the planning and listed buildings system, namely 'ecclesiastical exemption', although since 1986 in particular this has been eroded.

The cathedrals remain quite literally a law unto themselves. Neither the Department of the [...] agencies, in [...] could preven [...] of one at an [...] sounds unli [...] matter of degree and some recent schemes of over-restoration involve *de facto* destruction of old fabric. Neither the government nor many conservationists, even within the church, are content with this situation of total independence for deans and chapters. It is based on the old precept that he who pays the piper calls the tune, and cathedrals have never sought or accepted government finance. Even the sensitive and modest proposals

(a) and (b) (overleaf). [...]hristchurch, [...]ncaster Gate, London; an unnecessary demolition by the Diocese of London. All but the spire – itself only recently restored after war damage – has been replaced by an extraordinary block of flats

worked out over a period of ten years by a working party representing all interests for an advisory system of church-appointed experts in matters of ecclesiastical architecture, art, glass, furnishings, music, and so on, was at first rejected in the 1988 Synod by an unexpected coalition of deans and provosts. Questions of repair, conservation, and maintenance of cathedrals and great churches, exemplified by the controversial work on Wells west front (Chapter 11), need not detain us here. The more relevant matter is regarding the problems of redundancy followed by either demolition, conversion and reuse, or 'taking into care' – in effect 'museumizing' – church buildings no longer required for worship. There is also the matter of the effects of neglect and vandalism on church buildings and their furnishings during the period after closure and before acceptance of responsibility by new owners and/or users. Many years of successive church and then lay bureaucratic processes can result in there being little left to conserve or convert after theft and decay and wanton damage have prevailed.

Four-fifths of the 17,000 Anglican churches are parish churches and about 13,000 are listed buildings – 2,633 Grade I in December 1986. The Church of England's 1968 Pastoral Measure formulated a procedure for closure of churches no longer supportable by their parishioners. Over 1,000 have come into that category since 1968. If the Advisory Board for Redundant Churches considers the building to be of sufficient quality and interest, and – being realistic – if maintenance appears affordable, which it was not thought to be for some of the vast and rich inner-city Victorian churches like All Souls' Halifax until a consortium formed by SAVE had repaired the building, the Redundant Churches Fund may be asked by the Church Commissioners to take responsibility. The Fund has limited resources and has in the past been justifiably cautious. Now

finances are a little easier. In Summer 1988 the DoE allocated £600,000 to the fund for the next quinquennium. State input will now comprise 70 per cent of the total and Church of England input 30 per cent.

A sufficiently respectful and architecturally sensitive new use is a practical alternative to taking into care, and this would normally be welcomed. Such uses would be ones where minimum physical alterations for conversion would be required and day-to-day damage in use unlikely. Ideally that would mean some sort of art gallery or museum: examples of first-rate buildings thus adapted include St George's, Great Yarmouth, St George's, Bolton, and St Mary's, Gateshead.

Inner-city decay and population movements to suburban areas are causes for loss of places of worship. Also long gone are the days when a slate mining village in north Wales could support several chapels, and the same is the case in the coal-mining valleys of south Wales. But most places have not lost population so much as they have lost the habit of church-going. Perhaps never quite so universal as is now imagined, the proportion of people going with some regularity to some kind of religious service was nearer 50 per cent in the nineteenth century than the barely 5 per cent of a bigger population today. The Methodists closed some 5,000 chapels between 1940 and 1980. And the amalgamation of the Presbyterians and Congregationalists into the United Reform Church in 1972 resulted in a rationalization to about 2,000 places of worship for the twelve provinces. Several hundred were sold. Although there are some fine chapels dating from before 1700, the heyday for Congregationalist building in particular was the nineteenth century. Unlike some other faiths, the Congregationalists had few inhibitions regarding architectural ambitions, and leading architects – Mawson and Lockwood, even Butterfield and Waterhouse – were commissioned.

At Halifax the 210-ft spire of the Congregational church deliberately overshadowed the medieval parish church, only to be dwarfed in its turn by Gilbert Scott's Anglican All Souls' on nearby Haley Hill. At the opposite extreme in terms of architectural pretension are the meeting houses of the Society of Friends (Quakers), founded in the 1650s by George Fox. Of nearly 400 simple buildings still in use, a remarkable number are seventeenth- and eighteenth-century in origin.

The union of semi-autonomous Baptist churches has about 1,700 places of worship. Some attractive Baptist chapels survive from the eighteenth century and a handful from the seventeenth. These were of an almost domestic modesty usually. After a falling away in the very worldly period around 1750, there was a tremendous revival a century later when there were nearly 3,000 chapels, and building was continuing on increasingly extravagant lines. Examples are the magnificent Baptist Church of the Redeemer, in Birmingham (demolished 1975), and the cathedral-like Coates Memorial Baptist Church at Paisley, Strathclyde.

The Unitarians were less numerous and today have fewer than 250 churches. But they 'undoubtedly possess relatively the highest proportion of historic buildings. This is because the Unitarians inherited many of the best early buildings of the Independents, the Presbyterians, and the General Baptists.'[37] Unitarian churches of the late eighteenth century tended to be plain outside but with remarkably fine woodwork within. Binney and Burman speak of the 'comparative wealth' of Unitarians in the nineteenth century, of their building 'in a remarkable variety of styles', including 'a spiky filigree Gothic'.[38] Typical of the last was the Northgate End Unitarian Chapel in Halifax, dating from 1870 but incorporating fittings and monuments from the earlier Georgian chapel. The building and its contents, including monuments, were sold off separately in 1979. Some fine

tablets carved in bas-relief by Chantrey were bought by the Friends of Friendless Churches and have been resited in the neo-classical annex of the Walker Art Gallery, Liverpool, itself housed in a former cemetery chapel. The chapel itself was demolished. SAVE lamented at the time that

This sad case underlines the fact that the contents of Non-Conformist buildings are often of as much interest as those of the local parish church. The current situation where internal alterations may be made to even listed chapels which are in use, without consent, is resulting in the almost daily loss of fittings and monuments.[39]

92 (a) and (b). Christchurch, Spitalfields, London, by Hawksmoor; a superb repair of a Cyclopean-scaled building with major English Heritage aid. The Baroque interior is an ideal auditorium for pre-Romantic music

Most numerous of the Nonconformists were of course the Methodists. John and Charles Wesley held their first outdoor service for the Somerset colliers in 1739. By 1812 their followers had built 1,540 chapels – of which only 131 survived in 1970.[40] Nevertheless at the time of the union of all the Methodist sects in 1932 there were 14,500 chapels, a figure nearly comparable with Anglican churches. Little more than half survive now and in this increasingly secular world their Grade-I-listed Central Hall, Westminster, is far better known as a conference centre.

The Roman Catholic Church also has a considerable architectural heritage

throughout the country. Among its first post-Reformation churches are St John's, Bath (1685) and St Mary's, Bristol (1730), so again the preconception of essentially Victorian places of worship is by no means the whole story. However, it is true that the second half of the nineteenth century saw the richest period of building, its forms inspired by the more scholarly study of Gothic architecture introduced around 1840 by Pugin and the Ecclesiological Society. The latter part of the century, as Binney and Burman again point out, saw the Catholics, like the Nonconformists, building a number of adventurous Arts and Crafts Gothic churches. Today there are nearly 4,000 Roman Catholic churches and chapels. There is nothing like the falling away in numbers of churchgoers as with other faiths, but inevitably some Catholic inner-city churches, especially in the north-west where they were always strong, have been left in derelict areas and a few have been lost. St Francis Xavier, Liverpool, listed Grade II*, was saved from demolition and repaired.

While exemption from listed-building controls for churches in use apply to all the types of churches discussed above, it is a sad fact that there is no equivalent for any churches other than Anglican (not even for the Episcopal Church in Scotland) of the Redundant Churches Fund, which now cares for some 240 buildings in England. Otherwise, always excepting Anglican cathedrals, the legal position of all places of worship is similar. They are all slowly and inexorably being drawn into the secular machinery of controls.

As has been remarked, the pressure to go in this direction is financial. In its *1986/87 Report and Accounts,* English Heritage subtly conjoins the two thoughts: 'we planned to restore church grants to the level achieved before the middle of 1985 and to increase our involvement in the listed building consent process at a much earlier stage when many problems can be resolved without recourse to public inquiries'. In fact the

non-statutory public-inquiry system into proposed demolition of churches for which some interested parties considered an alternative could be found has not proved efficacious. It was established in 1979 as an informal *quid pro quo* for the first financial aid from the DoE towards churches in use (government has provided at least half the money for the Redundant Churches Fund since 1969). There have been four such inquiries: Holy Trinity, Rugby, by Gilbert Scott, which was demolished; the 1930s St Wilfrid's, Brighton, by Goodhart Rendell, which is to be gutted to provide twenty flats; St Alban's, Teddington, an impressive Gothic Revival church which is to be preserved; St John the Baptist, Avon Dassett, Warwickshire, a Victorian medievalist gem of 1868, where the inquiry determined that if a new use could not be found in a reasonable period the building should be vested in the Redundant Churches Fund. Significant changes in ecclesiastical exemption were announced in late 1986, and though somewhat vague, the state's control over partial demolition of places of worship was extended, as it was over 'significant external works'. English Heritage grants to churches totalled about £5.5 million in 1987/8.

This, then, is the historical, ecclesiastical, financial, and building-control framework, although the subject we are addressing is fundamentally more emotive than these discussions suggest. It is that since fewer people go to church, what is to be done with the redundant buildings? Writing of English churches in 1977, Patrick O'Donovan said:

On the whole they are probably more lovingly and subtly maintained than in any comparable country. Even non-churchgoers appear to treasure the presence of a fane and steeple in their street or village. The very presence of such a building seems to satisfy an instinctive need as well as representing the finest monument in almost any district.[41]

Discrimination in deciding what is to be done to which former religious building and how it is to be done is more crucial here than in any other area of redundancy.

At least there need be little concern here of discrimination in favour of modern church architecture of high quality since, with few exceptions, it does not exist. Other nations at least as pagan have produced some thrillingly beautiful and eloquent new places of worship – Le Corbusier (an atheist) at Ronchamp and La Tourette for example. The best in England is the handsome, recently listed church at Bow Common, east London, by architects Maguire & Murray, and a striking restoration of the fire-damaged parish church at Barnes by Edward Cullinan. In Scotland there is Coia's rugged concrete effort at Cumbernauld new town. There have been new additions to a number of historic churches, but they are not of a quality or interest to detain us. The near total failure of postwar architects in this sphere influences those arguing against demolition or change of use to the extent that even when a building is admittedly unsuitable or too big, or in decay, it will be tenaciously defended 'for fear of something worse'.

A perverted indication of the spiritual power of even an abandoned church building can be detected in the attraction it holds for vandals and desecrators. Two millennia of Christianity leaves a strong cultural legacy. Nor is it reasonable to expect even dwindling congregations to forget many centuries of converting heathens to the 'one true faith'. Half a century ago missionaries were traversing the globe and British architects had built Gothic cathedrals and parish churches in much of India, Africa, Australia, and even parts of China. The elderly who would rather see their beloved church destroyed than turned into a supermarket or restaurant, even a museum, even, indeed, a mosque, are expressing something which for them is deeper than mere negative or selfish pig-headedness. Thus before discussions reach the stage of discriminating about the architectural

quality of a threatened building, sensitivity about proposed uses is appropriate.

Discrimination in terms of architectural quality is, however, the key consideration. For the non-church authorities, the planning-permission and grant givers, the integrity of the building is more important than what some would consider the lack of integrity of the use. For a medium-sized church an art gallery or library is an ideal use – viz the Demarco Gallery in an eighteenth-century Edinburgh church, Lincoln College Library, Oxford, in the splendid English classical All Saints' of 1699, and St Edmund Hall Library in the part-Norman, mostly Gothic St Peter-in-the-East, also in Oxford. Fortunately the raising of the floor level by less than two metres in All Saints' to provide necessary accommodation in a semi-basement only brought the new floor to the base of the principal order and arguably even improved the proportions. The less lofty Gothic interior was subjected to no major vertical or indeed horizontal sub-division – and that is the most important decision of all – apart from the ultimate one of writing off the interior altogether (and even that has to be faced in some circumstances).

Also nearly ideal in what might be called spiritual as well as architectural terms are performing-arts uses: the circular St George's Tufnell Park, in London, has made an almost perfect Shakespearian theatre, and the octagonal Trinity Church, Irvine, is now a fine community centre; both are eccentric 1860s Gothic. Music has been even more closely related than drama to the life of the Church throughout the ages, and the volume and height of many church buildings, quite compatible with necessary reverberation times, have been invaluable in this field. There are many highly successful concert-hall or rehearsal-room conversions: notably Hope Park Chapel, Edinburgh, now the Queen's Hall, St Paul's, Huddersfield, a concert hall, Holy

Trinity, Southwark, an orchestral rehearsal hall, and the new St George's Brandon Hill, Bristol, a music centre.

Arguably sports-hall conversions do not score quite so high on the count of either suitability or retention of interior character. Some height is required for ball games, but there is usually a necessary sprung games floor insertion, with changing rooms and other facilities below. The proportions of Norman Shaw's former Holy Trinity, Latimer Road, West Kensington, are not improved by the new floor below the sills of the large, traceried east and west windows. And although these are protected by metal grills, there is an understandable temptation to screen off all but clerestory level windows in sports halls since it is almost impossible to retain sight of a moving ball against the filigreed light of a large and complicated window. Sports-hall conversions – for which a grant from the Sports Council may be forthcoming, incidentally – are appropriate for 'churches and chapels of a rather ordinary character' as Ken Powell writes: 'It involves the stripping out of every extraneous feature, the reduction of an interior to its essentials'.[42]

Conversion to disco, night club, even restaurant may, on the other hand, involve less radical internal stripping out, even the reverse as in the case of Sheikh's Indian restaurant in the former United Reform Church (a sect which, unlike Methodists, is not strongly predisposed against alcohol consumption in former places of worship) of St Andrew, Bradford. Potted plants have been imported to decorate the former font, converted into a water fountain. Only massive, but removable, lighting and sound systems have been added to James Cubitt's former Welsh Presbyterian chapel which, being hemmed in by the buildings of Charing Cross Road, London, on most sides, did not have large areas of low-level glazing anyway. A Stringfellow's club, whether in New York or London, intends intimations of decadence, among other attractions, and only

those for whom no lingering sense of sanctity attaches to mere bricks and mortar – intellectually a perfectly rational view – can be without a twinge of doubt about such a use for a former place of worship. The argument returns to matters of discrimination, of which there are several more dimensions to consider.

Precisely what are the particular qualities which justify the conservation of a particular church, ignoring for now the symbolic or spiritual overtones entirely? First and least is that here is a more or less large familiar object that exists, and it will be less disruptive, more economic, and simply quicker in most cases to reuse it rather than demolish and build something else or, as has happened in many inner-city areas, destroy it and leave the site barren. In most towns and cities there are quite a few mid- or late-nineteenth-century churches or chapels built very plainly, with cheap materials, no architectural distinction, possibly no architect, with decorations and fittings ordered 'off-the-shelf' from ecclesiastical furnishers. They can provide accommodation for retailers, furniture warehouses, or community centres without too much concern about internal changes, though it is to be hoped that the exterior, humble though it may be, will be decently maintained with the minimum of alteration.

The next category is the building which makes a significant townscape or landscape contribution. The collective attractions of the almost 'ordinary' buildings constituting the typical village or country-town street or neighbourhood was not widely understood until the 1960s. It was officially unprotected until Duncan Sandys' Civic Amenities Act of 1967 created the conservation area. Until then protective legislation had been historically or aesthetically elitist, quite rightly in its terms, for the whole idea was to preserve 'the best'. Once the idea is accepted that familiar areas should be cherished for all their haphazard detail, variety of scale, ornament, colour, and material, then areas are bound to be seen in compositional terms, if only to determine the boundaries of conservation areas. Many such compositions focus on church buildings: the square tower dominating the cluster of houses and farms in the Devon valley, the several steeples rising over the roofs of towns like Derby or Stamford, the soaring nineteenth-century spires vying to dominate Halifax, the cupolas and belfries hailing each other across the narrow streets of the City of London, even, and ironically, the empty Church of St Chrystostom, a beacon of hope as the sole standing building in the flattened wastelands of Everton in Liverpool.

But more than likely, the church or chapel which contributes to the town or country scene will be of architectural interest, might well be listed in the recent resurvey if not in the earlier ones which ignored many nineteenth-century examples, and must be preserved externally. The interior spaces and fittings of almost any church are worth keeping because they are essentially different to the rest of the 99.8 per cent of buildings in the country and so, other things being equal, a sympathetic solution of the type discussed above is suitable. But things are not always equal; the state of the building and the demand for space in a less than prosperous place may mean that its reuse will be marginal in financial terms unless in a conservation area. No grants will be available for the very reason that it is not outstanding, so in order to retain the contribution to the urban or rural scene, the inside may be gutted, that means stripped out, divided up, and made unrecognizable. This is the worst-case scenario apart from total loss.

If the decision is made that the interior must be preserved as far as possible, then it will be converted into a house if small, an office or studio if larger, in both cases leaving some full-height spaces and with floors that do not bisect windows and general alterations that might at some future date be reversible. Here again comes the matter of discrimination in size

and in reversibility. A small church may make a single house like All Saints', Langdon, Essex, or St Oswald, Fulford, Yorkshire. It can be largely undivided and retain many fittings and much character. A vast church like St Alban's, Teddington, could only be converted to residential use by inserting several floors and many apartments. A scheme to do just that was abandoned in 1988. As for reversing the process at some future date, this idea, based on the old SPAB gospel that 'we are only trustees for those that come after us', can be implemented by architects and their engineers in all but the largest buildings by designing new columns, beams, and floors as self-supporting 'cages' inside the original building but independent of it and by running plumbing, wiring, and other services through the new structure not the old. This can even be done with quite large churches, as architect Julian Harrap has recently demonstrated with the unlikely rescue and conversion into a museum of Victorian life of Teulon's semi-ruined and very isolated St Mark's, Silvertown, East London, built in 1862.

In every major conservation case the question has to be settled of 'what is it that is being preserved?'. What therefore is the irreducable minimum that must be retained for the sake of going to all the trouble in the first place and also for the sake of handing something to our descendants? There is very little point, except the very first, the economic use of an already-built volume, in keeping a church, or even, for example, a barn which is often a structure of comparable form, age, and internal space, if in so doing all the essence of a church or barn is destroyed.

Churches pose all the conservation dilemmas in their extreme form; it is unsurprising that when William Morris founded the SPAB in 1877 and with it the basis of modern conservation, he was moved to do so by an argument about a church. What is perhaps surprising is that the architect with whom Morris was in conflict over Tewksbury Abbey, Gilbert Scott, should also have designed buildings such as St Pancras Station Hotel and All Souls', Haley Hill, which Morris's successors a century later fought tooth and nail to preserve. And so outstanding are both of those that their interiors are to be retained as far as possible intact. For the best of every period and *every* essentially intact medieval building – of which churches comprise the outstanding stock – should be preserved unmutilated.

All Souls', Haley Hill, Halifax

Built in 1856–9 at the expense of a local manufacturer, Edward Ackroyd, by Sir George Gilbert Scott who considered it to be his finest church, All Souls' was declared redundant in 1977. There was a congregation, but a new minister felt that upkeep of the vast building was too much of a burden and had moved services to the church hall. The diocese had received an architect's report to the effect that the spire was dangerous and £200,000 would be required to repair it – but then such an opinion is very often available to a building owner who would find demolition of an old building convenient. It was certainly true that repairs to the whole church would cost at least double that figure.

Until the report *Faith in the City* was published, church authorities seem oblivious of the negative psychological impact of the continuing loss of marvellously prominent places of worship. All Souls' was indisputably magnificent, at the apogee of Victorian High Gothic church architecture. Intending to re-create the thirteenth-century peak of English building, with a spire to rival those of Grantham and Newark, Scott's lofty edifice is in fact slightly French in feel and very nineteenth-century. It is lavishly furnished with splendid stained glass, woodwork, and stone carving by the best

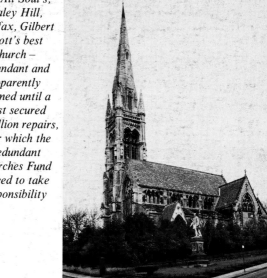

93. All Soul's, Haley Hill, Halifax, Gilbert Scott's best church – redundant and apparently doomed until a trust secured £1 million repairs, after which the Redundant Churches Fund agreed to take responsibility

craftsmen. The Church Commissioners Advisory Board had not recommended preservation, believing the great building to be beyond the means of the Redundant Churches Fund. The government's Historic Building Council had sent a deputation of the Great, Good, and rather elderly who concluded that All Souls' did not justify the huge grant necessary for repairs. By 1980 the shuttered building was dank, dark, and dirty but, thankfully, little damaged. Demolition appeared inevitable – except to Marcus Binney and others of SAVE Britain's Heritage, not a group put off by the sheer scale of a challenge. A new independent trust to save All Souls' received a tremendous boost when it was supported by Jennifer Jenkins, chairman of HBC, who had become 'enthused by the church because of its immense townscape value'.

Two events were crucial, the first a report by the experienced church architect Donald Buttress, working at first on a voluntary basis in combination with engineers Ove Arup; this proposed repair of the tower *in situ*. The second was a decision in June 1982 by the National Heritage Memorial Fund to grant £250,000 to this outstanding building. By the next year, with HBC help, the interior

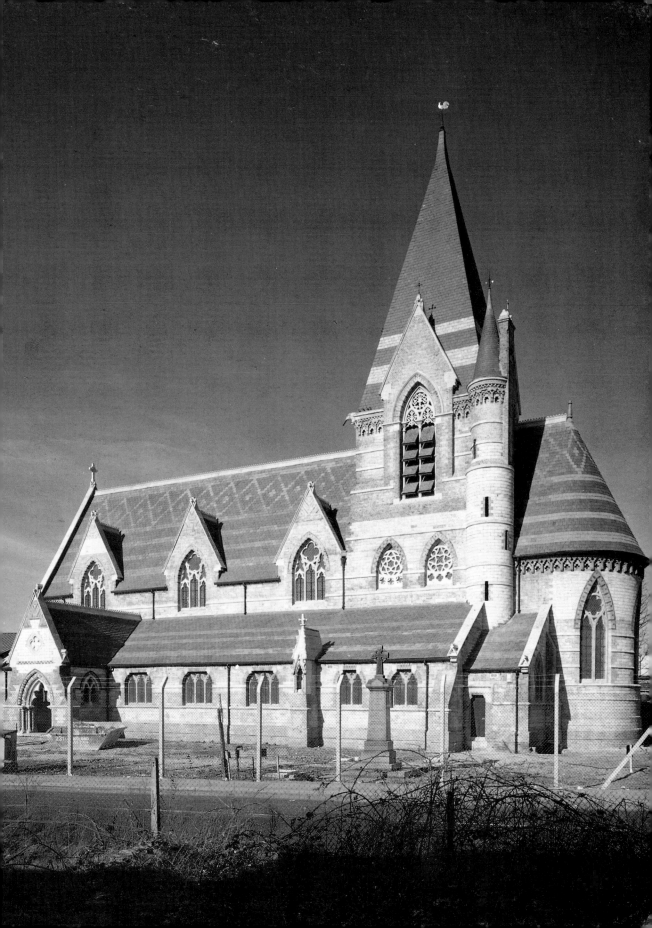

94 (a) (see p. 217) and (b). *St Mark's Church, Silvertown, London; a stranded masterpiece by the Victorian architect, Teulon, was vandalized and gutted by fire before reconstruction for museum use. The pitch-pine hammer-beam roof was reconstructed using old timbers and surviving ironwork*

95. Another imposing East London church, Hawksmoor's St Anne's, Limehouse, looks unaltered but its ceiling is now suspended from a delicate spider-web of structural steel installed by architect Julian Harrap within the roof void

and the churchyard had been cleaned up – always a boost for local support. Now, with a total of £500,000 spent, some of it from private trusts, the spire is repaired, and the Redundant Churches Fund has taken All Souls' into care.

St Mark's, Silvertown, London

The high Victorian architect, S. S. Teulon, was responsible for St Mark's, Silvertown, a compact, lofty, and crescendo-like building of contrasting stones, brick, slate, and polychrome-ornamented Gothic; it also has a striking timber roof of hammerbeam over an arcaded nave. Although only declared redundant in 1974, the building was apparently a lost cause ten years later, a derelict wreck severely damaged by arson, the fine roof a mass of charred timbers littering the floor. The London Borough of Newham, to whom ownership of St Mark's had passed, had intended it for use by the Passmore Edward's Museum, but the fire damage which included injury to the stonework as well as destruction of the roof would have put paid to this plan had not the

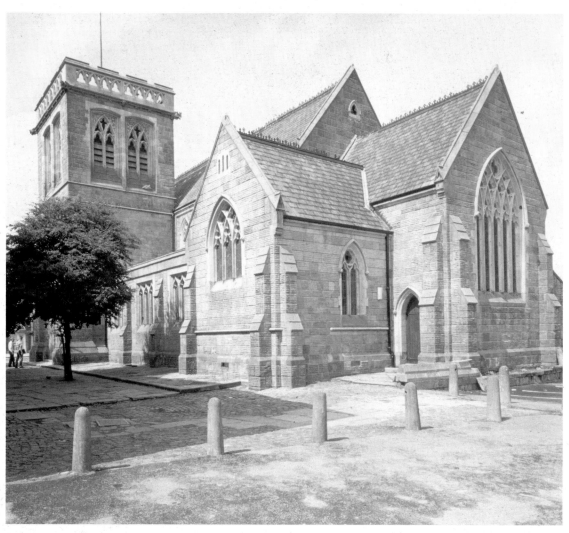

London Docklands Development Corporation, with its active conservation policies, come along and jointly sponsored the restoration, with the Passmore Edwards Trust, of a museum of Victorian life. LDDC is in the almost unique situation of having resources which, in relation to the number of important historic buildings within its jurisdiction, allow a comparatively generous approach.

Julian Harrap, whose work at St Anne's, Limehouse, another docklands church, had been described by LDDC itself as 'a very good example of high quality conservation techniques', supervised a contract starting in summer 1985

96 (a) and (b). St Michael's Derby; a decent Victorian church has been retained for streetscape value and converted into architects' offices

to repair the exterior envelope, including the replacement of much polychrome brickwork and not a little stonework. But the biggest task in this was the reconstruction of Teulon's hammerbeam roof, reusing quantities of salvaged iron fixings and bringing large timbers for the trusses in the form of perfectly preserved piles from the bed of the Thames which were shaped by the contractor in an on-site carpenters' workshop.

This first phase, which has raised the Grade-II-listed building at least to Grade II* status, cost £750,000, provided roughly one-third each by the LDDC, the London Borough of Newham, and the fire insurance compensation. Completion

and fitting out as a museum will require another £1 million which is not at the moment forthcoming. Eventually the building will house exhibition space in the nave, with a reading room in the gallery, recital space and audio-visual studio in the chancel, and substantial archives in closed cabinets on rails in the basement.

St Michael's, Derby

Completely lacking the extravagance, flair, and expressiveness of St Mark's, and nowhere approaching the scale of All Souls', this church has features in common: it is urban, stone, mid-nineteenth-century with thirteenth-century references, dirty, decayed, and *en route* to demolition. It has been converted by an architect into offices for himself and a couple of other firms.

Henry Isaac Stevens was the architect for this 'solid and serious'[43] and fairly small building. The chief merit of St Michael's has been recognized as being an event in the central area streetscape, its stumpy tower a sort of foothill to the soaring sixteenth-century tower of the cathedral just along the road and to Pugin's fine Catholic Church of St Mary also nearby. A dwindling congregation clung on during the 1960s despite the loss of city-centre population caused by redevelopments and an inner ring road which left St Michael's stranded on the edge of the commercial sector and razed another church in the area to the ground. Redundancy came in 1977; no one defended the building until a local architect, Derek Latham, secured a 'last-minute reprieve' in 1980. Vandals and neglect had taken their toll during the several years since active use, but church authorities did sanction emergency repairs in 1981, while a 125-year lease was being negotiated at a peppercorn rent, in order to make repair and conversion viable.

A six-month contract completed in spring 1983 cost £140,000. Many of the

fittings had been removed by the diocese for reuse and the west window went to the Ely Stained Glass Museum, but some memorials, choir stalls, and a screen were retained, although adapted and moved in some cases. Just as is intended at St Mark's, Silvertown, the new structural insertions are modern in spirit and carefully designed to expose the volume and character of the church interior while at the same time avoiding fixings or junctions with important original features.

The interior now provides open-plan offices on three floors; Derek Latham & Associates occupy the first floor and rent out the ground and second to design-related businesses. The entrance is at the west end of the church, indeed the reception area, formerly the vestry, contains Minton floor tiles and wall tablets from elsewhere in the building. The towerspace above reception has been left open to its full height so that visitors can immediately comprehend the full original volume. The first floor is at capital level but, as indicated, is kept back from the walls and columns. From the second floor, which is limited to two nave bays, the timber roof can be fully appreciated. Roof rafters have been cleaned and picked out in red following original paint traces.

Externally the cleaning and obvious reuse of St Michael's has had the classic

97 (a) and (b). St John's, Reading: the diocese sought demolition after an amalgamation of parishes, despite the wish of the local Polish church to take over the building

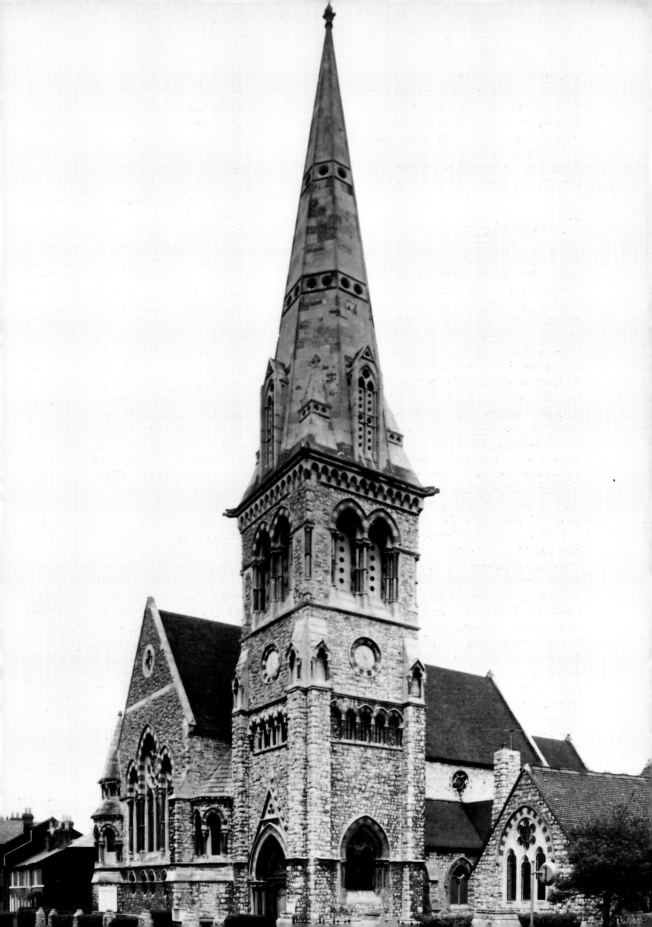

'conservation impact' in encouraging further rejuvenation of what had become a 'twilight area' of the city.

St John the Evangelist, Reading

Here another church was preserved in worship, always the best solution despite the explicit determination of the diocese to demolish in the face of local opposition. The Church Commissioners' Advisory Board for Redundant Churches had agreed to demolition in 1973 because 'of such small historic or architectural interest' shortly before the DoE spot-listed the building.

Built in 1872–3 by W. A. Dixon, St John's, now in a conservation area, is a vigorous Gothic building with a splendid spire, and a well known local landmark. It is a typical High Victorian church in the line of All Souls', Haley Hill, though not quite the same league in terms of quality. After a century of worship it was in sound structural condition. In 1978, when SAVE became involved, the building was still standing because as one of two churches in a recently united parish it was retained in use while a new 'multi-purpose church centre' was being built half a mile away. Upon its completion both vicar and diocesan authorities wanted St John's sold, not only to provide funds but also to make a clean break with the past. Thus they opposed two serious schemes put forward for reuse. One was for conversion to residential use at a cost of £250,000 which had already been earmarked by Reading Council. The interior would have been lost, but not the landmark. Greatly preferable, indeed almost perfect it might have been thought, was an offer to purchase on behalf of the active Polish Catholic Church which was in need of a building. The Bishop of Reading was adamant. But he was defeated by a stratagem adopted by the council. Demolition was physically

impossible unless plant could be got onto the site. This was only possible if the 3-ft-high church wall were demolished. Reading's planning committee refused permission for this. Stalemate was followed by a climb-down by the diocese and the Church Commissioners who agreed to sell to the Poles. After cleaning, redecoration, and a cardinal's blessing mass was being celebrated before the close of 1981.

98 (a) and (b). St Andrew's, Wood Walton, Cambridgeshire; a simple country church preserved 'as is' by the Friends of Friendless Churches

St Andrew's, Wood Walton, Cambridgeshire

This building is included to represent the picturesque county church, one of the basic images in our literature and culture. St Andrew's, which is essentially medieval, was sensitively repaired in the nineteenth century (a more common occurrence than is perhaps often thought). It is of particular architectural interest in that one nave arcade is Early English, that is, thirteenth-century in origin, and the other is perpendicular and of the fifteenth century.

It is now owned by the Friends of Friendless Churches – and is one of eighteen Anglican churches and one Nonconformist chapel which this entirely voluntary body cares for. The FFC was founded in 1957 by Ivor Bulmer Thomas who remains the honorary director. With a future guaranteed by a formal partnership with the Ancient Monuments Society, the FFC's churches are secure. As an unattached body it is able to take on churches in Wales and outside the Anglican fraternity, two things which the Redundant Churches Fund cannot at present do.

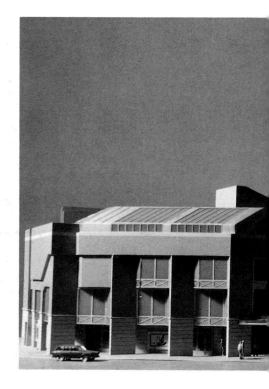

Chapter 13
The Way ahead

*Wimbledon
Theatre, London,
enlarged into
entertainments/
conference centre*

Generation gap

Leaders of architectural thought in the period 1930–60 were Modern Movement enthusiasts – Sir John Summerson, Sir Nikolaus Pevsner, even Sir John Betjeman, who wrote enthusiastically of internationalist work while on the staff of the *Architectural Review*. Like Sir Hugh Casson, they became in their maturity protectors of at least parts of what Summerson, in his dislike of pantechnicon phrases, declines to call 'the heritage'. Tastes, academic and nostalgic, added to circumstances such as the 1930s orgy of destruction of Georgian London, wartime losses, and the failures of the new architecture were all influential. Summerson helped to found the Georgian Group and the precursor of the National Monuments Record; Pevsner created Penguin's Buildings of England series; Betjeman virtually invented Metroland and was a great Victorian Society activist; Casson lent his name to many preservation campaigns.

They all shared the unashamedly elitist view that the best should be protected, but that if old buildings were to be indiscriminately preserved many of the masterpieces which we now revere and which occupy the sites of older structures, would not have been built. Their criteria were aesthetic and historic, in that order. They were uninterested in 'buildings as social documents', and unconcerned about the loss of the familiar and about the disruption and waste consequent upon demolition. Even arguments about tourist income would leave them cold. Nostalgia they would despise almost as much as revivalist or post-modern architecture. The arguments of these great men were irrefutable. If the modern architecture they espoused in the 1930s had been a popular success, their rigorous tastes would have become and remained those of the majority. Conservation is the only architecture-related cause that has ever been truly popular.

Local politicians have been among the

99. Euston Station, the hall, demolished in 1961. Hardwick's heroic neo-classical station and arch were judged unworthy of preservation

last to accept that popularity – they sometimes find it convenient to associate conservation with 'gentrification'. But in most parts of the country councils now support conservation policies. As indicated by the case studies, the situation is rich, varied, and mostly positive. Indeed, in some areas, notably not in Liverpool, some of the worst problems are the outcome of over-enthusiasm arising from success. Certainly the transformation in both attitudes and actions since 1975 is remarkable. The book accompanying the 'Destruction of the Country House' exhibition of 1974 – charting the toll of 400 major houses destroyed between 1920 and 1955 and illustrating the barely reduced haemorrhage to that date – seems like a document from another age.

Victorian values

It could be said that we have progressed a great distance – into the past. As suggested in Chapter 10, there is a stylistic free-for-all once more. Eclecticism in skilled hands can make as worthwhile a contribution to an environment composed of buildings from various traditions as it did a century ago. The 'morality' of the form-follows-function dogma has been rejected for the simple reason that its influence was malignant. Which does not mean that 'modernist' solutions are inappropriate in every context; far from it. It is no longer the *only* permissible answer however.

Another Victorian strain is the unabashed entrepreneurship abroad in the land again. It is not altruistic; if reused old buildings were not commercially viable, or if a combination of rising property prices and planning attitudes had not made them so, there would not have been a huge expansion in such work. But they were and there has. The almost single-handed saving of the Agricultural Hall in Islington by the head of a successful shopfitting company is a classic example. But that at about £10 million was small-

scale alongside the costs of other projects: more than £200 million budgeted for the conversion of Battersea Power Station into a leisure centre, £50 million on Billingsgate Market's transformation into an international banking headquarters, a similar sum for the conversion of St Pancras Chambers into hotel and retail uses, and the £120 million spent on Albert Dock in Liverpool into those and other functions. Hundreds of millions of pounds are in the process of being spent on the revitalization of London's docklands and a nearly comparable amount on the revival of the predominantly Victorian city of Glasgow. All these major projects, except Battersea, have involved nineteenth-century structures. All of them have been wholly or predominantly privately funded – although in both Glasgow and Liverpool there has been substantial public 'pump-priming' finance and in London's docks a certain proportion.

Increased lavishness has also shown signs of an almost Victorian refulgence. Polished marble, granite, bronze, stainless steel, and triple-glazed windows framed in hardwood have ousted exposed concrete, rusty metal, rotting softwood, and semi-detached tiling as finishes. The reconverted Langham and St Pancras hotels are specifically billed as designed to rival their nineteenth-century pre-

101. New Concordia Wharf, London docks: a monumental pillar-like chimney beside the inland entrance was restored with grant aid

100. Courage brewhouse, near London Bridge, detail of replacement cast lead on cupola

decessors in luxury. Showiness also manifests itself in less expected quarters. A letter in *The Times* from a retired stonemason complaining that the vaulted roof of Worcester Cathedral glowed with new gilding while it sagged to the point of collapse did not elicit a complete reply from the cathedral architect.

Worcester is one of many cathedrals seeking multi-million-pound funding for allegedly vital repairs; it is a matter of fashion. A visit to many of these indigent establishments reveals extremely costly interior redecoration. Southwark is now the epitome of gilded vulgarity. At York Minster there was a real problem in spending all the money donated to restore the fire-gutted transept, though the greatest difficulties were with the monies for specified items.

Antiquarian prejudice

Such profligate expenditure on at least some of the most prominent of historic buildings is but a manifestation of a national obsession with old artifacts of every kind from tram tickets and cocoa tins to red telephone boxes. Such criteria for preservation as 'outstanding' have long been bypassed. There is every sign of the triumph of what the late John Betjeman called 'antiquarian prejudice', that is, a conviction that whatever is older is better. What is undeniable is that older is rarer: fourteenth-century buildings are twenty times scarcer than seventeenth-century ones and they are a hundred times fewer in number than nineteenth-century examples. Not only has much less survived from earlier ages, but much less was built, and there were far fewer people.

At the end of the twentieth century anything that is genuinely handmade with natural materials is at a premium. But antiquarian prejudice can lead to far more bizarre decisions than our choice of expensive stone-ground brown bread in preference to the white loaves our ancestors regarded as the privilege of the rich.

It can lead to proposals to demolish a good Georgian terrace in Chester to reveal foundations of the Roman amphitheatre – and in a scholarly sense that may be right. It can lead to the chairman of the City of London planning committee determining that any redevelopment of Paternoster Square should return to the street pattern existing before the 1960s redevelopment, which has little historic validity but could well lead to a more pleasant environment.

As the founders of the Society for the Protection of Ancient Buildings realized a century ago – and there is added currency for the SPAB's Victorian values in this new period of restoration enthusiasm – the greatest danger is that in too zealous and incautious restorations we can 'kill the thing we love'. The most difficult thing is to do what is necessary and no more, especially if the architect's client is rich, again a more common occurrence now than for some decades past.

A more intellectual dilemma concerns the listing of ugly buildings. It is true that the least loved architecture is that which has just gone out of fashion. It is also remarkable how many of us have been taught to love such buildings as Battersea Power Station. There is now a lobby seeking protection for some of the most graceless, stained, leaking, uncomfortable, and unpopular of 1960s slabs – Alexander Fleming House at the Elephant and Castle, which was just turned down for listing, being one of the prettier examples. This is the sort of thing that could get even conservationists a bad name. Yet it is inescapable; every period has its historic significance and only the Georgian period was incapable of producing bad architecture.

Nostalgia as money-spinner

Robert Hewison in his critical book *The Heritage Industry* laments that 'the Heritage is the biggest growth industry in the country', and suggests that an obsession with the past will prevent Britain succeeding in the modern world. He produces laughable fakes among the fifty heritage centres established since 1975: Wigan Pier, for example. He seems quite put out that the country's 2,000 museums are being augmented at the rate of one a fortnight. But in an age when we are progressing, albeit falteringly, towards greater leisure, Hewison is hard-pressed to decry facilities which answer that need, provide a species of education and a large number of jobs, and swell a national annual income from tourism of £11,000 million; especially since the upsurge in conservation has coincided with a growth in prosperity which is not limited to the south. In all truth Glasgow *is* miles better since it stopped demolishing tenement blocks and laying waste its centre, and started to re-evaluate its Victorian heritage. Not only have Canterbury and Chichester found that 'preservation pays', but Halifax and Bradford are beginning to do so too.

But where Hewison is on stronger ground is where he joins with Peter Fowler in characterizing so much of the heritage industry as being not about the past but about the present. In other words it is about a sanitized and romanticized past which we have invented for ourselves and has much more to do with our values and tastes than those of our ancestors.

We all instinctively know that the 'cider with Rosie' world has gone for ever, that not only are our efforts to re-create it in our country cottages a charade, they are not even half serious. How many of today's cottages have earth floors, outside privies, no heating or hot water, no electricity or mains drainage, and a plentiful supply of lice? We are, or should be, aware of our good fortune in being alive in an age when we can sit in front of a log fire in a seventeenth-century hearth, listening to compact discs while eating food prepared in kitchens equipped with spin-offs from space-age technology.

102. (overleaf) Royal Free Hospital site, Islington: a modification to openings in the preserved 1830s façade allows a sufficiently dense layout of Housing Corporation financed units to achieve financial viability

Besides all the comforts there are the financial benefits to be gained from not pulling down old buildings, even though we are probably spending many times what they cost to put up in the first place to adapt them to our needs. It is just as well, however, if we do not delude ourselves into thinking that this way of life has anything to do with the past.

A lost generation

In the 1980s it has become fashionable to pretend that there were local 'communities' of 'ordinary working people' who resented being uprooted and moved into gleaming, hygienic tower blocks. Claptrap. It is difficult to exaggerate the unanimity of agreement on the need for a clean slate. Herbert Morrison in the government was at one with the architects department of the London County Council, an authority he had once led, in approving clearance policies. LCC architects, the largest department of the kind in Europe, were recognized as being in the vanguard, and architects could do no wrong. 'People were still content to be bespoken by the liberal intelligentsia', as Lionel Esher has written. LCC sociologist, Margaret Willis, polled tenants of the first eleven-storey blocks in London, and found that the higher off the ground they were, the happier. In Liverpool, council tenants wanted new flats instead of being 'fobbed off' with re-conditioned terrace houses.

The Festival Hall in London and Coventry Cathedral were popular, and modern architecture as a whole was widely admired. Hertfordshire schools were internationally acclaimed. Just as there had been little consideration of the idea of rebuilding Coventry Cathedral in its pre-bomb-damaged Gothic form, the rebuilt city centre around it was confidently – if by international standards rather provincially – contemporary. A handful of surviving medieval and Tudor structures were gathered up and rebuilt

in a pathetic little row. This was the spirit of the times.

Pevsner was laughed at when he started lauding some Victorian architecture in university lectures of the 1950s. Prime Minister Macmillan insisted on the unnecessary destruction of the Euston Arch in 1962 because he felt that concern for such relics would sap national vitality. The campaign to preserve the great arch and majestic hall of the station, both by Philip Hardwick, was a lively affair, conducted chiefly by a number of architects, including leading young modernists. It was by no means a cause with mass appeal. Conservation was a minority interest. The old Society for the Protection of Ancient Buildings clung on to life with a couple of thousand members. Even the National Trust had little more than 5,000 members, four staff, 59,000 acres and two country houses at the time of the last war. Now it has 1.6 million members and 2,000 staff, is the largest landowner in Britain, controls more than half (over 500 miles) of the country's unspoilt coastline, and owns over ninety major country houses and hundreds of smaller ones.

The past is another country

Just as we should avoid deluding ourselves into thinking that the brave new postwar world was something imposed on an unwilling populace, so we should clarify ideas about what we think it is we are preserving. Even more thoroughly than Bishop Berkeley's observer modifying by his presence the scene observed, so time and our particular viewpoint shapes our perception of the past. It is a truism that every age has its version of the past. As interest in all kinds of old things grows ever more inclusive, it is likely that there will be greater discrimination about what is really important. That which is rare and beautiful deserves more care than that which is merely quaint. A process was once described by Professor Gombrich, of how ordinary utilitarian rural dwellings decay over a period into 'picturesque' cottages.

This amounts to an elitist plea that what is truly important should be recognized and accorded a different species of respect from that given to what is little more than charmingly familiar. Not only is the architecture of every age identifiable by anyone who has travelled with a Buildings of England volume in his or her hand, so is the architectural restoration work of every period identifiable to the educated eye. The most difficult to discern – and Pevsner himself was baffled by the work of some 'conservative repairers' in west country churches – is that carried out by 'anti-scrape' architects, as members of the SPAB were called a century ago. The thoroughness of such gentle intervention is discussed here in relation to work at Wells Cathedral. In a general enthusiasm for conversion and reuse of buildings, it is important that our duty as 'trustees', merely, of the greatest monuments is fulfilled.

It is a big step from what has been called 'high conservation' here to the sort of work carried out at Prince's Square, Glasgow, or the Agricultural Hall, Islington. In Prince's Square, the 'ethos' may be conservationist, but in fact there is little pretence that the tubular-steel roof and balcony structures are anything more than Victorian-inspired or that the surrounding 'historic buildings' are anything more than restored façades. To what extent will Citibank's new headquarters in Billingsgate be regarded as a historic building? Surely it is more a creative synthesis of new and old. Much the same could be said – and with no more intention of denigration – of the Tobacco Dock shopping centre, New Concordia Wharf housing, and Albert Dock with all its entrepreneurial activities. The permissible amount of modification depends on the quality of the building. Country houses usually deserve and receive less

than radical conversions – depending always on the quality and condition of what has come to us.

The way forward

The burden of what has been said is that most dangers lie in the very success of the processes described in this book. Buildings of value will remain at risk, especially in country towns for example, and attractive environments will continue to be eroded despite conservation-area status, but the chief task is to see that what is done and approved as being in the common good really is of an appropriate quality.

103. St Mark's, North Audley Street, London. Enriched by the Dukes of Westminster, abandoned by the Church of England, the subject of a public inquiry at which SAVE opposed conversion to a hamburger restaurant, this opulent interior is to house an art gallery now

The purpose of a book like this, besides reinforcing the general approval of the retention and reuse of old buildings, is to remove as much as possible of the remaining sense of mystery about the shaping and reshaping of the familiar environment. Although the postwar redevelopments were carried out with a degree of consent, at least initially, that was partly because of a genuine belief that experts and authorities knew best. Among many crucial changes since then is a widespread belief that individuals, 'laymen' as architects call them, are as capable of helping to mould their environments as they are of 'doing up' their own homes. Many initiators of schemes described in this book were just such 'laymen'.

As has been repeated, 'high conservation' requires experts, and certain problem areas need the boost provided by publicly initiated and funded schemes with 'conservation impact'. And both such activities have met with public approval. But conservation as a whole is now a self-perpetuating process with immensely hopeful benefits for society. The perceptions and needs of the majority can once again find architectural expression. Having been for so long both causes and objects of alienation, buildings can be the objects of love once more.

Notes

1 David Lowenthal and Marcus Binney, *Our Past Before Us: Why Do We Save It?* (London: Temple Smith, 1981), contains essays by, among others, Tamara Hareven and Randolph Langenbach.

2 Matthew Saunders, *The Historic Home Owners' Companion* (London: Batsford, 1987).

3 English Heritage Monitor 1988, Max Hanna, London. English Tourist Board, 1988.

4 *Directory of Grant Making Trusts* (published from time to time by the Charities Aid Foundation).

5 Saunders, op. cit.

6 *The Times,* 15 July 1988.

7 Rosemary Richter, *Save Our Cities* (London: Calouste Gulbenkian Foundation, 1977).

8 *Sunday Times,* 7 August 1988.

9 Ben Weinreb and Christopher Hibbert (eds), *The London Encyclopaedia* (London: Macmillan, 1983).

10 Mike Jenner, *The Trinity Area of Frome* (Warminster: Mendip District Council, 1984).

11 Nikolaus Pevsner, *Wiltshire,* Buildings of England series 1, 3rd edn rev. Bridget Cherry (London: Penguin, 1973).

12 Jack Reynolds, *Saltaire: An Introduction to the Village of Sir Titus Salt* (Bradford: Bradford Art Galleries and Museums, n.d.).

13 *Architectural Review,* July 1988.

14 Robert Hewison, *The Heritage Industry: Britain in a Climate of Decline* (London: Methuen, 1987).

15 *Architect's Journal,* 6 July 1988.

16 Rowan Moore, *Terry Farrell in the Context of London* (catalogue to exhibition at the Royal Institute of British Architects, 1987).

17 *Architect's Journal,* 4 July 1984.

18 Marcus Binney, *Our Vanishing Heritage* (London: Arlington, 1984).

19 David Pearce and Marcus Binney (eds), *Off the Rails* (companion volume to exhibition at the Royal Institute of British Architects, London: SAVE Britain's Heritage, 1977).

20 *RIBA Journal,* February 1988.

21 Graham Thurgood, 'Silver End Garden Village, 1926–1932', *Thirties Society Journal,* 3 (1982).

22 Letter from Marcus Binney, *Guardian,* September 1980.

23 Nikolaus Pevsner, *Middlesex,* Buildings of England series (London: Penguin, 1951).

24 Joint press release from Thirties Society and SAVE Britain's Heritage, October 1988.

25 *The Times,* 25 October 1988.

26 Howard Colvin, *Calke Abbey, Derbyshire* (London: National Trust and George Phillips, 1985).

27 *Sunday Times,* 21 August 1988.

28 Marcus Binney, 'Castle crusader', *Landscape,* May 1988.

29 *Country Life,* 27 November 1980.

30 Ralph Dutton, *The English Country House* (London: Batsford, 1949).

31 *Country Life,* 23 April 1987.

32 Peter Richards, 'Barnyard renaissance', *Traditional Homes,* August 1988.

33 Deyan Sudjic, Peter Cook, and Jonathan Meades, *English Extremists* (London: Blueprint Monographs, 1988).

34 *Country Life,* 17 November 1983.

35 *SPAB News,* 5, 3 (July 1984).

36 Martin Caroe, *Wells Cathedral: Conservation of Figure Sculptures 1975–86* (privately published paper, 1987). I have relied on this and other reports by Mr Caroe.

37 Marcus Binney and Peter Burman, *Chapels and Churches: Who Cares?* (London: British Tourist Authority, 1977).

38 ibid.

39 SAVE Britain's Heritage press release, No. 198, 12 December 1979.

40 William Miles, *History of the Methodists* (publisher unknown).

41 *Observer,* 26 August 1977.

42 Ken Powell and Celia de la Hay, *Churches: A Question of Conversion* (London: SAVE Britain's Heritage, 1988).

43 *Country Life,* 17 September 1987.

Index